小学英语课堂教学的
20个细节

叶莲芳 ——— 主编

编写人员

叶莲芳 司 亮 常丹丹
吕 晗 马 艳 金晓吉
张煜瑜

南京师范大学出版社
NANJING NORMAL UNIVERSITY PRESS

图书在版编目(CIP)数据

小学英语课堂教学的 20 个细节 / 叶莲芳主编. —南京:南京师范大学出版社,2016.6
　ISBN 978-7-5651-2529-4

Ⅰ.①小… Ⅱ.①叶… Ⅲ.①英语课—课堂教学—教案(教育)—小学 Ⅳ.①G623.312

中国版本图书馆 CIP 数据核字(2016)第 011857 号

书　　名	小学英语课堂教学的 20 个细节
主　　编	叶莲芳
策　　划	姜爱萍　胡金平
责任编辑	王迎春
出版发行	南京师范大学出版社
地　　址	江苏省南京市宁海路 122 号(邮编:210097)
电　　话	(025)83598919(总编办)　83598412(营销部)　83598297(邮购部)
网　　址	http://www.njnup.com
电子信箱	nspzbb@163.com
照　　排	南京理工大学印刷照排中心
印　　刷	兴化印刷有限责任公司
开　　本	787 毫米×960 毫米　1/16
印　　张	15
字　　数	216 千
版　　次	2016 年 6 月第 1 版　2016 年 6 月第 1 次印刷
书　　号	ISBN 978-7-5651-2529-4
定　　价	40.00 元
出 版 人	彭志斌

南京师大版图书若有印装问题请与销售商调换
版权所有　侵犯必究

序

　　教学改革是一盘大棋局,需要改革者有大视野,做好顶层设计。然而,仅有顶层设计而没有实践操作层面对教学细节的关注、把握与研究,改革只能流于形式,坠入空洞,难达预期的效果。

　　课堂教学细节是课堂活动的外显行为和外部表现,"以生为本""先学后教"新理念固然使人激动,"问题探究""合作学习"新样态的确令人耳目一新,"有效教学""高效课堂"新追求获得了人们的普遍认同。但仅有宏观或中观层面的改革举措和大处着眼的整体布局,而没有见诸微观层面教学细节的小处着手的设计,则同样难有改革的成功。

　　所谓教学细节,一般有两种理解:一种是作为构成教学行为的最小单位,是教学行为的微观分解,犹如教学过程长链条中的一环节,表现为多样的形式和复杂的结构,形成于特定的教学情景中,具有独立的教学价值和意义。另一种是指教学过程中的关节点和关键点,对教学具有重要的推动和联接作用。本书所指的教学细节,既包含前面广义的理解,同时也涵盖后面较狭义的意涵,尤以后者为重。

　　教学是一门科学,但同时又是一门艺术。作为一门科学,它要求教学过程完全遵循教学规律运行,按照学生的认知规律设计,整个教学顺序、各个教学步骤之间有其内在的逻辑关联,教学细节的处理体现出科学性;同样,作为一门艺术,又要求教育者具有一定的教学机智、教育智慧,在面临不同教学现场和对象时,需要发挥其高超的教学艺术,细腻地处理一些教学细节。简言之,把握和研究教学细节,对追求教学实践的科学与艺术统一及进一步提高课堂教学质量有很重要的意义。

　　教学细节是可以从外部进行观察的具体教学行为或教学行为的组合,它看得见、听得到、摸得着,具有外显性和可观察性的特征。它可以是教师的言语、表情、肢体语言,可以是师生之间互动的行为组合,可以是特定情境中学生对教学的一种重要的行为反应,当然也可以是教师对某个关节点处理的方式方法。就此而言,教学细节似乎是一种"技术活",对于教学细节处理的成功与否,体现了教育者的经验多寡和教学技能技巧的水平高低,甚至亦反映出"生手"与"熟手"在具体教学行为方面的重要差异之一。可见,对于教学细节的管理有助于提高教师专业化水平、增强教学的适应性和针对性,提高教学水平,甚至形成教师个人的教学风格。

教学细节是师生内隐的、抽象的思维活动和内在情感的外显化、具体化和操作化,因此,教学细节在体现了教师"教学技术"的高低之外,也折射出教师所秉持的教学理念和拥有的教学智慧。一方面有什么样的教学理念就会有什么样的教学行为,另一方面教学行为在某种程度上亦体现了教学理念。教学细节作为更加微观的教学行为,当然亦体现着一定的价值追求。就此而论,教学细节似乎又不纯粹是"技术",而是教学理念的产物,是透视教师教学理念的"放大镜"。故而通过深度描述和考察教学细节,探究其中的科学与艺术,有利于真正树立正确的教学理念,提升教师的教学智慧,优化教师的教学行为。

教学是有目的、有计划、有组织的过程,因此,作为最小教学行为单位的教学细节一方面是预设的,具有计划性,但另一方面它又是在更为微观视域下的一个互动的动态生成过程,更具生成性。预设性与生成性的统一,构成了教学细节的特质,而生成性细节更反映出教师的教学智慧。苏联著名教育家苏霍姆林斯基说过,教育的技巧并不在于能预见到课堂的所有细节,而是在于根据当时的具体情况,巧妙地在学生不知不觉中做出相应的调整。

这套《课堂教学的20个细节》丛书,其主编及撰稿人均是有着丰富教学经验、充满教育情怀和教学智慧的一线教师。他们对于每个教学细节的剖析、品味、反思,不仅文字读来亲切、真实,引发共鸣,而且还能让人从朴实无华的文字背后感受到作者对课堂教学细节的感悟、反思、改造与重构,体会到作者令人难忘的教学智慧。是为序。

胡金平

(南京师范大学教育科学学院教授,博士生导师)

目 录

序 ……………………………………………… 胡金平（1）

细节 1　如何开展语音教学 ………………………………（1）

细节 2　如何开展词汇教学 ………………………………（13）

细节 3　如何开展语法教学 ………………………………（24）

细节 4　如何开展话题教学 ………………………………（32）

细节 5　如何开展句型教学 ………………………………（43）

细节 6　如何培养学生听的能力 …………………………（54）

细节 7　如何培养学生说的能力 …………………………（68）

细节 8　如何培养学生的认读能力 ………………………（78）

细节 9　如何培养学生的阅读能力 ………………………（88）

细节 10　如何培养学生写的能力 …………………………（98）

细节 11　如何激发学生玩英语、用英语的兴趣 …………（111）

细节 12	如何鼓励学生开口	(131)
细节 13	如何组织合作学习	(144)
细节 14	如何实施教学评价	(158)
细节 15	如何指导学生自主学习	(169)
细节 16	如何培养学生的思维能力	(178)
细节 17	如何促进学生语用能力的提高	(197)
细节 18	如何进行文化意识的渗透	(207)
细节 19	如何开展文化比较	(215)
细节 20	如何提升学生的跨文化交际能力	(221)

参考文献 ………………………………………………… (231)

细节 1
如何开展语音教学

细节阐述

在小学英语教学的过程中,中高年级的部分学生总是出现单词朗读或拼写比较困难的现象。因此,小学英语课堂也有必要进行适当的语音教学。

一、语音教学的作用

1. 促进词汇朗读和记忆

在学习语音之前,很多学生看见单词不会读,要记住单词的读音只能靠课外听音频或者课上多听老师的示范朗读。不过,由于遗忘规律,许多学生往往会很快忘记大多数单词的读音,这样就导致学习效率的低下。而语音教学是通过教给学生字母及组合的发音规律,促使学生独立进行大多数符合规律的单词的朗读,这样就有助于提高他们记忆单词读音的能力。

2. 改善词汇拼写

英语学习中词汇的拼写是重点之一,但很多学生的拼写却是靠反复朗读和死记硬背,还有部分学生连单词都还不会读就直接记拼写,这样的结果是背的时候十分辛苦,背完之后又容易遗忘。在英语教学中实施语音教学有助于学生将字母的音与形联系起来,根据读音拼写单词,这种方式能让学生大大提高记忆效率。

3. 帮助学生获得有效的学习方法

在英语学习中模仿是学生获得正确的语音语调的重要方式,在小学低年级学生主要是通过多遍模仿来记牢单词的读音,但如果教师到小学中高年级依旧提倡学生通过机械模仿来记忆单词读音的话,就难以帮助学生获得有效的学习方法。语音的教学能让学生了解字母的发音,同时提供丰富的实例让学生根据字母发音规律进行单词的朗读,这种拼读的过程包含了归纳、演绎、联想等学习方法的使用,它们对学生今后的学习有很大的帮助。

4. 增强学生的学习自信心

课程标准要求在英语教学中培养学生的学习兴趣,大多数时候学生的学习兴趣是与他们的成功体验密切相联系的。学生在学习、掌握字母发音规律后,可以通过它来学习新单词的读音,在学习完单词后,又可以利用字母发音规律来进行词汇的背诵。科学的方法使学生的学习效率得以提升,获得成功体验的几率增多,学习自信心就会随之增强。

二、语音教学的方法

美国学者斯塔尔等曾对语音教学活动做了以下的描述:在教学中,我们需要创设能够让学生意识到和理解语音的活动,比如,儿歌、词汇的配对练习、音和形的配对练习、首末字母的发音练习等。一种好的语音教学需要包含其中至少一项教学活动。

策略一:设计读音卡,关注易学性

学生完成26个字母的学习后,认识到字母在单词中的读音非常重要,教学时,教师可以利用汉语拼音的一些读音提示,先从与拼音接近的辅音字母的读音开始,如:字母 k, t, p, f, z, b 等,再过渡到辅音字母组合的读音,如:ch, th, sh 等,这种方法比较容易让中低年级的学生理解和掌握。在此之后,就可以转向元音字母的读音了,同样,也可以先从相对简单的单元音开始。

1. 制作读音卡

表一：辅音字母组合读音卡

辅音字母组合	ch	sh	th	wh	ng
读音	/tʃ/	/ʃ/	/ð/	/h/ /w/	/ŋ/
例词	chair	she	this	who, what	sing
你们的发现					

表二：元音字母读音卡

元音字母	a		e		i		o		u	
读音	/eɪ/	/æ/	/iː/	/e/	/aɪ/	/ɪ/	/əʊ/	/ɒ/	/juː/	/ʊ/
例词	cake	cat	he	egg	bike	big	nose	dog	use	put
你们的发现										

表三：元音字母组合读音卡

元音字母组合	ir/ur	er	or	ow/oa	ar	ou/ow
读音	/ɜː/	/ə/	/ɔː/	/əʊ/	/ɑː/	/aʊ/
例词	girl, nurse	sister	for	yellow, boat	car	mouth, cow
你们的发现						

2. 运用读音卡

读音卡片的设计是由教师完成的，但是完成的过程要学生自主参与。学生需要观察每张卡片内容的相关性，随着学习的进程，将新学的重点词汇自行整理到读音卡中。这样，读音卡的记录过程就成了学生发现式学习的过程。其次，在生成与更新卡片的过程中，学生还要对已经在卡内的词汇进行及时的巩固，如：教师可以运用每节课的前几分钟，通过给学生提供展示自己朗读能力的机会或者教师设计的 brainstorm 等教学活动，来对读音卡中的记录进行复现与运用，帮助学生牢固地掌握字母与读音的关系。

策略二：创设多种活动，关注趣味性

在语音教学中，教师可以设计一些形式多样、符合学生年龄特征与认知水平的活动,并且,这些活动要富有趣味性,能激发学生的参与积极性,只有这样,才能取得良好的效果。

1. 绕口令

在语音学习的过程中,绕口令的练习,不仅可以提高学生语音的准确性,还可以增强学生的语感,使学生在学习英语的起始阶段发声器官就变得灵活。另外由于绕口令具备一定的挑战性,它还能增加学生学习英语的兴趣。利用绕口令进行教学时,教师既可以进行单个语音的强化练习,也可以进行多个语音的对比强化练习。此外,教师还可以根据教学主题与语音学习的需要,自己创编绕口令。

如在学习译林版《牛津小学英语》2B Unit 9 Where's the plane? 的时候,主要句型是"Where's...?"。在教学完书本的知识后,教师可以利用与where含有相同元音/eə/的单词bear,pear,there来编写句子:

Where's the bear?

The bear is there.

Where's the pear?

The pear is on the bear.

以上的小对话读来朗朗上口。在练习句型的基础上,学生同时也学习了字母组合ear和ere在单词中的读音。通过这个绕口令的朗读,学生对特殊疑问句与陈述句的语调也有了一定认识。

当然,教师还可以采用陈述句的扩句练习,以从词到词组然后到句子的方式进行绕口令练习,如在译林版《牛津小学英语》2A Unit 3 Look at the moon的学习过程中,就可以用下面的例子来练习look at的句型:

Cook.

Good cook.

Look at the good cook.

Look at the good cook with the cook book.

在学习译林版《牛津小学英语》1A Unit 8 What can you do? 时,教师可以结合I can的句型进行绕口令练习:

Mum can run. Brother can jump.

Mum can't jump. Brother can't run.

Mum can run but can't jump and Brother can jump but can't run.

绕口令常常以两个物体或者两个人物作为内容,进行对比性的陈述,上面的例子最终合成了带有/ʌ/发音的长句,学生诵读时,既练习了语音,又达到了拓展运用含有情态动词 can 的句型的目的。

2. 儿歌

儿歌在形式上一般多以短句呈现,比较押韵,而且结构反复出现,易唱易记;内容上则多贴近学生生活,能引起他们的共鸣,所以,学生往往一听便记得住。儿歌的意义在于让学生在轻松的念唱中训练其说话发音的清晰性和准确性。

在低年级进行英语语音教学,儿歌的使用是必不可少的。儿歌对于保持学生高涨的学习热情和浓厚的学习兴趣起着十分重要的作用。儿歌的韵律性让学生随着节拍自由摆动身体,为他们的语言学习提供了丰富多样的形式。而且,儿歌尽管短小,但常常有故事作为背景,因而,容易使学生进入儿歌的情境中,此时,他们身心放松,情绪高涨,兴致盎然,诵读儿歌的时候就是他们使用语言、享受语言的时刻。

In the afternoon

Go to the zoo

Take some food

Have fun too

这首儿歌都以带有/u:/音的词汇结尾,简单的四个句子,却讲述了一个简短的故事,学生在念儿歌的过程中,似乎自己真的带着东西和小伙伴们去动物园玩耍了,他们在那儿是多么开心啊!

— Where is the cow? — The cow is down.

— How is the cow? — The cow is fine now.

— What color is the cow? — The cow is brown.

这是关于奶牛的一首儿歌,讲述了小奶牛的相关信息:"奶牛奶牛在哪儿啊?""哦,它在下面呢。""奶牛奶牛怎么样啊?""还不错啦。""奶牛奶牛是什么颜色的?""是咖啡色的。"学生在念这首儿歌的时候,似乎奶牛就在自己的身边,和小伙伴一起呢。

　　Father is in the car.
　　Aunt is on the farm.
　　Where are Grandma and Grandpa?
　　They're in the yard.

这首儿歌采用了陈述和问答两种方式,练习了带有/ɑ:/发音的词汇。儿歌中讲述了一大家人的活动:爸爸在汽车里。阿姨在农场上。爷爷奶奶呢? 他们在院子里呢。

策略三:将学习方法的指导融入语音教学

　　语音教学时,教师常常要引导学生去发现一些规律性的语音现象,除了常用的观察、讨论、推测等方法,教师还要向学生渗透其他几种学习方法的指导。

　　1. 归纳和演绎

　　教师通过提供多个含有相同字母或字母组合的例词,让学生观察、讨论,从中提炼出它们的读音规律。比如,教师列举单词 look, book, foot,让学生通过朗读思考字母组合 oo 在这几个单词中的读音;在此基础上,提供多个同样含有 oo 字母组合的新单词,如 cook, hook, took,让学生根据得出的读音规律来尝试朗读这些新的单词。需要注意的是,学生在归纳和演绎读音规律的时候出错是很正常的,教师要充分保护学生的学习热情和积极性,并给他们提供必要的帮助。

　　2. 联想

　　联想是指学生能够在新知识和旧知识之间建立起联系,或者能把多个知识的片段通过联想加以衔接,生成新的概念。联想能促进学生思维能力的发展。例如:教学时教师在指导学生朗读 student, study 等单词时,可以引导他们回忆曾经学过的单词,如 time, hat, between 中字母 t 的读音,然后通过比较,发现它们的不同,进而再结合单词 skirt, sport 中字母 k 和 p 的读音的学习,最终让学生掌握摩擦音后面送气音的发音特征。

> ◆典型案例1◆

译林版《英语》四年级上册　Unit 6　At the snack bar Story time 教学

本课时教师主要通过旧单词的读音提示来帮助学生朗读新单词，同时引导学生发现字母组合和读音间的关系。

Step One　导入主题

教师与学生讨论人物 Anna 的信息时，在进行了一些问答后，抛出一个问题：What does she have? 并在 PPT 上出示图片——一辆黑色的小汽车。

Ss：A black car.

T：You're right. She can drive a car. She drives the car to work. Where does she work? Please try to guess. Let me give you some hints.

（教师口述一些单词：hamburgers，juice，pies，coffee）

Ss：小吃店。

（教师在 PPT 上出示词组 snack bar，其位置对应在 black car 下面）

T：Can you read?

片刻的沉默后，举手的学生并不多。教师此时进行提示，重读 black，car，随后请一名学生来读，学生朗读比较准确。然后全班齐读 At the snack bar，进入本课学习的主题。

Step Two　词汇学习

在 snack bar 这个语境中，教师开始教授新的单词与词组：a glass of，a tin of，a bottle of。

T：（出示一杯牛奶的图片。出示单词 class，让学生朗读）

Ss：Class.

T：（再将 class 的 c 换成 g，变成单词 glass）Can you read?

Ss：Glass.

随后全班一起朗读词组 a glass of milk。

教师运用同样的方法教授 bottle 和 tin——首先出示 little,再学习 bottle;首先出示 in,再学习 tin。

◆ 案例反思 ◆

在本案例中,教师在教授 snack bar 这个词组的读音时,巧妙地将上一个教学环节中的信息 black car 作为教学铺垫。由于两个词组中 snack 与 black 都具有 ack 组合,而 bar 与 car 都具有 ar 组合,学生通过推测的方式,就十分容易地习得了新词组 snack bar 的读音。同样的教学环节也出现在了 glass, bottle 与 tin 的读音教学中。教师有意识的铺垫,为学生的推测做好了准备,简单的推测使学生轻松地学会了新的知识,学生学习自信心也会得到提高。

典型案例 2

译林版《英语》四年级下册
Unit 5　Seasons　拓展教学

本节课的授课对象是四年级的学生。教学的内容是自编的一个小故事。主要学习内容是音标/aɪ/与字母 i...e 组合与 igh 组合。

Step One　课前热身活动

T：Let's say a rhyme "I like my bike" together.

Ss：OK.

T：(播放儿歌)

I like my bike.

I like my kite.

I like my bike and my kite.

师生边念儿歌边表演动作,气氛热烈,很快投入学习情境。

Step Two　语音学习

1. i...e 组合的发音

在师生进行日常对话后,教师在 PPT 上出示了一张男孩的图片,

引导学生开始对图片进行提问,学生们提出了以下一些问题:

Ss: What's your name?

How old are you?

What can you do?

What do you like?

T: You did a good job. Do you want to know who he is and how old he is? You can find out the answers in the following sentences.

教师在 PPT 上出示以下句子:Hi! Nice to meet you. I'm Mike. I'm nine.

学生仔细观察以上句子,片刻后就有很多学生举手:

S1: He's Mike.

S2: He's nine.

在学生正确回答之后,教师邀请学生进行同桌之间的角色扮演:

A: Nice to meet you!	B: Nice to meet you!
A: What's your name?	B: My name is Mike. What's your name?
A: My name is...	B: How old are you?
A: I'm nine. And you?	B: I'm... Goodbye.
A: Bye.	

前一环节已经就问题进行了一些铺垫,因此,同桌问答的方式,既让学生了解了故事中人物 Mike 的相关信息,也将自己的信息融入进去,并将故事由描述式转换为扮演对话式,学生十分喜欢。

T: Can you read "nine, nice, Mike, like"?

学生在完成对话中已经运用到以上四个单词,所以都争先恐后地回答。这时,教师开始引导:

T: Can you find out the same letters in the four words?

Ss: Yes. 都有字母 i。

T: Look carefully.

(教师继续引导学生认真思考,培养学生的观察能力)

Ss：都有 e。

T：Where is the letter "e"?

Ss：在结尾。

T：What does "i" say? Read the words and guess.

（学生们开始朗读单词，推测 i 的读音）

Ss：/aɪ/.

T：You are right. And write down /aɪ/ on the blackboard. When you see letter "i...e", "i" says /aɪ/. I'd like to show you more words：bike, drive, ride. Can you read them?

学生都能准确地读出单词。在这一教学环节中，教师层层引导，学生观察推测，教师最后归纳总结，学生运用，通过这样的方式来学习语音，学生对语音的理解更透彻。

2. igh 的发音

教师首先出示故事部分内容，并给学生布置学习任务：朗读下列 3 句话。

In the morning, I drive a car.

In the afternoon, I ride a bike.

At night, I say "Good night".

然后给学生布置以下学习任务：

1) Read and match.

morning	drive
afternoon	ride
night	say

学生通过阅读然后连线的活动，将故事的关键词汇信息进行对应，既可以梳理故事的内容，操作的方式也符合学生的学习特点。学生很快就完成了这项任务。

2) Let's chant.

T：You did a good job. Now, listen to me first and then chant with me.

```
‖ ×    ×          ×      ‖    ‖ ×    × ×     ×    ‖
  In   the      morning,       I    drive a   car.
‖ ×    ×          ×      ‖    ‖ ×    × ×     ×    ‖
  In   the      afternoon,     I    ride a   bike.
‖      ×          ×      ‖    ‖ ×    ×       ×  × ‖
      At        night,         I    say   "Good night".
```

师生通过儿歌的方式,将故事的内容有节奏地唱出来,演唱的过程就是语言学习的过程,配以简单的动作如开汽车、骑自行车、道"晚安",帮助学生对语句的意义进行学习。

随后教师还采用对话的方式,引导学生对带有字母组合 igh 的单词的发音进行学习、推测与巩固。

light right high bright

Step Three 巩固总结

T: Now can you work in groups and try to retell the story in groups?

学生开始以四人小组形式进行合作,教师首先站在讲台上观察各组开展情况;随后走近各组,聆听并帮助学生解答在创编过程中的问题;最后邀请四组同学上台表演。

◆ 案例反思 ◆

这个案例中教师语音的教学始终融入语言的教学中,因而也就让语音的学习变得更有意义。而且,在教学过程中教师不断创造机会,让学生主动参与教学活动,如:让学生自己发现例词的共同特点,观察并推测开音节单词中字母 i 的读音,合作创编儿歌等等,这样的语音学习过程是学生获得学习方法的过程,也是学生学习能力得到提升的过程。

◆ 专家点评 ◆

提起语音教学,不少教师把它与音标教学画上等号,只要学生拼读单词能力弱,教师们就把它归咎为音标知识的匮乏。其实,学生的拼读能力是由他们自然拼读(Phonics)的能力决定的。根据 2011 年版《义务教育英语课程标准》(全书后文简称"《英语课程标准》")的阐述,小学阶段语音教学的主要目标是:① 使学生具备语音的意识,知道英语单词的拼写和读音是有规律的;② 掌握基本的语音技能,也就是能根据基本的读音规则拼写和朗读大部分单词,形成"见词能读,听音能拼"的技能。英语是拼音文字,多数单词的拼写都符合读音规则,一般来说只要读准单词,根据发音规则就能正确拼出单词,英语教师要做的就是让学生能感知并运用这些规则。上述案例中分别列出了在单词朗读和记忆时教师采取的一些做法:教授单词读音时,教师可以先让学生观察含有相关字母和字母组合的单词的读音,再带领他们尝试朗读新的单词;指导学生记忆单词时则可以使用分解单词读音的方式帮助学生拼写和记忆。对于教材中语音板块的教学,教师采用的是集中教学的方式,通过呈现某些字母和字母组合在不同单词中相同或不同的读音,让学生观察异同并尝试总结归纳读音规律,这种探究性的学习能够给学生留下深刻的印象。需要指出的是,这些案例中教师都没有就事论事地教授语音,而是把语音教学和语言教学紧密结合起来,让语音的学习变得有意义,这一点是非常值得提倡的。

细节 2

如何开展词汇教学

> 细节阐述

　　词汇学习是英语学习的重要组成部分,《英语课程标准》语言知识分级标准词汇二级标准中对小学阶段学生的词汇掌握规定了如下要求:"知道单词是由字母构成的;知道要根据单词的音、义、形来学习词汇;学习有关本级话题范围的 600—700 个单词和 50 个左右的习惯用语,并能初步运用 400 个左右的单词表达二级规定的相应话题。"面对词汇教学要求高而英语课时有限的矛盾,教师实施行之有效的英语词汇的教学,促使学生积极主动地习得英语,是小学英语教学的重要任务之一。

　　了解一个单词意味着知道它的音(pronunciation)、形(form)、意(meaning)和用(usage)。传统的英语词汇教学一般表现为:教师先带着读单词,接着通过不同的例句展示单词的用法,一条条为学生讲清楚,就好像在讲字典。遇到考试当中经常出现或者经常需要词义辨析的词汇时,教师会详细为学生讲解。然后,教师会要求学生课后抄单词、记单词、背课文。最后,教师通过听写方式检查学生的单词记忆情况。事实上,笔者通过多年的教学实践证实,传统的词汇教学效果并不理想。学生并不能达到满意的效果,往往是付出大于收获。事实上,词汇教学一方面要与语音、句型和语篇教学相结合,另一方面还要在听、说、读、写的活动中加以落实。所以,词汇教学中可以采用整体教学法,尽量减少教师解读语言知识的时间,把语言实践的机会留给学生,促使他们从感知到领悟再到最终能正确运用。

策略一：整体认读单词和自然拼读（Phonics）教学法相结合

整体认读单词不同于记忆、背诵单词，它是指能辨认单词，能说出它的基本意思。培养学生的认读能力是小学阶段英语教学的重要任务，认读能力的高低决定了学生今后阅读能力的强弱，所以，从小学低年级开始教师就要有意识地引导学生进行单词的认读。需要指出的是，从认读的规律和过程来看，学生不可能一次性全面掌握某个单词，他们需要在变换的语境中反复接触、滚动学习，才能最终牢固地掌握。基于这个原因教师要明确词汇的学习是一个反复和持续的过程，需要通过不同的形式贯穿于一个单元甚至几个单元的不同课时的教学。

从低年级向中高年级过渡的进程中学生逐渐开始背诵和记忆部分单词和短语，如果在整体认读的基础上能结合自然拼读（Phonics）策略的使用将起到事半功倍的效果。自然拼读（Phonics），《朗文当代英语词典》的词条解释是："a method of teaching people to read in which they are taught to recognize the sounds that letters represent"。其核心就是建立英语字母或字母组合与其发音之间的对应关系，让学生学会按字母的发音去认读单词。Phonics 教学让学生对字母建立两种概念，即 letter name 和 letter sound。letter name 是指字母本身的读音，如字母 a 读作/eɪ/；这个字母在单词 apple 中的发音是/æ/，/æ/这个音就被称为 letter sound。在 Phonics 教学理念当中，单词不是由字母组成的，而是由音组成的，而音是由字母或字母组合构成的。换句话说，letter 以 sound 形式合成单词，学生再通过拼读单词读音掌握单词，从而做到"见词能读、听音能拼"。

策略二：将游戏引入课堂词汇教学中

语言游戏，包括词汇游戏。游戏是小学生特别喜爱的教学活动，把枯燥的学习融入有趣的游戏中去，会收到事半功倍的效果。教师应采用多种形式刺激学生的感官，把单词教学贯穿到娱乐之中，让学生轻松愉快地学习单词，不断提高课堂教学质量和效率。因此，游戏的趣味因素可以使词汇更容易记忆。

下面就介绍一些可以尝试的词汇游戏。

击掌说词：学生站成一圈或坐成一圈，在教师的引导下，保持四拍的节奏——两手拍大腿三次(1,2,3)，然后拍手(4!)。游戏开始的时候要慢一点，拍手的速度可逐渐加快。按照顺时针的方向，依次在第四个节拍时，大声说出预先选定的词群(例如，水果和蔬菜的词群)中的词，所说的词不能重复。任何说重复的词、打断节奏或者什么都不说的人将被"淘汰"，余下的人重新开始游戏，直至剩下一个人。教师可以在关键点更换词群，并大声说出新词群的名称：Animals! Fruits! Jobs! 等等。

分类游戏：学生组成两人小组或多人小组，在一张纸上画出一些表栏，每个表栏都标有词群的名称，如：fruits, transports, clothes, animals, sports。教师说出字母表中的一个字母(如 b)，在限定时间内(如 3 分钟)，学生尽量在各栏中写出他们能想到的以该字母开头的单词(banana, berry; bus; bikini, blouse; bear, bat; baseball, basketball...)。写出最多(正确)单词的小组获胜。

宾果游戏：给每个学生发一个信封，信封内装有要练习的词汇类别的卡片(教师自己一个信封)。教师首先让每位学生从信封里挑三张卡片，放到课桌上，正面朝上。之后，教师随意从自己的信封里抽一张卡片，根据所教内容，提出一个有利于学习的问题。如，在学习食物方面的词汇时，教师挑一张三明治卡片，问学生："Do you like sandwiches?"持有三明治卡片的学生举起卡片说："Yes, I like sandwiches."然后他们将这张卡片翻过去放在桌子上。如果没人有三明治卡片，全班同学一起说"Nobody likes sandwiches."或者"I don't like sandwiches."。教师继续提问，一直到有学生三张卡片都翻过去了，这个学生可以说："Bingo!"宣布获胜。获胜者的奖励是得到主持下面游戏的机会。

词汇"同"：首先，准备若干单词卡片——例如，可从课堂词汇袋或者词汇盒中取出。学生分成小组，每个小组人数不要太多。每个小组收集尽可能多的成对的单词。一个学生摆放两张单词卡片，面朝上，以便每个人都能看到。第一个想出怎样联系两个词的办法的学生可以得到这两张卡片,然后再放上两张卡片。词汇的联系可以是:相同的词性、同义词或反义词、相同的词群或者只是可以用这两个词造一个有意义的句子。如果不能建立联系,这两个词就被放回去重新洗牌。当建立的联系有争议时,由教师做出决定。

我来猜:教师先设定活动所涉及的范围或环境,如教室里的相关物品。教师开始出题说句子,如:"I spy with my eyes, something beginning with letter 'b'."学生仔细听题后开始猜测以字母 b 开头的单词(答案是:blackboard)。"我来猜"还可以小组的形式开展游戏。教师将学生分为五人一组或六人一组,并选出小组长。在活动开始之前,每组由小组长先确定活动所涉及的范围,并由小组长开始出题说一个句子,如:"I spy with my eyes, something beginning with letter 'a'."组内其他学生开始猜测以字母 a 开头的单词(注意:被猜测的物品必须是可见的)。

背对黑板:这是一个猜词游戏,被选中的学生要通过向班级里的其他同学问问题来猜词。这位学生面向全班坐着,背对着黑板;教师在黑板上写一个最近学的单词、短语或者习语,猜词者看不到教师所写的内容。猜词者通过问不同的一般疑问句或者选择疑问句来猜测词汇。例如:Is that an animal?(Yes.)Is it big or small?(It's big.)Does it have a long nose?(Yes.)Is it an elephant?(Yes.)如果要简化游戏,教师可以在某些方面对备选词汇进行限制。

上面列举的并不是词汇游戏的全部种类,但却代表了一些词汇游戏的类型。如果能恰当使用的话,将词汇融入游戏中会是一种既有效又有趣的运用词汇的方式。

策略三:将小学英语词汇教学语境化

波兰的人类语言学家马林诺夫斯基(Malinowski)最早(1923)提出了语境的概念,他认为,"话语和环境互相紧密地结合在一起,语言环境对于理解语言来说是必不可少的"。《英语课程标准》强调要在语境中"理解和领悟词语的基本含义以及在特定语境中的意义"。因此,词汇要在典型的语境中呈现,这样学生就可以体会它们的意义、语域、搭配和句法环境了。

首先，教师可以将词汇学习和句子学习相结合。学习词汇的目的是掌握词义以及词的搭配和用法。词语只有组成句子或连成话语，才能实现交际功能。心理学研究也表明，把相关内容集中或联系起来学习和记忆，效果更佳。所以，教师在教学单词时应注意引导学生把所学单词联系起来，在有一定关联的句子和情景中去记忆单词。

其次，利用教材创设激发学生想象力的情景。例如，译林版《牛津小学英语》词汇教学编排在故事教学之后，教师可以在故事情景中进行词汇教学。教师可以针对不同年级的学生，对故事进行补充、整合和再创造，以促进不同学情的学生融入故事创造的情景中，在语境中理解、学习和运用词汇。教师也可以创设多种活动，让学生在情景中巩固所学语言知识，提高运用所学语言的能力。

而后，善于利用生活情景，强化词汇教学的语境。生活情景最能引导学生进行真实的语言互动体验，在生活情景中合理设置含有信息差的语言产出活动更能促进学生运用词汇。在自然语境中，教师和学生之间进行的有意义的交流，可以促使学生更快掌握所学语言。在日常教学中，存在着大量的自然语境，教师要善于借助学生熟悉的自然语境，让学生自己去体会词汇的意义和用法。

事实证明，语境在英语词汇教学中的作用不容忽视。教师应该坚持在语境中教授词汇，帮助学生准确地理解词汇，提高他们感悟语言的能力。这样，学生才能真正地学会运用并掌握语言。

典型案例

译林版《牛津小学英语》5A　Unit 8　A camping trip

本课主要教学内容为和野营相关的 7 个新单词（telescope, tin-opener, stove, pot, blanket, towel, tent）以及询问某人有什么物品的三组问答句型。

教学片段一 教师采用游戏形式,复习过去学过的水果类、文具类单词,激发学生学习兴趣,并唤醒其对已学单词的记忆,为下面的句型教学做铺垫

1. 教师与学生互相问候,并在交流过程中激发学生的学习热情

2. 以游戏形式复习已学单词

T:Can you read some English words?

Ss:Yes, I can.

T:OK, let's read.

屏幕上逐一呈现一些英语单词(如 pens, rulers, apples, pears, oranges, chocolate, hamburgers, cakes 等),并不时出现灰太狼的头像;学生看见单词就大声读出来,看见灰太狼就说 Bomb。

教学片段二 教师在一个具体的情境中,整体教授新单词,并始终注意到词不离句

1. 教师自我介绍,并说明自己喜欢野营,邀请学生一起去野营

T:Today I'm your new English teacher. I like going shopping and going camping.

(屏幕上播放几张与野营相关的图片)

T:Do you like going camping, too?

S1:Yes, I do.

T:Would you like to go camping with me?

S2:Yes, I'd like to.

T:Look, they have a tent. Do we need a tent?

Ss:Yes, we do.

(教师新授并领读单词:a tent)

2. 教师用课件呈现一顶帐篷,帐篷里有五件物品,学生根据提示猜测帐篷里的物品

T:Look, this is my tent. I have some things in it. Can you guess what I have?

学生根据提示用句型"You have..."猜测。

1) 课件呈现提示句型:"It's a fruit."

T:The first thing is a fruit. What do I have? Can you guess?

S1:You have an apple.

T:Sorry, it's yellow.

S2:You have a banana.

T:Yes, you're right.

2) 课件呈现提示句型:"I can drink it."

T:I can drink it. What do I have? Can you guess?

S1:You have some juice.

T:Sorry, I have no juice. Try to guess it again.

S2:You have some water.

T:Yes, you're right.

3) 课件呈现提示句型:"I can eat it. It is round."

T:I can eat it. It is round. What do I have? Can you guess?

S1:You have a hamburger.

T:Yes, I have a hamburger.

4) 课件呈现提示句型:"It is brown. It is sweet."

T:It is brown. It is sweet. What do I have? Can you guess?

S1:You have some sweets.

T:Sorry, I don't have any sweets.

S2:You have some chocolate.

T:Yes. I have some chocolate.

5) 课件呈现提示句型:"It is an animal. It can swim."

T:It is an animal. It can swim. What do I have? Can you guess?

S1:You have some fish.

T:Yes. I have some fish. I have a tin of fish.

T:Look, I have so many things. What do you have?

S2:I have...

教师先与几个学生用"What do you have?"进行示范交流,然后让学生自己拿身边的物品进行两两问答。

3. 教师提出野营中还需一些物品，引发学生积极思维，激活学生已有的经验知识，引出新知

T：I have some things for the trip. But I need more things. Look，I have a tin of fish.

（教师新授并领读 tin—a tin of—a tin of fish）

T：But I can't open the tin. I want to open the tin. What do I need?

S1：A tin-opener.

（教师新授并领读 a tin-opener）

屏幕上呈现五张图片。学生选择恰当的图片并回答教师的提问。

T：I want to cook food. What do I need?

S2：You need a stove and a pot.

学生自主朗读单词 hot，dog，lot，根据字母 o 的读音规律拼读单词 pot；学生自主朗读单词 student，close，根据字母组合 st 和字母 o 的读音规律拼读单词 stove。

T：（新授并领读 a pot，a stove）

教学片段三 教师通过句型操练，呈现新单词 telescope；紧接着教师根据新授单词特点设计了一个相关的游戏，不仅复习了已授单词 **pot，stove，tent 和 tin-opener**，还引出新单词 **towel 和 blanket**

课件呈现教材中 Part C 的第三幅图，并在图片下方给出提示句型，同桌学生根据图片内容和提示进行对话交流。

S1：What do they have?

S2：They have a Walkman.

Ss：What do they have?

T：They have a telescope.

学生自主朗读单词 telephone，go，根据字母组合 tele 和字母 o 的读音规律拼读单词 telescope。

T：（新授并领读 a telescope）

Ss：Telescope, telescope, they have a telescope.

屏幕远处出现一些模糊的物品,学生用肉眼几乎无法看清。此时教师让学生说出单词 telescope,用"望远镜"来看清物品,并说出物品名称。

T:Look at those things. Can you see them clearly?

S3:No, I can't.

T:If you want to see them clearly, please say:Telescope, telescope, telescope, go, go, go.

(屏幕中远处的物品逐渐放大,显示出锅的形状)

T:What can you see?

S4:A pot.

教师用相同的方法逐一呈现物品 a stove, a tent, a tin-opener,并让学生朗读这些词汇。

(屏幕中远处的物品逐渐放大,显示出最后一件物品)

T:What can you see?

S5:A towel.

学生自主朗读单词 how,根据字母组合 ow 的读音规律拼读单词 towel。

T:(新授并领读 a towel)

教师用课件呈现 Ben 和 Nancy,让学生猜测毛巾是谁的。

T:Look at Ben and Nancy. Guess! Who has a towel?

S6:Ben has a towel.

S7:Nancy has a towel.

T:Look, Nancy has a towel.(领读 has)

T:What does Nancy have?

S8:She has a towel.

T:Look, what does Ben have?

S9:He has a blanket.

学生自主朗读单词 lantern, jacket,根据字母组合 lan 和 ket 的读音规律拼读单词 blanket。

T:(新授并领读 a blanket)

◆ 案例反思 ◆

　　本节课新授是7个与野营有关的单词。教学片段一中教师注重新旧知识的衔接和积累。在本节课开始,教师设计了游戏:用课件呈现一些已经学过的食物类、水果类、文具类单词,让学生进行朗读,一方面激起了学生说的欲望,另一方面帮助学生复习了已学单词,为接下来的环节中"— What do you have? — I/ We have..."对话交流做了铺垫。在教授新单词时,教师立足于学生已有知识来引出新知,例如,以 open the tin 引出新单词 tin-opener,以 telephone 和 go 的读音教学 telescope 的读音,以 lantern,jacket 教学 blanket 帮助学生准确地朗读和记忆单词。

　　教学片段二中教师创设情境,注意整体教学。整节课都以"A camping trip"为主线,在这个情境中将单词和句型有机地结合起来,实施整体教学。教师在开始自我介绍时提到自己喜欢野营,自然引出本节课的主线"A camping trip",用猜测的方式让学生猜一猜老师野营需要带哪些物品,很自然地引出新单词 a tin-opener, a tent, a stove, a pot。

　　教学片段三中教师也设计了形式多样的教学活动,来达成本节课的教学目标。例如,教师在教授完新单词 telescope 后,设计了一个游戏,即屏幕上远处有一些物品,学生用肉眼几乎无法看清楚,这时课件呈现一个望远镜的图片,引领学生说:Telescope, telescope, go, go, go.课件中的物品也随之放大,以便学生看清这些物品,并说出物品的名称。这个游戏趣味性较高,既达到了复习单词的目的,又激发了学生学习的兴趣,促使他们积极主动地参与到学习活动中。

◆ 专家点评 ◆

　　在日常教学中部分教师有这样的认识误区:和词汇教学相比,语篇和句型的教学显得更为重要。这一认识上的偏差直接导致教学时教师只注重学生是否会朗读单词,是否知道了单词的中文意思。这样的教学造成的后果是学生记忆单词的时候耗时多且易遗忘,在语言实践时常常会因为不知道单词而"卡壳"。要想解决这个问题,就要从学生的认知特点入手。小学生的记忆特点是整体记忆,如果让他们离开具体的语境孤立地背诵、记忆单词,会事倍功半。所以,词汇学习过程应该是一个有意义的语言学习过程,也就是 meaning-based context。教师要将词汇教学与交际、文化、语言等多种元素相结合,充分发挥情境在词汇学习中的作用。实践证明:在模拟实际生活场景的情境中教单词不但有助于学生的理解,而且有助于学生把所学的单词在交际中得体恰当地使用,切实提高语用能力。另一方面,随着学生进入小学中高年级的学习,单词的背诵和记忆成为学生最感头疼的作业,好在多数英语单词的拼写是符合读音规则的,只要把单词读准了,根据读音规则就可以正确拼写单词。课堂上教师教授词汇时如果能结合单词的拼写告诉学生它们的读音或者就读音让学生尝试拼出单词,从最初的尝试拼出某一个字母过渡到拼写字母组合最后到拼写整个单词,久而久之,学生记忆单词的效率定会有很大的提高。

细节 3

如何开展语法教学

> ● 细节阐述 ●

语言是人类最重要的交际工具。语言之所以能够成为这样一种方便的交际工具，一个重要原因是它的系统性。系统性反映在它具有极强的规则性。语法规则是语言主要的组成部分，是语言得以成为语言的根本条件之一。

语法教学是语言教学中的重要一环，是每位英语教师无法回避的。但语法教学也是我们小学英语教师在教学中遇到问题最多的方面之一。在小学阶段语法教学应该摆在什么样的位置上呢？根据小学生的认知特点，在小学语法教学中，普遍不主张对一些语法规则或用法作过多的讲解，而提倡让学生在听、说、读、写中通过观察和感受并在教师的指导下逐渐意识到并懂得这些语法规则，因为语言的学习与运用不是一下子在一堂课上能解决的，它是一个缓慢的过程，是在不断地实践运用中才能实现的。小学阶段教师要避免让学生死记硬背语法规则，而应该注重培养学生的语法意识。

语法是语言形式、语言意义、语言用法的综合体，但是，就目前的小学课堂教学来看普遍存在的现象是过于强调语言的形式，基本能注意语言的意义，却往往忽视语言的用法。这种教学造成的后果是学生往往能模仿语言，却不知道应在什么语境下准确地表达自己的想法。所以，在小学初学英语阶段，一般主张语言的意义和用法应该先行，而形式的学习应该靠后，也就是强调理解，重视实践，让学生在听、说、读、写的实践中学习并掌握语言形式。

针对小学英语语法教学的特殊性，建议可以在语法教学中进行以下教学策略的尝试和探索。

策略一：创设语言学习和运用的情境，让学生感知语法

《英语课程标准》语言知识部分的要求是在具体的语境中理解语法的意义和用法。语言只有放在一定的情境中才能体现它的意义。《英语课程标准》还指出，鼓励学生在教师的指导下，通过体验、实践、参与、探究和合作等方式，发现语言规律，逐步掌握语言知识和技能，形成有效的学习策略，发展自主学习能力。所以教师应在教学活动中尽量创设生动活泼、贴近学生生活的有意义的情境，注重在情境中输入足量的语言，促使学生参与、体验、实践、合作与交流，把语言环境转变为真实的语言习得情境，让学生在具体的情境中感知语言的意义。因此，我们应该注意以下两点：

首先，创设的情境要尽可能真实。我们创设的情境应该是生活中可能存在的。所创设的情境只有与学生的生活经验相符合时，才能激起学生的生活体验，使他们从各自的生活背景出发，迅速投入到所创设的情境中，准确地体验和理解语言。如果所创设的情境不够真实，学生就不会有感觉，也不可能自然习得语言。

其次，创设的情境要有意义。有意义就是说情境中所发生的事或所做的事要有意义。情境中师生和生生之间的对话交流应该对彼此双方都是有意义的。比如："— Are you a student? — Yes, I am."等就是毫无意义的情境对话。

因此，教师在语法知识教学中应更关注语境的创设，对语法知识的教学要遵循"在语境中理解，在语境中认知，在语境中应用，在语境中迁移和巩固"的原则。

策略二：遵循语言习得规律，让学生领悟语法

小学生学习语言，特别是学习语法规则，可以通过两种途径，一种是隐性的途径，一种是显性的途径。所谓隐性的途径就是不直接讲规则,而是通过一些语句,通过语言实际的运用,或者通过所组织的一些活动,让学生有机会反复地接触到这些规则,在感受语言的过程中理解这些规则的意义和功能,包括语法形式。所谓显性的途径就是直截了当地把规则呈现给学生,并告诉学生这是什么规则,这个规则的结构如何,这些词型有哪些变化等。小学生学习外语,特别是学习语法规则的时候,应该以隐性方式为主,通过大量的英语实践,大量的接触、体验、理解和运用,逐步知晓这些规则。在教学中,教师应该根据学生不同的学习年段和年龄,把握好不同的"度"。小学中低年级以隐性教学为主,比如名词的单复数形式,如果学生只接触到名词后加-s 和-es 的几个单词,在归纳时教师就应只涉及这两条规则,不要拓展到 studies, knives, men, women, children 等。而到了高年级就可以根据学生的实际,给学生发现和归纳的机会,并增加显性的归纳和总结。

策略三:在交际活动中,让学生运用语法

语言的运用是语言学习中最为重要的环节,是实现语言知识向语言能力转化的关键一步,是语言学习的价值所在。我们平时的语法教学,其最终目的还是"用",即培养学生在实际交际中对语言的灵活运用。教师在教学过程中始终应该有创设机会让学生实践所学语言或语言形式的意识,使学生逐步从有意义的操练和实践过渡到真实的交际运用活动。教师可以设置一些有效的任务,实施真实的语言输出。真实的语言输出可以使学生所学语法知识得到巩固,也可以让学生体验到学习的快乐,从而激发他们进行更深层次的自主探究学习。

操练和实践活动,不能拘泥于教材上所提供的形式。教师可以根据教学的环境和学生表达的实际和需要,发挥自己的想象力和创造力,在内容和形式上进行增添和补充。此外,还要注意活动形式的多样性,注重开展两人或小组活动。同时,要注意指令清楚、目的明确、组织有效,让学生能广泛而有效地参与。

策略四:在归纳、总结中,让学生趣味学语法

归纳、总结语法规则或结构,是为了让学生形成比较明晰的概念,

也就是让他们在今后的学习和运用中对所学的新语言形式有所认识。在这个环节中,要进一步采用显性的方式让学生关注到所接触的新语言现象,如它的形式、它的意义、它的用法等。小学生年龄小,注意力的持续时间比较短,但对形象化、趣味性的东西比较感兴趣,若能抓住学生的这一心理特征进行教学,效果相当好。

例如,小学阶段讲到了数词的用法。数词分为基数词和序数词,序数词与基数词有一定的关系,但构成方法又不尽相同,如果让学生去死记硬背那么多的序数词,学生往往会感到厌烦。为了调动学生学习的积极性,也为了使这一语法项目简单化,教师可以为学生总结这样一则顺口溜:"一、二、三,特殊例,结尾各是 t, d, d; th 四加起,八少 t,九去 e, y 结尾改 ie; ve 结尾变 f, five, twelve 两兄弟;若是碰到几十几,只变个位就可以。"本来是很难掌握的内容,而通过这么一则富有节奏感、朗朗上口的顺口溜,学生很快便学会了1—100序数词的构成,可以说是事半功倍。又如在教"是"动词 am, is, are 与人称代词连用时的用法时,教师也可以这样总结:"我用 am,你用 are, is 用在他、她、它,凡是复数都用 are。"这样的处理简单易懂,较好地激发了学生的积极性,就连平时学习能力较差、不肯开口说英语的学生,也都说得津津有味,很轻松地理解并掌握了这一重要的语法项目。又如,在讲到情态动词 can 的时候,教师可以把 can 比作"照妖镜",告诉学生后面的动词碰到它就要"显"原形。这种趣味的学习方法不仅帮助学生掌握了语法知识,而且培养了学生的创新能力,有的学生还学会了自己编顺口溜,归纳、总结语言规律。

策略五:在合作探究中,让学生进行语法专项练习

儿童与同伴共同讨论问题、完成任务,也可以提高他们的认识水平。因此不同程度的学生可以在合作学习中相互取长补短、加深对问题的理解、促进学习质量的提高。小组成员只有共同承担责任,共同分享成果,才能在完成任务的过程中,为实现共同的目标而互相鼓励、互相帮助。小组成员会为了共同的目标,发挥各自的优势,取长补短,互相纠正语法表达上的错误,这对于语法基础较差的学生来说无疑帮助很大。他们可以借助同伴的力量更好地掌握和运用语法知识。例如在教授现在进行时的时候,教师事先准备好一个篮球,上课的时候教师边做拍球动作,边问学生:"What am I doing?"然后自己回答:"I am playing basketball."再把球传给另一位学生,让他拍球并同时问:"What are you doing?"学生回答:"I am playing basketball."然后继续传球,师问生答。通过一系列的尝试让学生小组讨论出现在进行时的构成"主语+be+v-ing",然后用 PPT 呈现几个动画场景,让学生描述"What are they doing?"。之后再做专项练习,要求学生用所给词的适当形式填空,并提醒他们做这一类题目时注意观察其中的特征词,做完后,学生分小组讨论得出答案:现在进行时的特征词有 now、look、listen 等,做题时须先找到这些特征词,然后根据主语确定 be 动词,再根据动词变化规则变成现在分词形式。只有学生自己发现了语法现象、归纳了语法规律,他们才会主动形成一种语言习惯,而且记忆深刻。

总之,小学阶段的语法教学,应该在语境下让学生学习,在有意义的活动中进行大量实践,再进一步运用,最后才是学生发现、感知、理解规则。

典型案例

译林版《牛津小学英语》6B
Unit 6　Planning for the weekend　A 板块

本节课的教学内容主要围绕"周末活动计划"这一话题展开,所涉及的日常交际项目有介绍、打电话、询问和建议等,其中以"What are you going to do...?"及"I'm going to..."为教学重点。

教学片段一　Warm up and free talk

Free talk

1) Enjoy a song *What are you going to do*?

2) T:Do you like vacation/summer vacation?

3) T:The song is about summer vacation. What's the name of the song?

Ss: "What are you going to do?"

T: Yes, what are the children in the song going to do?

S1: They're going to have a party.

S2: They're going to play with friends.

S3: ...

教学片段二 Presentation and practice

1. Presentation

T: Are we going to play?

Ss: ...

T: We are having an English lesson. And what are we going to learn today?

Ss: ...

T: We are going to learn Unit 6 "Planning for the weekend".

（教师领读）

T: What are we going to do in this lesson? Look at my teaching plan.

（教师呈现 plan）

T: When we talk about our plans, we can use "be going to". That is, I am going to do...

2. Practice

T: So we can use "be going to" to talk about our plans. What's my teaching plan for this lesson?

I am going to teach you the new words and sentences.

I am going to help you understand the dialogue.

I am going to help you talk about your weekend plan.

T: What are we going to do in this lesson? Please talk about your learning plan for this lesson.

S1: We are going to learn the new words and sentences.

S2: We are going to understand the dialogue.

S3: We are going to talk about our weekend plan.

3. Read and guess

T: We are going to learn Part A of Unit 6. But before that, let's play another game. Read and guess. What are they going to do?

1) Nancy sits in front of the piano. (教师呈现 concert)
2) My grandparents bought two tickets. (教师呈现 see a Beijing Opera)
3) Miss Li is asking the way to the library.
4) Miss Chang is looking for David's telephone.

教学片段三　Try to ask

T: You know they are going to see a Beijing Opera on Saturday. And they are going to a concert. What else do you want to know? Try to ask questions. First you can discuss in groups.

Ss work in groups.

T writes the questions on the blackboard.

e.g. Who is going to see the Beijing Opera?

When and where are they going to meet on Saturday?

Is there a concert in their school on Sunday morning?

Who is going to play the piano at the concert?

Are Wang Bing and Liu Tao going to play at the concert?

教学片段四　Consolidation

1. Try to say

T: After answering the phone, Gao Shan is having a QQ chat with his friend Jim.

What are they talking about? Let's look.

2. Make a plan for the weekend

3. Share your plan for the weekend

4. Check the teaching/learning plan

◆ 案例反思 ◆

将来时态是这节课的重点语法知识。在热身环节，教师通过播放歌曲《What are you going to do?》来让学生初步感知本节课的重点句型"What are you going to do...?"及"I'm going to..."；之后，再用PPT呈现了本课的教学计划(teaching plan)，引出关键词plan并顺势让学生谈谈自己的学习计划，介绍并学习使用句型be going to，为学生操练新语言搭建了语言支架和真实交流的平台。在新课导入环节，教师设计了猜谜游戏，通过游戏活动，与学生进行了真实的交流，使得学生很快就能熟练运用be going to句型，也处理了本节课的两个生词opera和concert。游戏后教师立刻揭示答案，对学生的猜测进行了反馈，保证了对话的真实性，促使学生们在真实的语境中更积极有效地开展对话。在本节课的教学中教师还对学生进行了学习方法的指导，先让学生感悟语言现象，在模仿使用中加深印象，然后从中总结将来时态的使用规则，举一反三。活动QQ chat, make a weekend plan拓展了语用平台，使学生在教师创设的语境中用将来时态进行语言的实践。最后，Plan show这个活动的目的是展示学生学习的成果，让学生进行自我评估，检测自己是否达到教学目标。

◆ **专家点评** ◆

日常教学中常常听到教师对学生说："这个语法知识我已经讲过很多遍了，你怎么还是错？现在我再讲一遍，你听好了……"可遗憾的是到下一次学生依旧照错不误。究其原因，并不是教师讲得不够多，也不是学生不能理解这些语法知识，而是教师给予的练习不充分，导致学生的语感不够强。所以，教学过程中教师要坚持从交际的角度去看待语法，把"语法的使用"这一技能教给学生，而不要把语法当作专门的知识去传授。

由此可见，教师不必在课堂上大讲语法知识，只要适时地引导学生发现规则，其余要做的就是让学生在教师创设的不同情境中反复进行语言操练和实践，促使他们逐渐形成语言运用习惯，最终牢固地掌握语法。

细节 4

如何开展话题教学

▶ 细节阐述 ◀

英语教学的重要目标是将知识目标和能力目标相结合,发展学生的语用能力,同时帮助学生认识生活和世界的多样性,在体验不同文化中保持对英语学习的兴趣,形成语言的感知能力。

现代外语教学注重语言学习的过程,讲求在语境中接触、体验和理解真实的语言,并在此基础上学习和运用语言。美国教育心理学家布鲁纳(Bruner)在他的"知识结构理论"中提出了组织最佳知识结构的适应性原则,即"学科知识结构的呈现方式必须与不同年龄学生的认知学习模式相适应"。随着课程改革的深入,小学英语教材呈现出贴近学生生活、注重语言实践的特征,选择的主题生动有趣,与生活密切相关,而且多以话题作为教学内容编排的主线。这样的编排有助于对学生综合语言运用能力的培养。教师在设计教学过程时,要以学生的认知发展水平和年龄特点为基础,设计科学、有效的教学形式。本章节我们就一起来探讨小学英语课堂教学中的话题教学。

一、话题教学的定义

话题,就是谈话的主题。话题教学是以教材某个或某块语言知识为基础,以一个单元或模块的教学内容为核心,围绕一个主题或话题展开广泛而多样的认知活动的一种教学方式。话题教学通常以教材文本为出发点,进行大量与话题相关的语料输入,通过一系列扩展、深化活动,在组织学生讨论、议论、延伸的过程中以潜移默化、逐步推进的方式帮助学生理解话题的内涵。

二、话题教学的功能

话题教学时教师创设的系列场景,使语言学习变得更为自然。学生在参与特定话题的各种活动时不但能习得新的语言知识,而且可以形成新的语言能力。在小学英语课堂中,教师要首先确立一个与小学生的生活和学习经验紧密联系并能引起他们兴趣的话题,以此为核心进行相关的听、说、读、写的训练,在此基础上还要注意培养学生的非语言能力,包括模仿能力、合作能力、逻辑思维能力、想象力等。

那么话题教学中教师如何能做到语言和非语言并举,既有能力的提升,又有智力的发展呢?

策略一:深入了解话题内涵　浅出开展课堂教学

小学英语的话题教学要根据小学生心理认知特点、兴趣和生活经验选择相应教学方式,使小学生通过学习,掌握基本语言知识、获得言语技能,达到初步运用英语进行日常简单交流的目的。像 shopping, holidays, sports, games 这些话题都非常易于激发学生的兴趣。在教学中教师也可以结合小朋友关注的流行事物创设话题,例如在学习衣物类名词的时候,可以引入当下小朋友很爱看的动画片《冰雪奇缘》作为话题,请主人公带领小朋友一起学习服装词汇,也可以请小朋友帮主人公选择适合的衣物。好的话题不仅能很好地体现语言在日常生活中的交际功能,而且更容易激发学生学习英语的兴趣,启发学生在学习中获取、处理和使用信息的意识,培养他们用英语与他人交流、解决问题的能力。

教师要根据教学内容和学生情况,设计讨论的话题,引导学生有目的地跟随主线进行学习。话题可以由一系列的问题组成,但话题不等同于问题。话题是教师清楚教学内容、明确教学目标后,经过设计提出的比较集中的问题。这些问题具有针对性和引领性,话题一提出,围绕它进行的讨论、交流能帮助全体学生快速有效地读懂、理顺文本。话题应具有趣味性,能激发学生参与课堂教学活动的兴趣。话题也应具有启发性,能引发学生思考,能帮助学生思维,能拓宽学生视野。

策略二:基于教材整合话题 解构教材创设话题

教材很大程度上反映和体现了教学大纲和课程标准的要求,但由于地域等因素,学习同一教材的学生有着程度和水平的差异,教材有时不能完全满足教学的需要。这时教师可以发挥主观能动性,对教材话题进行有益的整合、延伸,给学生提供多样而广泛的思维空间。以译林版《牛津小学英语》6A Unit 9 Shapes 的教学为例。这是一篇关于物品形状的课文。教师课前了解到学生们对常见物品形状已经有一定的掌握,课文仅仅讲述了一个包和一个风筝的形状,无法调动起学生的学习热情。因此,教师在教授课文的基础上扩充出一个"Super designer"的话题,请学生由课文中风筝和包的形状展开,用自己喜欢的形状为课本中的人物设计新的风筝和书包。这样的话题调动了学生们创作的热情,也锻炼了他们的思维能力,语言知识也在做与玩中转化为技能工具。

又如,教师可以通过自己对教材内容的解构和理解,对相关单元话题进行重组和整合,构成话题群:衣服、食品、购物三个话题是人们日常生活中最基本的话题,可以作为相邻话题,形成一个"My weekend"的话题,请同学们从衣服、食品、购物三个方面来说一说自己的周末生活。这种话题群经常被使用在几个单元结束后的复习课型上,帮助学生回顾和整合几个单元的知识。通过话题群的方式,教师也可以帮助学生了解某个话题可以从哪些方面展开讨论,进一步启发了学生的思维能力,促使语言知识在真实语境中被及时唤醒,转换为言语能力。

策略三:依托话题承载教学 借助话题引导思维

一个单元或者一节课的教学目标通常包含话题,但也不只是话题。例如,在教学译林版《牛津小学英语》4A Unit 1 I like dogs 时,除了相关动物的单词和短语,表达自己的喜恶以及询问他人的喜好等语言功能知识也是我们的单元教学目标。教师可以设计并依托"参观动物园"这个话题，介绍动物词汇，讨论自己喜欢和不喜欢的动物。教师也可以以"动物园的动物表演"这个话题为载体，带学生学习字母 g 的发音(My good little dog, go and get my big bag on the log)、朗读小诗、认识一些国家特有的动物，等等。在不同的教学内容和教学目标中设计出一个主线式话题，对整堂课或整个单元知识的学习会起到一个穿针引线的作用。

对教学内容进行话题式设计，是为了更好地调动学生学习的自主性和积极性，让学生有兴趣去自主地发现、探究、思考、解决学习中的问题，最终既帮助学生内化了语言知识，也帮助学生锻炼了思维能力。

➤•典型案例 1•◄

译林版《牛津小学英语》5A
Unit 2　A new house　A 板块

本课教学内容是介绍新家，教师从"家访"这个学生熟知的话题入手，带领学生进入到课文的情境中，最后又通过设计任务带领学生走出课文，回到学生自己的生活中。

Step 1　Warming-up

T：Do you like home visiting?（出示家访图片并询问学生是否接受老师的家访）

教师结合学校近期对学生展开的家访活动，询问学生是否喜欢老师家访，进而引入本课主题"介绍一个新家"，将学生的实际生活和教材内容结合起来并创设话题，使得不同程度的学生都可以有效地融入课堂。由于家访对学生来说是个很敏感的话题，大部分学生都有着自己对家访非常鲜明的态度。话题一经引出，就能吸引全体学生的注意力。

T：If you don't, today we'll do something differently. Be a little teacher, visit Yang Ling's house and then introduce it to our classmates.（邀请学生扮演"小老师"，介绍家访成果）

设计话题时教师应考虑学生的不同反应。有些学生害怕老师家访。这个角色扮演的环节,让学生扮演"小老师",参观课文主人公杨玲的新家并向大家介绍杨玲的新家。从学生到"小老师"的角色转换,可以充分调动学生的学习热情和新鲜感。这个环节的设计意在向学生展现本课的主要教学目标:了解杨玲的新家并掌握相关的词汇和句型。但是教师通过角色转换的环节将教学目标融入有趣的话题中,调动了全体学生的参与热情,消除了部分英语基础薄弱的学生对于学习新句型和词汇的抗拒感。

Step 2　Presentation

1. Lead in

(教师展示杨玲新家的图片,PPT 配合播放课文序言部分:"Yang Ling and her parents live in a new house now. It is near her school.")

T:Now you are "the little teacher". You will go and visit Yang Ling's new house. Where do Yang Ling and her father and her mother live?

Ss:They live in a new house.

T:Where is the new house?

Ss:It's near her school.

T:I think you are ready to be "a little teacher" to visit her home.

教师通过设定家访话题和设置家访"小老师"的角色,激发了学生的兴趣和主观能动性;通过家访前的问答,调动学生积极进入文本获取信息。

2. Look and find

1) 教师出示杨玲新家的内部结构图,请学生分组仔细观察并回答。

T:Now you have visited Yang Ling's new house. Can you answer my questions?

T:Is there a study in Yang Ling's house?(PPT 高亮书房区域并呈现单词 study)

S1：Yes, there is a study in it.

T：Are there any bedrooms in it? (PPT 高亮卧室区域并呈现单词 bedroom)

S2：Yes, there are two bedrooms in the house.

……

根据师生问答，逐步通过 PPT 展示重点句型和新单词：

— Is there... / Are there... in the house?

— There is a... / There are... in...

study   a large sitting-room   dining-room   kitchen   bathroom   bedroom

通过图片查找后的师生问答环节，引出本单元重点句型"Is there... / Are there... in...?"和"There is a... / There are... in..."并进行运用。因为学生是作为"家访小老师"在观察图片、回答教师的问题，所以无论是在获取信息还是表述上都显得非常主动。

2) T：What's on the ground/ first floor of Yang Ling's house?

教师通过提问进一步引导学生概括杨玲新家的布局：第一层有哪些房间？第二层有哪些房间？

Ss：There is a... / There are... on the... floor of Yang Ling's house.

使用重点句型归纳杨玲新家的布局，为后面的复述介绍杨玲新家做好铺垫。

3. Listen and complete

Yang Ling and her _____ live _____ a _____ _____. It is near her _____. There are three _____, two _____, a study, a _____, a dining-room and a large _____. But there _____ a garden.

学生完成练习并齐声朗读。

4. Learn and say

教师运用 PPT 向学生展示课文前半部分出现的重点句型和词组，要求学生根据课文内容和 PPT 提示，小组互练，作为"小老师"介绍杨玲新家,并请小组代表向全班进行展示。

There is a... in the house. There are some... in the house.	3 bedrooms 2 bathrooms a study a kitchen a dining-room a sitting-room

Step 3 Consolidation：Let's draw and talk

T：Now let's do a home visiting in groups and with ears.（顺着家访的话题,引导学生小组内用耳朵访问同学的家）

1）教师要求学生以小组为单位,一位同学运用PPT上呈现的本课重点句型和单词,讲述自己家的布局和陈设;其他几位同学作为"小老师",听着他(她)的陈述在纸上把这位同学家的布局和陈设简单地画一画;然后小组集体评一评谁画得最准确;最后邀请一位同学代表小组向全班介绍一下同组那位同学的家庭布局和陈设。

2）当一个小组的代表在介绍的时候,请其他组同学边听边画。比一比哪组同学听得准确、画得准确。

◆ 案例反思 ◆

新课标施行以来涌现了许多教材,它们大都以单元主题为中心进行教学内容的编排。这些教材为我们提供了许多生动、实用的话题,所以,在实际教学中教师不需要刻意地脱离教材单元主题,进行文本再构。以本案例为例,单元主题是 A new house,主要知识点是使用 there be 句型结构用英文表述屋子各个房间以及房间内物品。这是一个非常完善的话题。课堂教学时教师结合学生实际情况,以他们熟悉的家访活动作为切入点,让他们以"小老师"的身份去杨玲家家访,先看一看图片、读一读课文,然后向其他同学介绍杨玲家的布局。这样可以帮助学生更好地融入课文学习,加深理解。这种对教材话题背景的丰富和补充贴近学生的生活经验,因此有助于他们语言运用能力的提高。由于操作简单有效,这可以作为教学中常用的方法和形式。

另外,在话题教学过程中,坚持一个角色或者话题贯穿始终,可以帮助学生更好地明确学习目标、紧跟教学节奏、完善知识体系。以本案例为例,教师在进行各个房间名称表述时,采用了 TOP-DOWN 的教学模式。教师首先设计"Is there.../Are there...?"的问句向"小老师"发问,引导学生主动观察图片并自然地使用"There is/are..."句型结合房间名称回答问题。在学生初步掌握房间名称后,教师又提问"小老师":杨玲家的第一层有哪些房间呢?促使扮演"小老师"角色的学生更主动地去理顺各个房间在屋子中的布局,帮助学生在脑子中将散乱的房间名称形成一个知识网络去记忆。教师最后要求学生完成小短文并向大家介绍杨玲的新家,由于前面几个步骤的层层铺设,"小老师"们已经掌握了房间名称、理顺了屋子每一层都有哪些房间,加上自己作为家访"小老师"的身份,学生们在课堂上既有了知识的准备又有了情感的需求,复述活动就开展得热烈而有效。在进行完第二部分的教学任务以后,教师要求学生们以小组为单位,继续扮演"小老师"的角色,用耳朵听听其他同学对自己家布局的描述。

►•典型案例2•◄

冀教版《小学英语》第七册
Unit 4　Lesson 25　Christmas Is Coming!

背景介绍:

本单元讲述了一些圣诞节的传统,单元教学内容为与圣诞节相关的基本单词和句型。圣诞节是西方文化中一个十分重要的节日,在这一单元,Li Ming 与 Danny 和 Jenny 的家人共度圣诞节。Lessons 25 Christmas Is Coming! 是这一单元的第一课,为了把圣诞节更生动地呈现在学生面前,课前教师用圣诞老人、圣诞树等卡片装饰教室。课上教师借助多媒体课件将西方国家过圣诞节的视频和图片呈现给学生,营造出浓厚的节日氛围,激发学生的学习和认知兴趣。

本单元和本课话题是圣诞节的一些风俗习惯,这和学生的日常生活有一定的联系,在四年级的时候他们已经接触了一些节日,如:New Year's Day, Children's Day, Teachers' Day 等。另外,学生在日常生活中对西方节日也有一定的了解。

教学过程:

Step 1　Warming-up and revision

1. Enjoy and follow the tune:a Christmas song

2. Greetings

3. Play a game "What day is it?"

T:I have some beautiful pictures. Look! Can you guess what festival it is? (Show pictures of New Year's Day, the Spring Festival, Teachers' Day, National Day and Children's Day)

T:These are holidays. What other holidays do you know? In Canada, there is an important holiday in winter. It's on December 25th. Do you know?

教师通过圣诞节歌曲和教室布置营造节日氛围、引起学生对单元话题的联想;同时通过游戏复习学过的节日,再现旧知的同时将话题引到 holiday 上。教师在热身环节的设计,不论是歌曲还是游戏,甚至是教师语言都紧紧围绕单元主题,层层铺垫,最后顺利将学生的思维和表达引到本课主题圣诞节。

Step 2　Presentation

T:Just now we heard a Christmas song. We have Christmas lights decorated in our classroom. And we can see pictures of Father Christmas:Santa. What else can we see on Christmas Day?

Ss:(Discuss in groups)

教师利用课件或教室实物呈现本课涉及的单词:Christmas tree, Christmas lights, Santa, Christmas song 等。这个环节教师并没有简单机械地进行单词教学,而是提出话题"What else can we see on Christmas Day?",引导学生分组合作学习,进行思考、参与话题。由于现实生活中圣诞节的流行,学生对话题参与度很高,词汇的掌握程度也很好,教师在这个环节只扮演旁观者和帮助者。

Step 3　Consolidation

T：Discuss in groups and find the answers of the following questions：

1. What is Christmas?

2. Why is it special?

3. Who is Santa?

4. When is Christmas?

5. In Canada, what do they do at Christmas?

在教授完课文之后教师要求学生分小组讨论以上问题并完成短文：Christmas is a (Western) holiday. It's on (December 25th). It's special, because it has (Christmas trees, lights and Santa). Santa is (a merry man in red clothes). Children like Santa, because he (brings toys). In Canada, they invite their (family and friends) to their (house). They bring (gifts). They sing special (songs). They are happy. 任务完成较好的小组会受到表扬和奖励。这个环节由学生扮演的圣诞老人发奖,领奖的学生要和圣诞老人相互问好。

这是一个巩固课文内容的环节,但是教师通过请学生扮演圣诞老人、与圣诞老人相互问好等教学设计很好地将课文话题引入学生的真实生活,既富有趣味,又促进了学生语言运用能力的发展。

Step 4　Further reading

1) T：Do you want to know how Santa sends gifts? Now let's read a story.

教师通过课件讲述圣诞节时孩子们准备长筒袜,并在睡觉前将长筒袜放在床头,圣诞老人从烟囱钻到家中,派送礼物;通过延伸阅读,帮助学生进一步了解圣诞节的习俗。

2) T：Say the differences between Chinese festivals and Western holidays.

如:食物(dumplings, turkey)、祝福语等,使学生了解中西文化差异。

◆ **案例反思** ◆

常规教学很难使学生了解圣诞节的相关知识和背景,所以教师选择了用多媒体课件来解决这个问题,通过呈现生动活泼的动画、视频、图片,把学生的积极性充分调动起来,给学生以乐趣,更给学生以启迪,让他们整体感知圣诞节的节日氛围,拓展了他们的文化视野。教师还为学生创设了自主学习情境,提高了教学效率。通过本课的实际教学,教师比较成功地完成了教学任务,达成了教学目标。

◆ **专家点评** ◆

概括来看,目前小学英语教材中出现的话题主要有以下两类:① 与日常生活密切相关的,如:My family, Hobbies, School subjects 等。② 与地域文化密切结合的,如:Halloween, At Christmas, Chinese New Year 等。针对第一类话题,教师要充分考虑学生的生活经验和认知水平,围绕课文主题用接近学生生活实际的话题导入,激起他们学习语言的热情。在第一个案例中教师以学生熟悉的话题"家访"为切入点,让学生扮演一位到杨玲家中家访的"小老师",并且布置了解杨玲新家的任务,这种把生活话题和课文话题相结合的教学设计可以促使学生在熟悉的场景中表达自己的思想,变客观地学习为主观地运用。对于第二类话题,如果教师觉察到学生对这些背景知识比较陌生的话,教学前就有必要借助图片、多媒体等辅助手段对相关话题进行补充和说明,只有背景知识的问题解决了,学生的学习才会更加顺畅。如第二个案例中的圣诞歌曲,它起到了广而告之的效果,促使学生很快将注意力投向将要学习的话题;随后的图片、课件和实物则起到了营造氛围、推进教学的作用。有时,出于丰富语境的考虑,教师可以暂时抛开课文的主题,创造性地引入一个话题来继续单元内容的学习,新话题会让学生颇感新鲜,起到很好的效果。不过,要避免离题过远的情况发生,毕竟,话题还是得有助于语言的学习!

细节 5

如何开展句型教学

▶ 细节阐述 ◀

句型也叫句式。顾名思义,句型就是从口语和书面语的无数实际句子中概括出来的句子模型或模式。句型是有代表性的、常用的。句型的数量是有限的,而以句型为依据所衍化或生成的句子数量是无限的。

在教学中,句型是独立的。它和语法规则、例句有关系,但又不是一回事。语法规则是知识性的,语法例句是为描述语法规则服务的;句型是模式性的,是为使用语言进行交际服务的。语法规则首先要求认识,句型首先要求模仿。所以在小学英语教学中不能把句型材料完全当成语法材料对待。那样,学生识辨和组织句子的基本功就可能不过硬,以句子为单位进行听、说、读、写的技能就会受到影响。句型操练(pattern drill)是一种综合性的操练,它对于提高使用英语的综合性,减少分析性,从而增强学生的直接理解和表达的能力,有明显的积极作用。

一、句型教学的作用

1. 句型教学起到化繁为简的作用

将句型作为一个支撑点,把语法规则、词汇搭配等包罗其中,将语言知识的学习融于句型中,会让学生感到语言学习不是单调、乏味的。如教授教材中涉及的进行时态、将来时态以及陈述句、疑问句等知识时,教师如果花大量的时间来谈论这些时态的结构、语序,把语法当作一个领域的知识去传授,不仅费时,而且效果不好,这时,不如给学生创造机会,让他们在练习中感悟、使用。

2. 句型教学能促进学生语言实践能力的提高

句型教学注重让学生模仿,所以,句型教学时教师不需要花很多时间给学生讲解语言知识,只需要做到把时间尽可能多地留给学生,为学生提供语言实践的平台,让他们在模仿、练习的过程中逐渐感悟并内化。

但是,需要指出的是,尽管句型教学离不开机械的操练,教师在设计活动时要做到把句型置于有意义的情境中练习。句型教学要扎根在语言情境的土壤中。句型呈现在学生面前的是句子的骨架,只有赋予其血和肉时,它们才有生命,在学生头脑中"存活率"才高。因此教师在教某个句型时,一定要结合出现该句型的生活场景。学生对该句型所依附的情境越熟悉,对该句型的理解就越深入,记忆也越牢固,使用的时候也会更加得心应手。在此基础上教师再把该句型骨架提取出来进行套用和扩展,学习效果会更好。

二、句型操练的策略

策略一:句型操练要关注语意

句型操练从根本上说就是模仿和套用,教师可以让学生根据教师提供的基本句型框架和结构反复进行练习,达到熟悉句型的结构、语序和搭配的目的,最终做到能脱口而出。但同时,句型学习的目的是产出能交际的语言,学生要通过句型的学习获得在日常交际场合中得体地使用语言的能力,因此,句型教学时教师要做到以表意为重,既关注语言的形式,又关注语言的意义和用法。例如:在教授句型 Put on…前,教师可以借助图片进行介绍:"Look at the sun! It's very hot today. So I put on a hat. I put on glasses. I put on a T-shirt…"这样,学生就能了解 put on 这个句型是如何在日常生活场景中发挥作用、表达意义的。

有时,出于强调语言形式的考虑,教师会采用机械的操练形式,但是,即使是这样的情况,也应尽可能避免完全脱离意义的教学。我们以This is...的句型教学为例。教师请学生用此句型来向伙伴们展示自己的文具。

首先是老师示范。

T:This is my book.

然后,学生轮流练习。

S1:This is my ruler.

S2:This is my school bag.

S3:This is my pencil.

S4:This is my rubber.

同时,看图说话也可以作为句型操练的一种形式。例如,学习There be 句型时,可以出示下面的图片让学生通过描述图片来练习此句型结构。

T:What is in the room?

S1:There is a table in the middle of the room.

S2:There are three umbrellas beside the window.

S3:There are some cars under the table.

S4:There is a bear on the chair.

策略二:句型操练要在情境中感知与练习

就小学生的特点来看,他们听觉灵敏,善于模仿又富有想象力,对直观形象的内容接受能力较强,但同时他们活泼好动,有意注意的时间不长。因此,在句型教学中,如果教师能做到始终将其与语言情境结合,让学生在真实的交流中感知、学习语言,就能收到意想不到的效果。"感知"主要是教师通过设计具有典型性的语言使用场景向学生进行语言的输入,让学生能"感受与了解",由于这种输入是置于情境中的,对学生而言理解起来就更为容易。情境的创设可以运用实物、体态语、电教、表演等多种活动和手段。

1. 借助实物

在小学英语课堂上用实物创设情境进行句型操练可以起到非常好的效果,这是因为相对于图片而言,实物既看得见又摸得着,它拉近了学生和课堂的距离,更能激起学生的兴趣。

以译林版《牛津小学英语》1B　Unit 4　My nice ruler 中句型 This is.../That is...的教学为例:

Step 1　Lead-in

(教师分别出示实物:an apple, a banana, a toy cat and a toy dog)

T:What's this?

Ss:This is an apple/a banana/a cat/a dog.

(教师在活动前用实物名字为各小组命名)

T:"Apple" has a letter "a". So today I give an apple to Group A and you will be the "apple group". And a banana for Group B. You will be the "banana group" today. And Group C, you are the "cat group". The "dog group" will be Group D.

Step 2　Three tasks

T:And you should help me to finish three tasks. Are you ready?

Ss:Yes. We are ready.

T:Let's go to the first room. Look! That's a note. What does it say?

T:(把几样水果分别放在布袋中,让学生摸一摸,然后猜一猜)

Is this an apple?

Is this a banana?

Is this a peach?

Is this a pear?

Ss：Yes. This is an apple.

This is a banana.

This is a peach.

This is a pear.

T：(把实物分别装在不同的袋子里，让学生根据袋子里实物的轮廓猜测)

Is that an apple?

Is that a banana?

Is that a peach?

Is that a pear?

Ss：(教师指导学生说) Yes. That is an apple.

That is a banana.

That is a peach.

That is a pear.

T：(用 this 和 that 来描述近距离和远距离的实物，引导学生边听边想)

This is an apple and that is an apple.

This is a banana and that is a banana.

This is a cat and that is a cat.

This is a dog and that is a dog.

Now can you tell the difference between "this" and "that"?

Ss：…

2. 利用图片和简笔画

有时句型学习需要依托于特定的生活场景，教师如果使用语言来描绘这些场景，既浪费时间又难以让学生产生现场感，但是，图片则能立刻把学生带入教师创设的情境中，让学生有"身临其境"的感觉。例如在教学 I can see... on/in/under... 这个句型时，教师可以给学生呈现一幅动物园的挂图,里面有各种各样的动物分布在动物园的各个角落,有远有近,有清晰的有模糊的,这时教师就可以指导学生边看图边练习句型。

相比现成的图片而言,简笔画有即时生成的特点,教师可以根据课堂上学生的反馈情况及时进行教学调整,而且将简笔画与图片交叉使用,能避免学生产生审美疲劳。例如,译林版《英语》四年级上册 Unit 5 Our new home 教学片段(本课主要学习各房间的英语表达及句型"— Where's the...? — It's.../— Where are the...? — They're...")中,教师先在黑板上画一只猫,然后问:"Look! Where's the cat?"接着在猫的下面画一个房顶,引导学生说:"Oh! It's on the house."接着,教师在房子里画出若干个房间,边画便问:"What room is it?"最后分别在每个房间添加不同的物品,问:"Where is the...?/Where are the...?"图片就在师生的互动中不断变化,极富趣味性。

3. 利用表情和体态语

在小学英语的教学过程当中,教师的每一个表情、动作都能给学生提供很大的想象空间。如在学习"Apples are sweet. Grapes are sour..."时,教师可以尝试用夸张的表情或体态语来演示:吃一口苹果,表示很开心的样子;吃一口葡萄,捂着脸,表示很酸的样子。学生则通过观察教师的表情和体态语来猜测句子的意思。接着教师还可以要求学生参与表演,用体态语"说出"句子,而其他同学则根据他(她)的表演用所学的句子进行描述。

策略三:句型操练要采用多样的形式

句型操练相对机械化,时间久了,学生未免觉得枯燥乏味,教师可以设计一些趣味性强的活动,调动学生参与的积极性。

1. 听读

教师可以通过转换听读方式带领学生朗读。如果教师大声读,学生则小声读;如果教师语速慢,学生则语速快。此方法通过反复刺激小学生的听觉神经,达到使其掌握句型的目的。

2. 诵读歌谣

歌谣往往节奏优美，朗朗上口，深受学生们的喜爱。教师可以通过自编歌谣的方式来进行句型巩固。如：

Running, running, I am running.

Singing, singing, he is singing.

Dancing, dancing, she is dancing.

Reading, reading, who is reading?

Reading, reading, you are reading!

3. 学唱歌曲

通过歌曲学习句型能使学生在轻松、愉快的气氛中掌握句型。许多歌曲旋律优美动听，学生耳熟能详。随着歌曲的旋律，学生们唱出所学句型，不但巩固了句型，而且使学生对学习英语产生美感。

4. 仿写练习

小学中高年级的句型教学往往不仅要求学生会说，还对他们提出了书写的要求，对此，教师可以在让学生口头流利表达的基础上，把句型的练习再落实到笔头，通过让学生按照例句仿写的方法，促使学生关注语言表达的准确性。

➤·典型案例 1·◄

译林版《英语》四年级下册 Unit 3 My Day 活动板块

本课主要通过对 I... at... 句型的复习和巩固使学生学会用第一人称 I 来描述一天的生活。

Step One 学习歌曲《When do you get up?》

理解歌曲：

T：We have known something about Mike's day. Do you want to know about his friend Peter's day? Let's enjoy a new song *When do you get up?*

歌曲内容如下：

When do you get up, Peter, hei-lo-li, every day?

When do you go to school, hei-lo-li, every day?

I get up at six thirty, hei-lo-li, every day.

I go to school at seven thirty, hei-lo-li, every day.

之后,师生有如下问答:

T: Now who can tell us when Peter gets up every day?

S1: At six thirty.

T: And when does Peter go to school every day?

S2: At seven thirty.

Step Two   创编歌曲

T: From this song, we know what Peter does in the morning. But what else does he do in his day?（指向表格）Look at the form. Now, please try to change the time in the song and then sing your new song in your group.

get up go to school	6:30 7:30	in the morning
_____	_____	in the afternoon
_____	_____	in the evening
_____	_____	at night

Peter's Day

When do you _____, Peter, hei-lo-li, every day?

When do you _____, hei-lo-li, every day?

I _____ at _____, hei-lo-li, every day.

I _____ at _____, hei-lo-li, every day.

教师要求学生四人小组合作,先将 Peter 的作息表补充完整,然后组内成员以自由选择展示的方式,将补充后的内容用原来的旋律演唱出来。

◆ 案例反思 ◆

教材中的歌曲板块通常是比较受学生欢迎的,在演唱的时候由于旋律动听,即使歌词多遍重复,学生也不会感到厌烦。所以这节课句型复习时教师就设计了听、唱歌曲与回答问题相结合的活动,把歌曲资源作为练习句型的素材,提高了学生学习英语的积极性。而且创编歌曲的活动充满了趣味性和挑战性,还拓展了学生语言实践与运用的空间。在自编歌词的过程中学生的创新思维也得到了培养。

►•典型案例2•◄

译林版《牛津小学英语》2A Unit 10 Put on your coat 课文和句型的教学

本单元的课文和句型主要围绕"Put on your.../Take off your..."展开,为了增强学生的语境意识,使其能结合语境准确地解读词汇和语句的意义,教师采用了简笔画创设情境的方法。

T：Tell the story of the snowman.

Winter comes, it's very cold and snows all the time. But Mike and his friends are singing and dancing happily. Look! Here is the snowman. Snowman："Cold, cold, I'm so cold."

T：Boys and girls, can you help the snowman?

S1：Put on your hat.

S2：Put on your gloves.

S3：Put on your scarf.

S4：Put on your sweater.

Snowman：Thank you.

(教师用简笔画分别给雪人戴上帽子、手套、围巾,穿上毛衣……)

T：The snowman feels so warm. Now he's singing and dancing with the children.

But the sun comes out. Snowman："Hot, hot, I'm so hot."

T：Boys and girls, can you help the snowman?
S5：Take off your hat.
S6：Take off your gloves.
S7：Take off your scarf.
S8：Take off your sweater.
Snowman：Thank you.

（教师把雪人的帽子、手套、围巾、毛衣一样样擦去）

◆ 案例反思 ◆

这个教学片段中教师首先利用英语小故事为枯燥的句型教学创设出了真实的情境。学生在听故事的过程中很容易自己也置身其中，感受到雪人的寒冷，这时，"Put on your gloves."，"Put on your scarf."，"Put on your sweater…"这些句子就不再是学生口中蹦出的毫无意义的符号，而是成为他们自己真实想法的流露与表达。接着教师又借助简笔画即时生成的特点，创设了太阳出来、雪人感到热了的情境，引导学生使用句型"Take off your gloves."，"Take off your scarf."，"Take off your sweater…"，使句型练习从机械操练走向了意义操练。

◆ 专家点评 ◆

通常，说话人是根据自己所处的情境和想表达的意思来决定使用什么样的句型的，所以，教学时教师要解决好句型的三个相关问题：形式、意义和用法。从上面的两个案例来看，教师在进行句型教学时都尽量做到了通过情境的创设让学生进一步体验句型的表意功能：案例一从教师的导入"Do you want to know about his friend Peter's day? Let's enjoy a new song *When do you get up*?"到就歌曲中 Peter 的一天进行讨论并完成任务，一系列的活动都依托于情境，属于有意义的操练活动。当教师引导学生关注语言的形式时，采用了借助原有歌曲旋律自编歌词的方法，由于歌词中的句子基本结构相似，学生在编写、演唱的同时就强化了对句型结构的印象。不过，这个案例中的教师要真正检查学生能否学以致用，还需要把情境重新切回到学生的日常生活，设计真实的或接近真实生活的任务,例如教师可以通过在课堂上设计"健康生活大讨论"的活动,安排学生们谈一谈自己的作息时间,然后再进行讨论,从中选出比较健康的生活方式,这样,语言的学习就和学生的实际生活相联系起来,让学生感觉他们说的是自己的语言,表达的是自己的想法。比较而言,第二个案例中的活动更能吸引学生,一方面,教师选择了雪人这个形象,让学生很有新鲜感;另一方面,教师运用简笔画即时回应了学生的指令:给雪人增减衣物。这样,学生既感受到交流的乐趣,又拥有了学习的成就感!

细节 6

如何培养学生听的能力

> ❧ 细节阐述 ❧

美国新生儿专家佛尼所进行的研究指出:正常的胎儿在母亲子宫里的时候,听力就开始发展了。孩子呱呱坠地之后,更是时时刻刻在自觉不自觉地接受着来自各方面的听觉刺激,他们用自己的听力来感知世界,感知来自世界的不同信息。这些有声刺激就为孩子日后的语言学习和发展奠定了至关重要的基础。此外,对孩子语言学习经历的关注让我们发现:孩子们从牙牙学语,到说一些简单的句子,再到越说越流利、越说越清楚,在这个过程中,父母并未刻意对小孩子进行语言的训练,并未教过孩子们语法,更没有让他们查过字典,他们好像天生就会说话了。其中很大一部分原因就在于:孩子们是在父母或者周围人说话的氛围中长大的。他们几乎每时每刻都在"聆听着"不同的声音,自觉或者不自觉地将储存在脑海中的"记忆碎片"进行内化和整合,最终以他们自己的形式"表达"出来。孩子们就是在这样一个不断"吸收""内化""产出""纠正"的过程中学会了运用语言、输出语言。所以,听力是口语突破的第一个重要环节。

《英语课程标准》指出:"语言技能是语言运用能力的重要组成部分,主要包括听、说、读、写等方面的技能以及这些技能的综合运用。听和读是理解的技能,说和写是表达的技能。它们在语言学习和交际中相辅相成、相互促进。"在交际的过程中,交际的参与者首先要听懂对方说的是什么。由此可见,听的能力对于外语学习者来说,不仅是一种目的,更是一种学习手段。因此小学英语教学在很大程度上都采用了"听说领先"的教学模式。

《英语课程标准》中对于小学阶段学生应当达到的听的能力也有明确的规定:

"一级:

1. 能根据听到的词句识别或指认图片或实物。
2. 能听懂课堂简短的指令并做出相应的反应。
3. 能根据指令做事情,如指图片、涂颜色、画图、做动作等。
4. 能在图片和动作的提示下听懂简单的小故事并做出适当的反应。

二级:

1. 能借助图片、图像、手势听懂简单的话语或录音材料。
2. 能听懂简单的配图小故事。
3. 能听懂课堂活动中简单的提问。
4. 能听懂常用指令和要求并做出适当的反应。"

对照《英语课程标准》中小学阶段英语听力能力的培养目标,教师在小学英语的教学过程中应该着重培养学生的英语感知能力,运用听力策略的能力,课堂交流过程中的倾听能力,并帮助他们养成良好的听力习惯。对此,课堂教学时教师可以从以下几方面入手:

策略一:发挥学生听的主动性

教师必须把学生作为课堂教学的主角,让他们的主观能动性在课堂中得到最充分发挥。教师在设计课堂教学内容或者设计听力练习的形式时应当最大限度地激起和保护学生的学习兴趣。小学英语听力的培养应当注意视听结合,教师可以利用实物、图片、简笔画、教师的动作或教师的面部表情等来创设情境,让学生通过耳朵听结合眼睛的观察和大脑的思维进行理解。这样,学生在跟不上所听内容时,也能够通过猜测对所听内容有大致的了解,不至于完全听不懂而失去听力学习的兴趣。

策略二：重视听力技能的形成

在听力教学的过程中，教师应该将其分为听前—听中—听后三个阶段，各个阶段重点解决的问题有所不同，各有侧重，环环相扣，共同促进听力任务的达成。听力是听和理解能力的总和。没有一定的语言知识基础，学生要听懂是十分困难的。因此，在听前阶段，教师应当通过一定的语言渗透、知识讲解或者讨论等导入活动，激活与话题有关的背景知识，从而引导学生对听力话题进行猜测和联想。教师还可以提出听力的任务，让学生有目的地进行听力练习。听力活动开展的过程中（听中阶段），教师应当培养学生掌握一定的听力技巧，如善于捕捉重要信息、能够找出关键词；能够从所给的文字材料中找出背景线索；善于利用听力笔记，归纳问题答案等。在听力内容完成之后（听后阶段），教师还可以利用听力材料中所获取的信息，进行一些"输出性"的口头或者笔头活动。

策略三：注重倾听习惯的养成

小学英语听力教学是贯穿每节课教学过程的始终的。在小学英语课堂中，学生的听、说活动占据了大部分时间。这实际上也是对学生听的内容的无形渗透、对听的能力的潜在培养。然而，教师往往发现，学生更多关注自己的表达，不太关注同学的发言及教师与他人的交流。在这种情形下，大量语言"输入"的流失就显得非常可惜了。经过深层次的思考，我们就会找到问题的根源：学生之所以不注重倾听，是因为缺乏英语语言的环境，学生对于纯英语的输入还不能够完全接受和理解。因此，教师在教学过程中要充分利用课堂为学生创造一个听英语、学英语的环境。教师应当坚持尽可能多地使用英语，包括课前问候语、课堂用语、评价、布置作业等都尽可能说英语。

只要教师坚持每堂课都尽量多使用英语，经过长时间反复听、经常练，学生就会逐渐适应英语教学的课堂氛围，师生配合也会越来越默契。长此以往，不仅教师能够提高自己的口语表达能力，学生也能够逐步养成听英语并用英语思维的习惯、不断提高听的能力，收到教学相长的良好效果。

策略四：区分精听和泛听

要培养学生听英语的学习习惯，教师首先要了解听力的种类。听力大致可以分为三种：泛听、精听和有选择地听。

所谓泛听，就是大致了解所听内容的相关信息。比如，所听内容的种类、大致结构、参与者、参与的不同时间以及地点等，泛听的目的在于创造英语学习的氛围，扩大学生听力的接触面，使学生的英语学习更加贴近生活，不拘泥于课本；精听一般都是以泛听为前提的，即通过泛听先确认所需要精听的信息出现在什么位置，然后再注意倾听确切的内容；当学生对所听内容的某一部分感兴趣或对教师某一部分有听力要求时，学生就会专心地听这一部分，这就是有选择地听。

▶·典型案例 1·◀

译林版《英语》四年级上册
Unit 5　Our new home　Story time

本单元整体教学主要围绕 Su Hai 和 Su Yang 搬到新家后的活动展开。

Step 1　Free talk

Activity 1：Play a word game

T：Hello, boys and girls. I'm your new teacher today. My name is Candy. I like playing games. Do you like playing games?

Ss：Yes, we do.

T：Good. Let's play a word game now. Let us talk about colours first. You may count numbers one, two. If you should count three, please speak out one colour instead. The group which speak out eight colours will be the winner. Now, please go in groups!

Ss: One, two, red. One, two, yellow…

T: Great! You know colours very well. Let us talk about animals this time. Are you ready?

Ss: Ready.

T: Let's go!

Ss: One, two, cat. One, two, dog…

(设计意图:通过玩单词游戏,不仅舒缓了学生紧张的情绪,也为下一步话题的谈论做好了铺垫)

Activity 2: Make a guess

T: OK. You know many colours and animals. Do you know what my favourite colour is? If you are not sure about something you can ask some questions. You can ask: "Is it…?"/"Do you…?"

S1: Is it yellow?

T: No, it isn't.

S2: Do you like blue?

T: Sorry, I don't.

S3: Is it white?

T: You are right. I like white. What's my favourite animal?

S4: Do you like monkeys?

T: No, I don't.

S5: Do you like pandas?

T: They are lovely but they aren't my favourite.

S6: Do you like cats?

T: You are clever. I like cats. So I have a white cat.

(设计意图:通过引入一张手绘的猫的卡片吸引学生的注意,并且引出课文单词和句型的教学)

Step 2 Presentation and practice

T: Look! My white cat is very naughty. Where's my white cat now?

Ss: It's on the house.

T: Yes, it's on the chimney of my house. (教师在黑板上简笔画出一所房子)

Please read after me: Where's...? It's...

Ss: Where's...? It's...

T: Look at my house!

Ss: It's big/nice/beautiful!

T: Thank you. Would you like to go in?

Ss: Yes.

T: Let's go. How many rooms are there in my house?

Ss: Four.

T: (教师拿出一张床的简笔画卡片) What's this?

Ss: It's a bed.

T: Yes. And my bed is in this room. What room is it?

Ss: It's a bedroom.

T: Yes, it's a bedroom. There's a bed in the bedroom. We can sleep in the bedroom. (教师拿出一张冰箱的简笔画卡片) What's this?

S3: It's a fridge.

T: Yes, I have many ice creams in it. What room is it?

Ss: It's a kitchen.

T: Great. It's a kitchen. Look, I have a sofa and a TV. I can sit on the sofa and watch TV in this room. What room is it?

Ss: It's a living room.

T: Yes, you are right. And I like having a bath. This is a bathtub. What room is this?

Ss: It's a bathroom.

T: Now please read these words after the tape. Bedroom, bathroom, living room, kitchen.

Ss: (Read the words) Bedroom, bathroom, living room, kitchen.

（教师将单词卡片贴在简笔画相应的房间上，便于开展接下来的活动）

（设计意图：通过房间里的标志性物品，让学生弄清楚各个房间的功能）

T：Where's my white cat？（教师故意将白猫从烟囱上拿下，放在了厨房的卡片上）

Ss：It's in the kitchen.

T：Meow, a black cat comes. Where's my black cat?

Ss：It's in the kitchen.

T：So where are my cats?

Ss：They are in the kitchen.

T：Read after me：Where are...? They are...

（设计意图：通过引入另外一只猫，引出复数句型的表达）

T：The cats are very happy. They want to play hide-and-seek with you. Look! Where's the white cat? （教师将白猫卡片置于房间卡片的后面，让学生猜测）

S1：Is it in the bathroom?

T：No, it isn't.

S2：Is it in the living room?

T：Yes, you're right. Please come to the blackboard and help the cats to hide. Then make other students guess.

S2：Where's the white cat?

S3：Is it in the bedroom?

S2：Yes, you are right.

S3：Where are the cats?

S4：Are they in the living room?

S3：No, they aren't.

S5：Are they in the bathroom?

S3：Yes, you are right.

（设计意图：让学生动手隐藏猫的卡片，并对其他学生提问，不仅复

习了句型,也帮助学生养成倾听的习惯)

T：Do you know why my cats are so happy?（教师边问边对简笔画的房子进行装饰）

S6：Your house is nice.

T：Thank you. But that's not the answer.

S7：You have a party in your house.

T：You are so clever. I want to have a party in my house. Would you like to join in?

Ss：Yes, we'd love to.

T：I also want to invite my friends Su Hai and Su Yang. Let's go to their new home.（教师简笔画一所大房子,里面有五个房间）

Look! This is Su Hai and Su Yang's new house.

Ss：It's big/nice/beautiful!

T：Let's knock at the door.

C：Welcome to our new home.（电脑录制出苏海和苏阳的声音）

T：Today, we will learn Unit 5 "Our new home".（揭示课题）

C：Please come in.

This is our bedroom.

This is our parents' bedroom.

This is our living room.

This is our kitchen.

（通过人机对话,创设真实环境,让学生切实体会到英语在日常生活中的用途）

T：Would you like to go to my party, Su Hai and Su Yang?

C：Yes, we'd love to.

T：I think they need some things. What do they need? Please listen to the tape.

Task 1：Listen to the text and try to find what they need

Ss do Exercise 1.

（设计意图：让学生初听课文,为学生设置一定的任务,让学生学会

找出听力内容的关键词,引导学生有重点、有选择地听)

T: Now, let's check the answers. (教师在黑板上贴上五种物品供学生选择)

Ss: They need a bag, some skirts and a white cap.

T: Yes, you are right. Now let's try to find where they are.

Task 2: Listen to the text again and try to find where the things are

Ss do Exercise 2.

(设计意图:让学生再听课文,为学生设置更难的任务,让学生在听出关键单词的基础上听出关键的介词短语,并将物品与所在位置的图片进行连线。学生完成了语音输入,语音筛选,音、义、图结合的过程)

T: Now, let's check the answers. I will choose one student to come to the blackboard and tell us the answers. You may ask him.

Ss: Where's the bag?

S8: It's in the bedroom.

Ss: Where are the skirts?

S8: They are in the living room, on the sofa.

Ss: Where's the white cap?

S8: It's in the kitchen.

(设计意图:请一位同学与全班同学通过问答形式将图片贴在相应的房间里,刺激了学生英语学习的兴趣,也对句型再次进行了操练)

T: Now, let's watch and read after the tape.

Task 3: Watch and read

Ss watch and read the story.

T: Now, please read in groups.

Task 4: Read in groups

Ss read in groups.

(设计意图:小组朗读,可以增进同学之间的感情,也有助于进行同学互助学习,是一种很好的合作学习方式)

T: Now, let's recite the story according to the pictures and the words I gave you.

Task 5: Recite the story

Group 1 recite the story one by one.

Group 2 recite the story together.

(设计意图：不同的复习方式增加了趣味性，为枯燥的课堂增添了一些生机）

Step 3　Consolidation

T：OK. You help Su Hai and Su Yang find their things. Would you like to go with us?

C：Sure. My cousin Jack wants to go too. But he can't find his clothes. Would you like to help him?（电脑录制并播放苏海和苏阳的声音，形成人机对话）

Ss：Yes.

T：Now, let's listen to a song and please put the pictures in your groups in order.

Task 6: Listen and order

Ss listen and order the pictures in groups.

(设计意图：小组成员每人分得两到三张图文结合的图片，根据所听的歌曲内容将其排序，最后形成一本完整的图画书。本次活动是对学生听力的综合训练，学生通过聆听歌曲、研读文本，完成了语音输入、文本理解、音义配对的过程，最后通过小组合作，共同完成任务）

T：Look! This is my picture book. Please read after me and check your answers.

Where's my T-shirt?

(It's in the drawer.)

Where's my shirt?

(It's on the shelf.)

...

Ss read after the teacher.

T：You have your own picture books. I know there are some new words in the picture books. You can look them up in the dictionary. And you are good helpers. Jack can go with us. So after class, you can go to my house and have a party, OK?

Ss: OK.

(设计意图：学生通过自己的努力，小组合作共同完成了一本图画书，这不仅可以为学生的英语学习提供更多的资源，开拓他们的视野，而且提升了学生英语学习的成就感)

◆ 案例反思 ◆

课堂的导入部分，教师以简笔画的形式结合卡通图片进行了语言的渗透和单词、句型的教学。这种活泼、自然的教学手段打破了传统PPT以图片吸引学生的特点，使学生更加关注教师的口语表达。在教师形象化的语言及图片和简笔画的辅助下，学生的听力得到了训练，倾听习惯得到了培养。

在主要教学内容的教授过程中，教师设置了听选、听后连线、看读、组内朗读、背诵这五个层层递进、环环相扣的教学环节，引导学生发展从听关键词到听关键短语，再到图义结合的能力。整个教学过程流畅，衔接紧密，设置的任务都遵循"最近发展区"原则，学生持续保持学习的兴趣，学习效果较好。

在复习巩固环节，教师仍然采用"以听促学"的教学方法，让学生通过聆听一首英文歌曲完成小组合作对图片进行排序的任务。完成后，教师引导学生认真阅读图画书，以大量阅读巩固所学句型，并且在课后对不认识的单词通过查阅字典等方式进行学习，将新知识的学习内化到已有的知识体系中，更将听力学习的内容延伸到了课外。这样的听力学习是有效的，是能够激起学生持续的学习兴趣的。

▶• 典型案例2 •◀

"On the farm" 话题教学

教师精心设计边听边演、边听边选择、判断情况真伪、边听边说等几个层次的多种教学活动，让学生分辨、认读农场动物名称 horse, cow, sheep, chicken, pig, duck 的单复数及其在句型 There's.../ There are... 中的运用；同时，通过与人合作、积极参与，体验学习的乐趣和成就感。

Step 1 Warming-up

1) Ss say the names of the animals they know and imitate their sounds or actions.

2) Talk about the objects in the classroom, using the sentence patterns "There's..." or "There are..."

3) Listen to a new song *Old McDonald's farm*.

（在 Warming-up 这一环节里，孩子们说到了熟悉的 cat, dog, monkey, mouse, bird 等动物名称，饶有兴趣地模仿了这些动物的叫声和动作；谈到了教室物品的存在，如：There's a computer. There's a TV. There are six fans. There are green curtains. There are thirty five yellow and white chairs. 孩子们通过自己说说、演演、实际运用语言，为新的学习过程做了热身准备。歌曲《Old McDonald's farm》能让学生一开始就感受到课文话题，并引起注意从而产生兴趣）

Step 2 Presentation activities

Ss look at the picture and listen to the record and talk about the subject："On the farm".

（在这一环节中，倾听是主要任务。学生可以集中注意力听，形成深刻的印象，这是形成准确发音和良好语感的基础）

1) Listen attentively without looking at the words.

静听发音。用图片逐一介绍这些动物，教师走近学生，清晰地重复发音，在英语薄弱或者胆小的孩子面前多停留，多鼓励。学生静听，回忆并模仿老师的发音。

2) Connect the sounds and the words.

音形结合。将词贴在黑板上，标上序号，教师每读出一个单词，学生根据教师的发音及语音规律，找出所听到的词。

3) Listen and compare the sounds of words ending.

听音，猜测，对比复数名词词尾发音。

4) (Books closed) Listen to the tape of the text twice. Ss recall what they've heard and answer the questions:"How many ducks are there? How many sheep are there?" Then repeat after the tape.

听课文材料回答。

Step 3　Practice activities

Level 1：Controlled practice

1) What can you hear?

（播放 PPT 上单个动物的声音，快速让所有学生说出自己能听到的声音后，再显示文字、图片，进行对照和检查）

2) Play the game of "Simon says".

（听指令做出恰当的反应）

3) What's on the farm?

（看图片、听描述、做判断，用句型 There are... 和 There is... 描述农场动物）

Level 2：Free practice

……

（本案例选自《小学英语教学活动设计案例精选》）

◆ 案例反思 ◆

　　本案例取材的背景在农场。虽然大多数学生对农场的情景并不熟悉，但是对动物的话题却十分感兴趣。其主要教学内容是动物的名称及其单复数在 There be 句型中的运用。教师通过设计一系列的优质教学活动，将教学内容变得趣味横生。它打破了传统以听力教学为主的"聆听—做题—检测"的枯燥的教学模式，让学生边听边演、边听边说，在轻松愉快的情景中进行了高效的学习。

◆ 专家点评 ◆

　　斯蒂芬·克拉申（Stephen Krashen）关于语言的输入说认为：语言学习有必要让学习者理解略微高于其现有语言水平的语言项目，学习者可以通过情境线索来理解那些语言，简单来说就是要给学习者提供

"可理解性的语言输入"。而"听"被认为是可理解性的语言输入的主要来源之一。综观日常教学中各种听的活动和任务，其中的绝大多数是要达到两个目的：为了听力理解和为了习得。如果是为了检测学生的理解程度，那就需要教师根据所听的材料先划分出表层信息和深层信息，并据此设计不同形式的任务，如：Listen and number, Listen and match, Listen and choose, Listen and answer, 等等。需要注意的是，考虑到班级中不同水平和层次的学生，教师还得设计不同层次的任务，以便让听懂却说不出来或者听懂却写不出来的学生同样有参与的机会。此外，正如教师在案例中陈述的那样，为了帮助学生提高听的实效，教师要帮助学生养成良好的倾听习惯，并且在完成各种任务的同时尝试运用听的策略：听前预测、听时推测与记录、听后归纳总结。除了听力理解，语言习得是课堂设计听的活动的又一目的。想要促使学生积极主动地聆听，教师要尽量挑选那些略微高于学生现有语言水平的听力材料，因为根据经验法则，大脑处理低难度的内容时需要的时间最少，这意味着在这种情况下学习者很可能会忽略对英语语言信息的处理。但是，难度过大的语言也容易让学生由于听不懂而放弃，达不到语言习得的目的。

细节 7
如何培养学生说的能力

➤• 细节阐述 •◄

心理语言学家认为,外语学习和母语习得有很多共同之处,都应先从口语即从说开始。另有研究表明,听说占人类语言交际活动的75%。当前小学英语教学中对"说"的能力的要求是:学生从小养成大胆开口说英语的习惯,进而达到语音标准,语调优美,说话自然。

进行口语教学时,选择适合教学目标的活动很重要。教师所选择的具体教学技巧和教学活动应该基于教学计划的目标和学生阶段发展的特点。

策略一:学儿歌说英语

《英语课程标准》明确指出:听是理解的技能,说是表达的技能,这两项技能在语言学习和交际中相辅相成、互相促进。学生应该通过大量的专项和综合性语言实践活动,形成综合语言运用能力,为真实语言交际打基础。

根据学生的年龄特征,在小学低年级的英语课堂中,教师可以充分发挥儿歌和童谣的功能,让学生在唱一唱、诵一诵的活动中潜移默化地学会说英语。为了营造一个轻松的氛围,教师可以带领学生们一边跟着节奏或旋律唱儿歌和童谣,一边配以各种肢体动作。在儿歌和童谣中常常会出现一些复现率很高的用语,学生在反复的吟唱和动作演示中能牢牢地记住歌谣的内容和意义。如：

歌谣 1： Just like me!

    Everybody put on your hat,

    Put on your hat, put on your hat.

    Everybody put on your hat!

    Just like me!

    ……

对于年龄稍大些的中年级的学生，为了避免学生在多遍练习说唱的内容后产生疲劳感，教师可以采用多样的活动形式，在学生熟悉歌词或歌谣后让他们自己改编、填词或表演。例如：

歌谣 2： We are singing.

    We are dancing.

    It is very interesting.

下面是学生改编时可能出现的版本：

We are playing.

We are swimming.

We are climbing.

It is very interesting.

策略二：在游戏中说英语

游戏适用于小学不同年龄段的学生，因为喜爱游戏是孩子的天性，把语言的学习融入有趣的游戏中去，会收到事半功倍的效果。《英语课程标准》明确指出：学生应能在教师的指导下用英语做游戏并在游戏中进行简单的交际。

下面就介绍一些可以尝试的教学游戏。

1. Ball with questions

请学生们围成一个大圈，一个学生(S1)站在圈的正中并且手拿一个球。S1边掷球边提问，接住球的同学必须回答出 S1 的问题，并把球掷还给S1。比如：教师先宣布今日游戏主题是"Jobs"。

S1：What do you want to be when you grow up?

S2：I want to be a teacher.

S1：What's your father's job?

S3：He's a doctor.

S1：What do the nurses do?

S4：They help sick people.

直到 S1 提不出问题，可以换人，游戏继续进行。

2. Action time

请学生们围成一个圈或者站成一排。从第一个同学开始，轮流进行口语练习。规则是一边说句子一边要配合做出有意义的动作，并且重复说出前一个同学所说的句子。如：

S1：I'm Peter. I like jumping.（做跳跃的动作）

S2：He's Peter. He likes jumping. I'm Rose. I like dancing.（做跳舞的动作）

S3：She's Rose. She likes dancing. I'm Kerry. I like drawing pictures.（做画画的动作）

……

等所有学生都说完以后，教师带领学生从头开始回顾每一个学生的名字以及他们的爱好，当然学生们可以用动作进行提示。

3. Learn and return

教师准备好一篇语言逻辑性较强的文章并且将其分割成一句一句的纸条。教师把纸条分给小组成员，每名成员拿到一张纸条，即文章中的任意一句话（其中有一名成员的纸条为空白）。每人记住自己的那句话，并把纸条交还给教师。小组成员围成一个圈，轮流说出自己所拿到的纸条上的句子，如果有人忘记了，可以回到教师那里去看，但是不能拿着纸条朗读。小组成员通过互相听同伴说的句子，调整站圈的位置，最终合成一篇文章。拿到空白纸条的同学，展开合理想象，为文章加一个结尾。

4. What do you know, Joe?

这是个十分简单又易于操作的游戏，但是却能很有效地锻炼学生们的口语表达能力。对于中年级的学生,教师可以让学生自选主题,不间断说话 30 秒。在练习了一段时间之后,教师可以给出 5 个话题,让孩子抽签选择话题进行不间断说话。教师可以根据教学需要及学生水平对不间断说话的时间进行相应调整。

策略三:在情境中说英语

《英语课程标准》明确指出:"本标准以学生'能用英语做事情'的描述方式设定各级目标要求,旨在强调培养学生的综合语言运用能力。各种语言知识的呈现和学习都应从语言使用的角度出发,为提升学生'用英语做事情'的能力服务。"

教师要创设接近实际生活的各种语境,开展循序渐进的语言实践活动,以各种强调过程与结果并重的教学途径与方法,培养学生"用英语做事情"的能力。例如,学生都喜欢扮演成年人的角色。教师可以创设在餐厅点餐这一场景,让学生通过扮演服务员与顾客来练习目标语言。这种类型的活动对学生来说是真实而有意义的,因为这些活动给予了他们练习不同语言表达的机会,而这些语言表达在今后的生活中就会用到。

此外教师还应考虑到学生在特定情境中使用的语言类型。例如,如果学生要进行角色扮演的活动,内容是寻找自己的衣物,他们就需要知道如何用 where 提问,以及一些方位介词如 in,on,under,beside,behind 等。再比如,教师组织学生进行棋盘活动时,他们要会说 first,next,last 等。如果学生要谈论周末活动,他们需要知道常用的动词词组以及一般将来时态的用法。

交际语言教学注重传达意义和帮助学生流利地交流。教师需要调整语言的难度以适应学生的语言水平。教师还可以以图片、句式等形式给予学生一定的语言支架,让他们更自然地表达自己的思想。

○ 典型案例 ○

译林版《英语》三年级上册
Unit 5　Look at me　第二课时

Step 1　Free talk

教师与学生互相问候，在交流过程中激发学生学习热情，同时渗透表示赞美人物或事物美丽、可爱的形容词：lovely，beautiful，nice，pretty等。

T：Look at the girl.（指向班级中某位女生）

She's beautiful.（板书）

And look at the girl on the beach!（教师出示PPT）

Ss：She is beautiful.

T：Yes, she is beautiful. We also can say she is pretty.（板书）

Now follow me：She is pretty.

Ss：She is pretty.

T：Now, look at that girl's dress.

Ss：It's beautiful/pretty.

How beautiful/pretty!

Step 2　Revision

T：Yes! That girl has a pretty dress. How about Yang Ling? She has many pretty dress, too.

（引导学生回忆story time课文中杨玲展示了哪些衣服）

Ss：A cap, a T-shirt, a skirt.

（教师从杨玲的衣柜里拿出这些服装的图片贴在黑板上）

T：This is Yang Ling's wardrobe. Can you guess what else there is?

（指导学生如何进行猜测）

T：When we guess, we can ask like this：A coat? Is it a coat?

S1：Is it a sweater?

T：Yes, you're right. But what colour is it?

S1：A yellow sweater?

T：Oh, no. Try again.

S2：A brown sweater?

S3：A white sweater?

……

T：Yes, it's a pink sweater. And I think this sweater is very smart. （从柜子里拿出服装图片，展示之后，贴在黑板上）

（教师领读 a sweater, a pink sweater, a smart pink sweater）

同法猜测 dress, jacket, hat, 并且学习形容词 cool。

T：OK! There is only one left. I'll open the door. Let's count.

Ss：Three, two, one. Open.

T：What's this?

Ss：皮带。

T：And we call this "belt". Belt, belt. Can you spell it?

（为了引导学生根据读音拼写单词，教师用学生学过的单词 bell 予以提示）

T：This is bell. And the word "belt" also has four letters.

（PPT 呈现 ___ ___ ___ ___）

T：Can you spell it out?

Ss：B-E-L-T, belt.

T：（领读单词 belt）

T：Great. We have found out all the clothes in the wardrobe.

T：（领读单词 clothes）

T：Listen to me, and look at my tongue：/ð/, /z/, /ðz/.

（学生跟读，进行练习）

Step 3 Presentation

T：Yang Ling has many clothes. They all look great! How do you think of these clothes?

(PPT 呈现句型：They all look _____ .)

Ss：They all look nice/beautiful/cool/smart/pretty...

T：Bobby's mother has many new clothes, too. What are they?

Ss：A skirt, a T-shirt... （根据 PPT 回答）

T：What colour is the skirt?

Ss：It's red.

T：What colour is the T-shirt?

Ss：It's yellow.

T：Yes. They all look nice.

（PPT 呈现 Cartoon time 的插图，并圈出妈妈的面部表情）

So, look, Bobby's Mum is very happy in Picture One and Two. But is she happy in Picture Three, Four and Five?

Ss：No.

T：How does she feel?

Ss：She's angry.

T：Why?（通过问题激发学生讨论的热情）

T：Now, let's watch the cartoon and find the answer.（观看动画，验证学生们的各种猜测）

T：Mum is angry with Dad. Because Dad isn't listening to her. Can you read and imitate?

Ss：（跟读录音，模仿语音语调，读出妈妈开心与生气时的心情）

T：Mum is angry. Try to use your body language when you imitate.（引导学生想一想自己妈妈生气时的表情与动作）

T：Now let's try to act the whole story.

（学生两人一组，戴上头饰，使用服装、报纸等道具进行课文表演）

T：From your performance, we know Mum is really angry. Dad is very sorry for that. Why does Dad feel sorry?

Ss：...

T：Because he is impolite. What should Dad do then?

(师生共同总结:First, he should listen to and look at someone carefully. Then he can use his body language, such as, clap his hands, show his thumbs and smile...)

T: Dad says, "Oh, I see. I'm sorry."

(转换场景,进行故事的续编)

T: Next day, Mum is showing her clothes again. Can you make a new story?

S1:(扮演 Mum) Look at my new hat.

S2:(扮演 Dad,放下手中的报纸,站起来,看着 Mum 说) It's smart.

S1: Look at my new dress.

S2: How beautiful!(竖起大拇指)

S1: Thank you, dear!

Step 4　Consolidation

1) T: Here is a rhyme about "nice clothes". First time, only listen, but you can clap your hands. Enjoy the rhyme.

2) 教师指导朗读,强调重音、升调、降调等。

3) T: Read after the tape.

4) Ss read in groups.

5) T: Read and also use your body language.

6) 全体学生边诵读,边表演。

7) 教师指导学生运用自己的衣物,进行歌谣的改编。

Nice clothes

Look at my _____.

Look at _____ _____.

Look at _____ _____ and _____.

They all look _____.

8) Show time:学生个人展示或者小组合作一起展示。

Step 5　Homework

1) Try to know more words about clothes.

2) Listen and imitate, try to act. (Cartoon time, Rhyme time)

♦ **案例反思** ♦

本节课以学会展示自己的服装及对他人的服装进行赞美为主要内容。服装类单词学生在低年级时已经接触过,并且这个主题也与学生的日常生活紧密联系。因此,在本节课的开始,教师就设计了一个 Guessing game,即猜一猜本单元主人公杨玲的衣柜里有哪些衣服。教师通过这一个活动,一下子激活了学生的思维,唤起了他们对旧知的回忆。此外,教师又不仅仅局限于词汇的学习,同时也给出了语言支架:"A coat? Is it a coat?"指导学生用升调来表示猜测,在猜的过程中又不断地丰富语言,如:"What colour is the coat?""Look at this sweater!""How cool!"等等。一下子使师生间的对话"活"了起来。

其次,在学习 Cartoon time 的教学内容时,教师引导学生通过观察图片,模仿体会 Bobby 妈妈的心情变化。在常规的角色扮演之后,教师又创设了一个更为真实的情境,即:爸爸学会了如何有礼貌地赞美妈妈。第二天当妈妈又向爸爸展示新衣服时,他们的对话又会是怎样的呢? 这个引导学生自主创编对话的活动,真正培养了学生的综合语言运用能力。

最后,Rhyme 的教学设计层次分明,层层递进,从中可以看出教师是有计划地对学生进行口语训练。从一开始的听录音、拍手感知节奏,到通过强调重音、升降调等指导朗读,从表演诵读到创编歌谣,教师给予学生的帮助越来越少,而学生的语言输出越来越真实且有意义,达到了课标中提出的"用英语做事情"的最终目标。

♦ **专家点评** ♦

对大部分学生而言,课堂是他们学习说英语的主要场所,如果教师能为学生营造一个安全的环境,就能够提高他们参与的积极性,激发他们用英语表达的欲望。所谓"安全的环境"指的是学生在用英语表达的时候不会因为过于困难或者害怕出错而不敢开口。根据语言学习的规律,学生开口说英语之前会有一段"沉默的语言习得"时间,这可以解读为在要求学生使用新的语言之前要给他们足够的时间去听,这时,教师的话语是学生最重要的语言输入来源。上面的典型案例中,教学伊始,教师就借夸奖班里同学漂亮的时机,多次向学生输入了语言:"She is beautiful."这就为后面要求他们输出语言打下了基础。需要注意的是,学生尝试使用新的语言时常会发生错误,教师对这些错误要区别对待:在关注语言连贯性的基础上关注准确性,有时教师需要忽视错误,有时只需要处理主要错误,有时需要纠正所有的错误。而当学生有了一点小小的进步时,教师要给予充分的正面反馈,以帮助他们建立用英语表达的自信心。另外,课堂活动的设计是否能激发学生说的欲望也很重要,那些与学生的生活经验和兴趣密切相关的活动更容易让学生产生情感上的共鸣,也就更容易让学生融入其中!

细节 8
如何培养学生的认读能力

◆ 细节阐述 ◆

　　小学教师在低年级的课堂教学中,常常会发现这样的现象:翻开书本,在图片的提示下学生都能够流利地朗读课文中的句子和对话;但是,当合上书本,把课文中的句子和对话以板书的形式呈现时,大部分学生的朗读就有困难了。其实,产生这个问题的根源在于这些学生对单词、短语或句子的认读能力的缺失。与其说他们是在朗读课文不如说是在图片的帮助下背诵和复述课文。因而,他们的朗读并不是建立在认读的基础上的,当没有图片的支持时,他们就无法回忆单元课文的内容,自然也就"读"不出了。

　　那么什么是认读能力呢?所谓 recognition,就是指辨认出某一个单词或者是词组以前是否见过,并且能够指出它的基本的词义。所以,通常意义上的 recognition,指的就是对单词或者是简单词组的一种辨认。

　　许多语言学家也对认读能力有论述。王蔷、程晓堂和陈琳在《新课程远程研修》一书中对认读能力分别有如下的解释:认读能力首先是一个快速准确的识字能力。认读是一种初步的识别单词和单词意思的能力,以及识别句子或意群的能力。认读有三个层次,最高层次是联想认读。

　　认读教学是单词教学中的一个组成部分,在单词教学的过程中需要包含认读教学,以此来培养学生的认读能力。认读能力是学生开展阅读的前提，认读能力较好的学生会更快进入阅读的阶段。认读教学需要关注两个层面，一是单词的认读，将单词的音、形、意进行紧密联系；二是句子的认读，学生能够整体感知句子，而非将句子拆分为一个个单词进行朗读。如何才能在英语教学中培养学生的认读能力呢？

策略一：活动激趣

《英语课程标准》中对一级的读写能力有这样的描述：能够看图识词，在指认物体的前提下认读所学的词语。学生的单词认读能力的培养需要一个长期的过程，需要在趣味的活动中练习、运用与检测。下面介绍几个单词认读的相关活动。

1. 掷色子

在进行单词的形义结合教学时，教师可以采用掷色子的活动。一般来说，低年级的英语教学中，每课时学习的单词数量不多。以译林版《牛津小学英语》为例，B 部分 Look and learn 一般为四个单词。在掷色子活动前，教师需要制作好一个六面的色子，每个面上贴上图片；每个学生都准备好相应的四张单词卡片。

在课堂教学时，可以采用学生一起念"Dice, dice, go, go, go"，教师扔色子的方法。色子停止后，学生根据色子面上的图片出示自己手中的单词卡片。活动过程中，还可以结合竞赛的方式，比比谁出卡片的速度最快。在教师大色子掷完之后，每个小组也可以发小色子，进行小组的练习。

2. 表演秀

低年级词汇教学中，有很多单词都可以用形体动作来进行表演。TPR(Total Physical Response，全身反应法)是低年级英语教学中常用的一种教学方式。表演秀"COPY 不走样"就是结合 TPR 教学来进行词汇的认读教学的一种活动。

活动以四人小组为单位，在学习完单词之后，教师请几组同学到教室前面。每组第一位同学面向黑板，其余成员则面向班级同学。活动开始，教师拿出写有单词的卡片(卡片内容是否统一教师可以根据教学对象而确定)，教师向每组的第一位同学呈现单词卡片后，大家一起喊：

"Copy, copy, go go go."看到单词卡片的同学将单词的意思以做动作的方式传达给第二位同学,以此类推,到最后一位同学时他(她)需要取下黑板上相应的单词卡片。动作快并准确的小组获胜。

在这个活动中,第一位同学需要辨认出单词的含义才能做出正确的动作,而最后一位同学要根据动作理解单词含义,并准确与单词进行匹配。

3. 找朋友

低年级的教材都是按主题来编排单元的,每个单元学习相关的一类单词。教师在教学过程中,可以采用"找朋友"的活动,帮助学生在活动的过程中将词汇进行归类,在培养学生认读能力的同时,潜移默化地使其在单词间建立联系。

例如,如果学生已经学习了文具类的单词和水果类的单词,那么教师就可以在黑板上画两个方框,里面分别写上 pencil 和 banana。方框外面张贴两张单词卡片 ruler 和 apple,让学生将这两个单词贴到相应的方框里面。当然,随着学生的认读能力和词汇量的提升,活动中分类的单词可以适当增多,种类也可以增加一到两项,可以是文具、水果、颜色、家庭成员等等。

策略二:语境表意

小学低年级英语教学除了词汇教学之外,还有一个重要的教学内容——短语和简单的句型。所以,认读的范围也就从单词扩大到了短语和句型。不同于单词的认读,短语和句型的认读应该逐渐摆脱指读的方式,扩大学生的"视距"。也就是说要引导学生从关注字母组合发展到关注以意群为单位的多个单词的组合,因为这种发展可以提升阅读的速度与质量,并有助于学生形成良好的语感。那么具体到课堂上如何开展短语与句型的认读教学呢?创设语言环境是一个有效的方式。

1. 结合仿说认读

一般仿说都是围绕一件事或者一个物体展开的,这就为学生创设了一个简单的语境。以结合单词的复习帮助学生认读句子"They

are..."的教学为例,教师可以采取下面几个步骤:

(1)教师出示图片并提问:"What are these?"学生回答:"They are trees."于是教师拿出写有"They are trees."的卡片,带领学生朗读:"They are trees."同时将卡片贴到对应的图片下面。接着用同样的方式完成"They are green.","They are in the park."这两个句子的学习。

(2)接着教师移走图片,带领学生看着句子朗读。这个活动的设计就是围绕 tree 这个单词来讨论颜色与地点,在这个简单的语境中,将单词与句型 They are... 相结合。教师通过问答,首先让学生知道句子的意思,随后出示卡片,帮助学生进行认读:"They are trees. They are green. They are in the park."

(3)最后,教师出示内容为公园里有许多红色小花的图片,同时呈现六张句子卡片("They are red/black. They are ants/flowers. They are in the park/on the farm.")。经过前两个教学环节,学生已经进入了语境中,明白接下来要讨论的是花的颜色与花在什么地点。教师要求学生模仿上面的活动,在六个句子中快速选择正确的句子,并组织好顺序做如下描述:"They are flowers. They are red. They are in the park."

2. 结合绘本认读

绘本在培养学生的认读能力方面起着非常重要的作用。这种作用主要体现在绘本使语言的学习变得有意义。无论绘本的语言多么简单,它结合图片所呈现的大量信息总能为学生展现丰富、有趣的故事情节,学生也就更加乐意去阅读。而且,大多数面向低龄儿童的英语绘本中所使用的句子结构复现率极高。以英文绘本 *The very hungry caterpillar* 为例,绘本中写道:"On Monday he ate through one apple. But he was still hungry. On Tuesday he ate through two pears, but he was still hungry. On Wednesday he ate through three plums, but he was still hungry..."其中多次出现了"ate through","but he was still hungry"这样的结构,学生阅读时每翻一页就能读到它们。尽管多次重复,但由于故事情节是在变化的,学生就不会感到乏味。这种依托故事的绘本阅读可以极大地优化认读效果。

策略三：生活复现

当然，除了在课堂教学中进行认读教学活动外，还可以通过在学生生活与学习的环境中提供认读机会的做法，让词汇与句型有复现的平台。

1. 英语角

教室环境布置是低年级教育的一部分，可在其中创设英语角，在课堂教学之后，教师可以开展布置英语角的活动，比如，要求学生对近阶段所学单词进行自我创作。如，学生可以选择单词 chocolate，将它写在卡纸上，并画上一块巧克力。然后在班级进行展示与评选，并将获奖同学的作品布置在英语角中。英语角的使用给学生营造了学习英语的氛围，潜移默化地提升了学生的认读能力。

2. 物品标签

在低年级的教学内容中，大多数都是与学生生活紧密相关的词汇。例如，译林版《牛津小学英语》2A Unit 4 中的单词包括 window, chair, desk, door，教师可以将单词制作成卡片，张贴在各个物品相应的位置上，如窗户上贴上 window，门上贴上 door。课后教师还可以要求学生制作单词卡片 table 和 sofa 贴在自己家里的餐桌和沙发上。这些物品标签，可以提供给学生将这些物品与张贴的单词卡片进行联系的机会。这些活动，就是学生在学习生活环境中自然认读的表现。

3. 单词游戏牌

单词游戏牌具体的做法是，在学习完每单元之后教师都布置这样的活动型家庭作业：将本单元所学的单词制作成纸牌，一面画上图片，另一面写上单词。活动时以两人或多人为一个小组。游戏的规则是，一位学生先出示纸牌写有单词的一面，指定小组内的某一位成员朗读并要求他（她）说出其中文意思，如果回答正确，就可以拿走该纸牌。游戏结束时持有最多数量游戏牌的同学胜出。这个游戏活动的设计意图是：首先，制作纸牌的过程有助于学生加深对所学单词的词形与词义的印象；其次，要想在活动中胜出学生得在课后经常练习，这样，他们就会有复习巩固的动力。

▶·典型案例 1·◀

译林版《牛津小学英语》2A
Unit 7　Here you are　Part A and B

Step 1　Warming-up

1. Sing a song：*Head，shoulder，knees and toes*

2. Play a game："Simon says"

欢快的英语歌曲迅速地吸引了学生的注意力，学生在演唱过程中加上了动作，边唱边跳；紧接着游戏"Simon says"让学生复习了学过的一些动作类单词，营造出轻松愉快的课堂气氛。

Step 2　Presentation and practice

1. Present words

T：(做出喘气与劳累的样子，并摸肚子，表示饥饿) I'm very tired and hungry.

I have some things here. Can you help me to select something to eat?

教师用PPT出示一些单词：

carrot　bean　tomato　potato

ant　butterfly　flower　tree

学生选择食物类的单词朗读：carrot, bean, tomato, potato。

教师适时回应：Thank you. They are nice.

T：I also want to have some snacks.（出示 snacks)

Teacher says the Chinese meaning.

Students read together.

2. Present a pie

T：(Take out a pie, taste it and ask) What's this?

Ss：派。

T：Pie.

Ss：(Pass the pie and practise the pronunciation)

在学生拿着派传递并朗读时，教师在黑板上贴上pie的图片，随后拿出单词卡片pie，让学生进行朗读，读完之后贴到黑板上pie的图片旁。

T：(Show pies) How many pies?

One, two, three. Three pies.

Pies, pies, I like pies.

(Ask the students to follow)

T：(Show a box) There are many snacks in the box. What's in the box?

(通过猜小吃的方式教授 cake, hamburger, hot dog；通过数数来讲解其复数形式 cakes, hamburgers, hot dogs)

3. Practice

1) Play a matching game.

教师带领同学朗读黑板上的 4 个单词。随后，将 4 张图片和 4 张卡片随机发给 8 位同学，做配对游戏。8 个小朋友很快就配对成功。游戏玩 4 个回合。

2) Play a guessing game.

T：(Show four boxes with PPT) There are different snacks in the four boxes. Look and remember.(教师快速地点击盒子,盒子下的小吃图片与单词迅速出现并迅速消失)What is in the first box?

Ss：...

T：What is in the second/third/fourth box?

Ss：...

Step 3　Drills and practices

1. Practise the dialogue

T：(手拿 pie) I like pies very much. I'm hungry. A pie, please. Now we are in the shop. There are many snacks. What would you like?

S1：A..., please.

T：Here you are.

S1：Thank you.

T—Ss：(Practise the dialogue)

2. Say a chant

"A pie, a pie, a pie, please.

Here you are. Here you are.

Thank you."

教师首先带领学生一起念这段儿歌,随后出示以单词 cake 为核心的一段儿歌,请学生照着念,现场略显沉寂。教师进行提醒,并请同桌合作。最后呈现良好。

"A cake, a cake, a cake, please.

Here you are. Here you are.

Thank you."

随后,教师请学生自编一个儿歌,学生们四人一组开始用 hamburger 和 hot dog 进行创编。

3. Play a passing game

学生边说儿歌边传递盒子,教师说停时,盒子在手的一对同桌要表演买卖的场景,表现好的可以从盒子中取出小吃作为奖励。学生们十分投入,表达也比较流畅。

Step 4　Consolidation

1. Do a survey

T:(Ask the students to do a survey with the following dialogue and then fill in the blanks)

A: Hello.

B: Hello.

A: Do you like hot dogs/hamburgers/cakes/pies?

B: Yes, I do. /No, I don't. A..., please.

A: Here you are.

B: Thank you.

Name	Hot dogs	Hamburgers	Cakes	Pies
Mr Jin	✓		✓	

口头表述：

Mr Jin likes hot dogs and cakes. _____ likes _____.

2. PPT presentation

（多媒体出示 a little pig and some snacks）

T：My friend the little pig likes snacks very much. So he eats many snacks.

Ss：(Read the words about the snacks)

T：(Show a fat crying pig and say) Now the little pig becomes very fat. He has something to tell you. (Show the sentence："Don't eat too many snacks.")

3. Homework

1) Point and read Page 30 and 31.

2) Make the cards and show them to your father and mother or make your own story book *At the snack bar*.

◆ 案例反思 ◆

以上案例是二年级上学期的词汇与句型教学。课题为"Here you are"。新授了四个关于食品的单词以及在小吃店买卖需要的日常用语。

在导入部分，教师借助歌曲和动作以及"Simon says"游戏，自然地导出累与饿；随后出示了关于蔬菜的单词以及关于公园中各种事物的单词，在复现与巩固已学知识的同时，给学生布置了新的学习任务：帮助老师选出小吃。随后导入主题 Snacks，将学生引入新的学习语境中。

在新授单词的过程中，教师遵循了认读教学的一般模式，先出示实物，教师示范读，学生跟读，感知音与义的联系；随后出示单词卡片，进行形和音结合。在练习单词的过程中，教师根据低年级学生的学习特点，设计了游戏活动，将图片和单词分别发给了8位不同的同学，然后请同学们快速地 match。这样的活动用时 15 分钟左右，既通过活动让学生放松了身体，活动的趣味性也吸引了学生注意力，最重要的是通过活动达成了形义结合的认读教学目标。

在对句型"A... please."以及"Here you are. Thank you."进行练习时候,教师也层层递进,从示范念儿歌,到出示新的儿歌,让学生同桌尝试朗读,到最后小组合作创编儿歌,其实就是一个从扶到放的过程,学生在模仿的过程中,逐渐完成了认读句子的学习过程。最后的采访活动,就是在语境中运用句子的过程,是综合语言运用的活动,其中也包含了认读这一教学目标。

课堂教学在情感教育中结束,但这并不等于教学的结束。教师布置的家庭作业,第一个是指读第30页和31页。这是一个基础性作业,但是教师特别强调了 point and read,不仅仅是读,而且需要指着读,帮助学生将句子的读音和句子的形式联系起来。第二个是制作卡片或制作主题为 snack bar 的绘本,这是一个拓展性作业,具有选择性。制作卡片或绘本的过程,就是复习单词与句型的过程。

◆ 专家点评 ◆

研究表明:学生的认读能力会对他们今后的阅读速度和效率产生直接的影响,如果学校从低年级就开设英语课,那么教师应该从一开始就对学生进行认读能力的培养。同时,无论采取哪一种教学方法对学生进行单词认读能力的培养,结合语意和语境是首要条件。上述案例中的多种做法,都以创设语境为基础,对学生提出从最初的单词认读过渡到后来对短语和句子的认读的要求。比如,go to school 这个短语不能把它分成三个单词 go, to 和 school 让学生分辨,而是要把它作为一个完整的意群来认读。

细节 9

如何培养学生的阅读能力

➤ 细节阐述 ◄

目前大多数小学英语的阅读教学仍然停留在传统的"梳理文章信息—语言知识讲解"的阶段。受到教学观念的影响,阅读的文本在有的教师眼里就是单词、短语和句型等"知识点"的载体。学生阅读的目的是为了完成教师布置的多个任务,如判断正误、回答问题或者完成表格等,阅读者仅仅是信息的被动接受者,他们享受不到阅读的乐趣。还有些时候,为了追求阅读课流程的"完整性",教师会设计纷繁复杂的教学环节和活动,牵着学生匆匆走过场,这样的教学导致学生没有充足的时间静下心来体验思考的过程,也无法深入理解文本的内容,久而久之,学生就会产生疲劳感,失去阅读的动机和兴趣。在小学阶段如何依托教材中的主题篇章开展有效阅读教学,做到既能激发和保持学生的阅读兴趣,又能初步培养学生阅读的策略,是值得我们广大一线教师探究和实践的。

策略一:理清阅读教学思路

1. 准确定位教学目标

在阅读课上,每个文本都涵盖了不同的内容,反映了不同的主题;在形式上也各不相同,有的是对话,有的是短文,有的是故事;在难度上也有所差异。因此,要根据具体的文本内容,具体设计教学目标,使目标定位得更为具体、明确。

2. 抓住文本主线

阅读教学所涉及的词汇、句型、语法等更多、更广、更深，要求也更高。在阅读教学中，许多教师很想抓住阅读教学所涉及的所有东西，但往往思路不清，效果不太理想。因此，面对不同形式的文本，依据话题抓住一条主线，帮助学生理清文本的思路，显得很关键，它能起到提纲挈领、辐射全文的作用。

3. 突破语言重点

在阅读教学中我们强调对文本的整体理解，但不意味着文本中的词汇等重要的语言点可以忽略不计。新的语言点同样是文本学习的重要组成部分，一方面它们是学生学习文本的价值所在，另一方面也给文本学习带来了困难，如果学生对文本中的语言点理解不够充分，那么他们对文本的理解必然就会不到位、不透彻或不全面，从而在整体上影响文本学习的质量。例如，在执教译林版《牛津小学英语》6B Unit 6 Planning for the weekend 的 A 板块时，有位教师为对话文本中的语言项目 be going to 和本语篇的核心词 plan 创设了一个真实的教学情境，让学生正确理解。教学片段如下：

T：What are we going to do in this lesson? Can you try to guess? When we are talking about our lesson, we can use "be going to".（用手指着自己）I'm going to...（用手指着一个男孩）He's going to...（用手指着一个女孩）She's going to...（用手指着部分学生）They're going to...

根据该教师引出的话题，学生运用以往的课堂学习经验与教师展开了如下的交流：

S1：Maybe we're going to listen to the dialogue.

T：Maybe you're right. But what else are we going to do?

S2：I think we're going to write some new words.

T：Anything else?

S3：Maybe we're going to read Part A.

S4：Maybe we're going to do some exercises.

T：What exercises are we going to do?

S5：Maybe we're going to learn what people in Part A are going to do.

S6：Maybe we're going to make sentences by using "be going to".

S7：Maybe we're going to talk about our plan.

T：Well, I'm going to show you our plan about this lesson.（教师呈现本节课的教学计划）

T：So I think you know our teaching plan. And we can use "be going to" to talk about our plan.（引导学生归纳并板书）

策略二：构建阅读教学的指导模式

小学英语阅读教学一般可以使用阅读前（Pre-reading）、阅读中（While-reading）和阅读后（Post-reading）三段阅读教学模式。其教学目标和教学活动在三个阶段有着各自的特点。

1. 读前（Pre-reading）教学——激活背景、激趣导入

阅读前教学的核心任务就是为阅读做准备。读前准备包括背景图式的激活，话题的导入，任务的介绍，兴趣的激发和语言、策略的准备。在这一阶段，教师往往借助视频资源和图片，采用预测和讨论方式引入话题，激发学生学习兴趣，扫清部分生词障碍，构建文本与学生过去经验和知识之间的联系，为学生迅速进入阅读状态做好铺垫。

（1）阅读前创设情境，引入目标词汇。教师在设计教学时需要根据课文标题、课文内容以及生词表确定主题词和核心词，通过创设真实语境，设计有意义的、开放性的、适合交际的活动，在生动、自然的交际活动中引入目标词汇，扫清部分生词的障碍，为学生快速参与阅读活动做好铺垫。

（2）阅读前应初步激活学生思维。教师应利用背景知识设计开放型的任务，引发学生思考，鼓励和引导学生积极探索，积极参与教学活动，并积极思维。

2. 读中（While-reading）教学——了解全文、以读促知

读中教学是阅读教学的核心，各种阅读能力的培养都是通过读中阶段的教学完成的。从具体信息的识别，到推理判断能力的培养，再到

各种逻辑关系、篇章结构的分析,阅读能力中知识层面、理解(领会)层面、分析层面一般都应在读中阶段完成。阅读策略的培养活动也属于读中活动。因此,读中教学一般由多个教学活动组成,而不是简单的判断正误、回答问题或图表填充。同时,活动必须具有层次性,从知识到领会,从分析到评价。这就给教师设计教学活动提出了更高的要求,也给教学过程的安排提出了更高的要求。

(1)阅读教学应体现整体性。阅读教学的重点应放在指导学生从篇章的角度整体把握所学语言材料,遵循整体—部分—整体的路径,即从篇章到句子,再到词汇、语法点等语言知识点,最后落实到对所学语篇的整体理解。

(2)阅读任务应具有针对性。在整体设计阅读任务的基础上,应依据文本段落层次分层设计细节性的任务,让学生有针对性、多角度地进行文本阅读,理解文本细节内容。

(3)阅读任务应凸显层次性。语篇教学一般都有一条主线,教学中要围绕主线,设计有层次的阅读任务,使学生思维循序渐进,对所读文章的理解逐渐深刻。

(4)阅读过程要充分。在学生阅读的过程中,教师要学会等待,要给学生留有充分阅读、思考和交流的时间,要把话语权还给学生,让学生静下心来真正阅读,并在学生阅读时尽可能多地为学生提供阅读信息、进行语言交流的机会,这样才能有利于学生对文本信息的理解,并促进学生实现真实、高效的阅读。

3. 读后(Post-reading)教学——检查评估,学以致用

读后活动一般侧重知识的应用和综合。读后活动是对阅读质量的检查和评估,也是对文本内容的延伸与运用。读后活动设计应基于文本内容和话题,检查学生对所学内容的掌握情况,并拓展学生的思维。

(1)读后活动应呈现渐进性。阅读后练习的设计应该循序渐进,先基于文本,后超越文本。

(2)读后活动应体现综合性。综合性包括两层意思:一是教师所设计的活动需要学生综合运用文本知识来完成;二是教师要通过设计听、说、读、写等多种语言实践活动,培养学生的综合语言运用

能力。

（3）读后活动应具备实践性。阅读后活动要打破课本的束缚,使英语学习真正向生活延伸。教师要通过创设真实的语境、运用真实的语言材料、提供真实的语言信息鼓励学生进行真实的语言交流。

策略三：在阅读教学中有效渗透阅读策略

阅读策略应该作为阅读教学内容之一,那么什么是阅读策略,教学中又应该如何培养学生的阅读策略？

根据竺小思和周龙兴等人的阐述,阅读策略就是读者用来理解各种文本的有意识的、可灵活调整的认知活动计划,以及在阅读过程中为完成阅读任务而采取的一切有效方法与手段,包括对学习方法的选择以及怎样组合、操作使用等方面的决策。常用的阅读策略包括预测、推理、猜词、寻读、细读等。

1. 预测——理清文章脉络

预测是一种有效的阅读策略。在教学中,教师可以借助图片、标题、生词呈现来让学生进行预测,形成主动思考。在此过程中,教师要努力让学生打开思维,不要过度关注学生预测的准确性。预测技能的培养有助于调动学生阅读的主动性,激发学生强烈的好奇心和浓厚的兴趣,能够更加有效地形成文本和阅读者的互动过程,使学生进入读的状态,提高读的目的性。

2. 猜词——猜测词义,化解词汇学习难点

阅读时,如果遇到难以理解的词语,教师应引导学生根据不同情况选择忽略、查字典或进行猜测等策略。词义猜测的教学方式很多,常见的有：

（1）利用上下文线索。引导学生根据上下文线索来推测词义,有助于提高学生的阅读速度和阅读能力。

（2）巧用近义词和反义词。恰当地使用近义词或反义词可以降低词汇学习难度,让学生更容易接受新词汇。

（3）英语释义。用英语解释词汇能有效地增加学生的英语输入。

典型案例

译林版《英语》六年级上册 Unit 2 Healthy food

这是一篇以健康饮食为主题的语篇阅读教学。执教老师是南京拉萨路小学的李磊老师。教师在课堂教学中充分利用学生已有的知识和生活经验，创设生活化的真实情境，引导学生在运用语言中学习语言，并能够创造性地使用语言。

Step 1 Pre-reading

1. Get to know each other

T：Glad to be your new teacher today. Would you please introduce yourself?

学生组织话语简单介绍自己。

T：Good. Do you want to know me? Try to ask me some questions.

学生发问，了解新老师。

教师用PPT逐一快速呈现描述学生与教师信息的句子，要求学生仔细观察、聆听，对这些信息迅速做出判断，并用"Yeah! Yeah! Yeah!"或"No! No! No!"作答。最后，教师总结自己是Big Eater，并引出与food and drinks这一主题相关的词汇。

2. Talk about food and drinks

T：You know I enjoy eating and drinking different kinds of food and drinks. Do you have the same hobby? Great. Let's talk about food and drinks. What food and drinks do you have every day?

学生六人一组，围绕关键词food and drinks进行头脑风暴活动。

3. Talk about my diet

T：Here's my diet for today. What do you think of it? Healthy or unhealthy?

小组完成任务后，教师通过"What is healthy food?"这一问题引出本课话题"Healthy food"，并板书该话题。

Step 2　While-reading

1. Read and ask

T：Let's read a story about healthy food.

用PPT呈现文中Mr Green和学生交谈的场景图后，教师先向学生交代故事发生的背景，再通过"What else do you want to know from this story?"这一问题启发学生积极思考，鼓励学生根据图片提出自己想要了解的问题。学生六人一组进行讨论，并提出了如下问题：

S1：What food are they talking about?

S2：Where are they talking about healthy food?

S3：What is healthy food?

S4：How much should we eat?

S5：Why should we eat healthy food?

S6：How can we eat?

……

在学生提问的过程中，教师及时对学生的思考与表达给予激励性评价，并板书what，where，how，why等关键疑问词。接着，师生共同解决较为浅显的问题，如含有where的问题就可以从PPT的图片中直接获得答案。最后，教师辅助学生梳理与整合遗留问题，并提炼出"What food and drinks are mentioned? How much should we eat? Why should we eat like this?"这三个具有梯度的问题，让学生在后续阅读文本的过程中逐一解决。

2. Watch and circle

教师让学生观看课文动画，并圈出动画中提到的食物和饮料，解决"What food and drinks are mentioned?"这个问题。在核对答案的过程中，教师在黑板上粘贴相关食物和饮料的图片，引导学生根据图片、上下文的语境理解部分新词，如vegetables，meat等，指导学生掌握它们的音、形、义。

3. Read and match

教师呈现第二个问题"How much should we eat?"后，要求学生快速浏览课文，完成食物金字塔的匹配任务，进而帮助学生理清课文的层次。

学生阅读完毕后，教师先引导学生用"We should eat..."这个句型进行表达，而后师生共同核对答案。教师在此过程中将食物和饮料的图片粘贴至金字塔合适的位置。然后，教师通过夸张的语音、语调和丰富的肢体语言，帮助学生理解食物金字塔各层所代表的不同含义，弄清 plenty of, a lot of, some 和 not too much 的用法。最后，教师引导学生根据食物金字塔，运用文中的关键句和数量词进行简单的语言输出。

4. Read and underline

教师呈现最后一个问题"What should we eat like this?"，要求学生阅读文本并画线找出答案。师生核对答案后，教师围绕健康饮食话题表达自己的观点。

5. Read and judge

1）Ss read aloud.

2）T：Here I write some sentences about story. Please read and judge.

教师通过 I can judge 和 I can say 这两个游戏检查学生对文本掌握情况。

6. Try to retell

T：Now, let's try to retell the story according to the notes on the blackboard.

Step 3　Post-reading

1. Task—Design a healthy diet in four

T：Now, you know I have an unhealthy diet. Could you design a healthy one for me?

Ss work in four.（学生四人一组合作，设计一份健康的食谱）

2. Homework

1）Read the story after class, and try to introduce the Food Pyramid to your family.

2）Design a healthy diet for the school dinning hall.

◆ 案例反思 ◆

本案例采用阅读前—阅读中—阅读后三段模式展开教学。

1. 分析教材，确定主题，精心设计读前活动

教师在读前活动中设计了两个环节，一是游戏热身，了解彼此信息。教师利用信息差设计了猜测判断游戏，该活动既增进了师生间的了解，又巧妙地引出了教师是 Big Eater 的身份，为学生在读后环节完成任务做好了铺垫，同时将学生的目光聚焦到以 food and drinks 为主题的词汇上。二是头脑风暴，引出本课话题。学生六人一组，围绕关键词 food and drinks 进行头脑风暴活动。此活动不仅激活了学生头脑中与话题相关的知识储备，也让其在与同伴的互动交流中丰富了自己的知识。同时，学生在小组讨论中讨论了自己所了解的知识，这也是经验分享的过程，由学生传授知识给学生。在所有讨论结束后，教师再呈现本课话题"Healthy food"就显得自然、得体。

2. 围绕主题，分析文本，整体设计读中活动

教师依据文本内容依次呈现阅读中要解决的三个主要问题，并设计了① Watch and Circle——观看动画，了解大意，② Read and Match——略读课文，理清脉络，③ Read and underline——精读课文，读明细节的任务。学生带着问题读，逐层完成阅读任务。在学生理解文本、掌握阅读策略的基础上，教师又让学生跟读模仿和自由朗读全文，促使学生整体理解文本意义。教师又以游戏和小组合作学习的方式，一方面检查了学生对文本的理解情况，另外一方面也为学生提供了表达机会。学生在游戏中既强化了对细节信息的理解，也内化了文本的语言知识。

3. 基于文本，回归生活，巧妙设计读后活动

在本节课后的读后活动中，教师一方面要求学生复习课文及故事，并向家人介绍食物金字塔，帮助学生在语言输出的过程中巩固和总结所学知识；另一方面，要求学生给 Big Eater 和学校食堂设计食谱。这些活动是对文本的适度拓展，让学生运用文本知识在真实的语境中进行综合性的语言输出，增强了学生的语言体验，培养了他们的综合语言

运用能力。

♦ **专家点评** ♦

现在，小学的英语教材通常把课文安排在单元的第一板块，通过课文来引出和介绍单元的语言知识，使学生在阅读课文、获取信息的同时能够感知、理解语言并逐渐获得语言运用的知识。因而，教师要改变以往先解决生词再学习课文的做法，从让学生了解课文中的信息内容开始，同时依托课文这个知识的载体部分解决学生词汇、句型和语法方面的困惑并引导学生在语言知识的支撑下进行信息的交流，提升语言运用能力。上面的案例能很好地诠释这个方法：上课伊始，教师借助师生间 Free talk 的契机促使学生把注意力转移到要学习的话题"Healthy food"上面，调动了他们相关的知识储备；当进入课文学习的时候，教师又通过呈现图片和提问的方式让已知和未尽信息之间产生的信息沟激起学生学习课文的兴趣，接着，试听和阅读活动的安排使学生有机会运用到不同的学习策略，其间还穿插了词汇和句型的学习，让学生在语境中猜测单词的含义，感知句型的用法；在完成课文的学习之后，教师随即带领学生以小组合作的方式一起设计健康的食谱，从而让语言学习和语言运用达到了完美的结合！

细节 10

如何培养学生写的能力

细节阐述

从认知角度来看,英语学习主要涉及语言输入和语言产出两方面的内容。写和说同属语言产出技能,它们能反映学生的综合语言运用能力。同时,写和说还是学习语言的有效方式,因为学习语言的最好方法莫过于使用它。但和说的活动相比,写的难度更大,因为它对语言精准度和逻辑性的要求更高,而学生的拼写、单词形式以及句子结构等方面的错误在口语表达的时候并不容易反映出来,即使被发现也比较容易得到听者的宽容。《英语课程标准》中对小学阶段写的要求作了如下阐述:能正确书写字母和单词;能模仿范例写词句;能写出简单的问候语和祝福语并能根据图片、词语或例句的提示,写出简短的语句等。课标从英语教学的起始阶段就对写的要求作了明确的规定,这是因为有研究表明,写的技能是需要一个长期的发展才能趋于成熟的,而且,在写的训练过程中,学生口头表达能力会随之而有潜在性的发展,读和听的能力也会间接受益,所以写能够带动学生综合技能的发展。

小学英语课堂上比较常见的做法是将写的训练融入词汇、句型、课文等板块的教学中。由于写是学习中的一个难点,学生往往因畏难而害怕写。要让学生对写的活动感兴趣,教师有必要给学生创造一种自由的、支持性的氛围。首先,教师要努力让写的内容变得更加有意义。教师可以在写之前进行有关的背景介绍,让它与学生的生活相联系:布置班级宣传栏、为学校图书馆设计标语、给远方的朋友寄一张明信片等等，这些越是接近学生生活的话题和内容就越能激发学生写的动机。其次，教师可以灵活设计写的活动，将独立写和合作写两种不同的形式交叉进行。尽管大部分时候写是一项独立的活动，但是，合作的形式有利于给学生创设一个宽松的氛围，而且合作讨论的过程中成员的思路能得以拓宽。最后，教师还要注意对学生写的信心的培养。一方面可以用各种简单有趣的活动吸引学生，让他们能够有机会体验成功，这样，学生们就会充满热情地参与到写的活动中；另一方面教师还要避免因过度的批改而引起学生的挫败感。教师可以用圈出精彩词句的方式来取代纠正每一个拼写、每一个语法错误甚至每一个标点的做法；对于文章中反复出现的错误，教师可以用评语的方式提醒学生自己纠正，如：请注意动词第三人称单数形式的使用，试着找出你文章中的拼写错误等。

策略一：选择合适的任务

写的活动并不是只有在高年级才能进行，即使是中低年级，只要教师注意方法、精心引导，同样可以很好地实施写作教学。刚开始写，学生的困难一定会比较多，这就更加要求教师讲求教学方法，特别是讲求教学的系统化，无论是形式还是内容，都要按照从易到难，由简单到复杂的原则有序安排，不能一开始就要求学生自主写出成段成文的内容。下面提供的三个活动设计分别适用于低、中、高年级。

1. 活动内容：抄写

教学对象　低年级

活动目标　能根据教师提供的生活情境选择、制作英语贺卡

准备材料　卡纸一张

活动过程　出示图片，图片内容为教师节那天一名学生向老师送上一张自制的贺卡的场景。教师先让学生看图说话，说说图片中的学生可能对老师说什么，然后请学生在"Happy Birthday"、"Happy New Year"、"Merry Christmas"以及"Happy Teachers' Day"中挑选一个符合图片场景的句子，写在卡纸上，到教师节那天赠给任课老师。

说明　这其实是一项抄写活动，但由于教师把它与生活密切联系

起来,就避免了让学生感到枯燥乏味的情况,更重要的是语言的交流功能通过这种形式得到了凸显。

2. 活动内容:仿写

教学对象　中年级

活动目标　能用所学的句子描述自己喜爱的一种动物

准备材料　动物的照片一张

活动过程　教师呈现一张小狗的照片后,让学生小组活动进行外貌描述,然后教师出示并请学生朗读教师写的一个片段:"This is a dog. He has big ears. His eyes and nose are small, but his mouth is big. He is my friend."最后,请同学们拿出准备好的动物照片以教师的范文为例模仿写话,完成后交流分享。

说明　该活动的目的是巩固有关描写动物外貌的句型,但是中年级的学生自主写作尚有困难,所以教师就设法提供帮助,给他们可以参照的模式和框架,消除他们的焦虑感。

3. 活动内容:续写

教学对象　高年级

活动目标　通过续写故事的活动培养学生想象能力,激发学生的写作兴趣

活动过程　课文"Goldilocks and the three bears"的故事结尾是:"Goldilocks finds three bears in front of her. She is afraid and runs out of the house."教师请学生们进行小组讨论,就 Goldilocks 跑出屋子后的情节展开联想;然后全班学生一起交流,教师同时提供语言方面的支持和帮助,以板书的形式呈现给学生;最后让学生们以组为单位续写故事,完成后交流分享。

说明　该活动目的不在于巩固语言知识,而是让学生享受用语言表达思想的过程,但是,受语言水平的限制,学生想自由表达还有困难,所以教师就通过全班交流时给予学生语言帮助的方式,为学生的续写活动搭建支架。当然,具体在写作的时候学生肯定还有疑问,教师可以随时施以援手。

策略二：采用趣味化的形式

教师要通过设计形式多样、富有趣味性的活动让学生知道写是为了交流，为了分享，为了表达自己的感受，而不是为了应付考试，为了完成一项任务。小学阶段的学生大多喜欢绘本，有时还喜欢临摹几笔绘本上的图案，教师可以充分发挥学生的这个爱好，将写和画的活动相结合，调动他们参与的积极性。例如：低年级学生学完关于家庭成员的单词后，教师可以设计制作家庭画册的活动，要求学生在每一张纸的上方画自己的一位家庭成员，下方分别写上 my grandpa，my grandma，my father，my mother……完成后装订成册，班级进行传阅。高年级的学生则可以把改写或续写的故事制作成连环画和大家分享。这样，学生就会发现他们是在用英语和图画表达他们的所思所想，也就更容易享受到写的乐趣。除了绘画，还有一些比较受学生欢迎的活动形式，如：改编歌词和小诗、制作海报、设计菜单等。这些趣味性的活动能促使学生对写的活动满怀期待，让他们觉得写是一件乐事。

策略三：提供足够的帮助

要让学生乐于写，还离不开教师的指导和帮助。教师在要求学生实施写的活动前要充分考虑学生可能会遇到的困难。归纳起来，学生的困难主要体现在语言知识的匮乏和思路的局限上。对于语言知识匮乏的情况，教师可以在活动前和学生积极互动，帮助学生整理曾经学过的与所写话题有关的词汇和句子，在此基础上还可以根据学生的需要补充、拓展一些词汇和句型，以供参考使用；如果是因思路局限而造成的难以下笔，教师则可以组织学生开展小组讨论，促使学生在相互的交流中迸发出新的想法和构思。另外，为了能更有针对性地给学生帮助和指导，加快学生的进步，教师可以自己先写一篇"下水"作文，也就是立足于学生的知识层次和语言能力，写一篇同话题的作文，这样教师就能更加清楚地了解学生的需求，这种"现身说法"对于小学生而言是最有效的指导方式。

◢ 典型案例 ◣

苏州工业园区唯亭学校王丽琴老师的课堂实录

本课教学内容为译林版《牛津小学英语》6A　Unit 5　On the farm,通过教学要求学生能熟练运用句型"There was.../ There were...","— What did you do last week? — I...","— What else did you do? — I..."并能用这三句话来描写自己的一段活动经历,做到语法准确,描述清晰。

Ⅰ.预热

1) Flash the pictures(学生秋游的照片).

2) T：Class begins. Good afternoon, boys and girls.

Ss：Good afternoon, Miss Wang.

T：Sit down, please.

Ⅱ.导入

T：Boys and girls, I like playing games very much. Do you like playing games?

Ss：Yes.

T：OK. Let's play a game.

T：What can we do on the farm? What can we do in Taihu Wetland Park? Let's have a group competition. Team 1, 2, 3, 4 and 5 will be Group 1, Team 6, 7, 8, 9 and 10 will be Group 2. First discuss in groups. OK?

Ss：OK.

(说是写的基础,"说话"这个活动形式既打开了学生的思路,又能为他们顺利地"写话"打下基础,同时,竞赛的形式极大地调动了学生的参与积极性)

T：Boys and girls, are you ready for "30 Seconds' Non-stop Talking"?(小组内说属于这一类的单词,30 秒内尽量不要间断、不要重复。全班分成两组,哪一组说得多就哪一组获胜)

T: Group 1, are you ready?

G1: Yes. (Say the phrases one by one)

T: Now, Group 2, are you ready?

G2: Yes. (Say the phrases one by one)

T: Wow. Group 1, you're the winners. Congratulations, big hands!

Ss: (Clap hands)

Ⅲ. 复习与新授

1. 复习

T: Boys and girls, I was very busy last week. Do you want to know what I did last week? You can ask me.

Ss: What did you do last week?

T: I had an autumn outing on Wednesday.

Ss: What else did you do?

T: I cooked some food and cleaned my house.

T: What about you? What did you do last week?

S1: I...

T: What else did you do?

S1: I...

T: Ask and answer in pairs: "A: What did you do last week? B: I... A: What else did you do? B: I..."

2. 学习 Part E

1) T: I know all of you were very busy. You had a good time last week. Wang Bing and his friends had a good time, too. What did Wang Bing and his friends do last week? Please listen and judge. (Show four pictures) Which pictures are right?

Tip 1：在听之前,先浏览一遍图片。(Play the tape)

Ss: Picture 1 and 4.

T: What did Wang Bing and his friends do last week?

S1: They played football and walked in the mountains.

T：(Show the new word "mountain")

Ss：(Learn the word "mountain" according to the pronunciation of the word)

T：(Show the picture of a hill) Is this a mountain?

S2：No, it's a hill.

T：Can you tell me what they didn't do? (Show the words "plant", "father", "dance")

S3：Plant trees, planted trees, sing songs, sang songs.

Ss：(Read and learn the phrase "plant trees")

2) T：Where were they? What did they do? How did they feel?（板书）Please open your English book at Page 43. Read the dialogue with your partner loudly, think about the questions, and then underline the key words and sentences.

Tip 2：同桌分角色朗读对话，思考问题，并画出关键词句。

Ss：(Read and answer)

T：Where were they?

S1：They were at a camp.

T：What did they do?

S2：They played football and volleyball, walked in the mountains and played a lot of games. Mr Green cooked a lot of food.

T：How did they feel?

S3：They were tired. It was fun.

T：Boys and girls, who were they in the dialogue?（板书）

S4：Wang Bing and his friends.

T：When was it?（板书）

S5：It was last week.

3) T：Boys and girls, please retell the dialogue with three parts：Beginning, Main body and Ending. Retell the dialogue in pairs first.

Ss：(Retell in pairs)

T：Who wants to try?

S1: Wang Bing and his friends were at a camp last week. They played football and volleyball, walked in the mountains and played a lot of games. Mr Green cooked a lot of food.

They were tired. But it was fun!

（教师在教学时始终围绕本课的核心句型与学生积极互动，在一个个真实的听和说的活动中帮助学生加深对这些句子的印象；教师提醒学生复述时要注意三个部分——Beginning, Main body 和 Ending 的方式促使学生说话前整理思路，让他们能有条理地叙述，并为条理性地叙述做准备）

3. Let's imagine

1) T: Wang Bing and his friends had a camping trip last week. It was very fun. It was very interesting. Do you want to go and join them? If you were Liu Tao, what did you see at the camp? Let's imagine.

For example: There were some tents at the camp. The trees were very tall.

There was/were...

I saw sth.../I saw... doing sth...

The... was.../The... were...

These sentences will help you.

Ss: (Imagine what you saw at the camp with these sentence structures)

T: What did you see at the camp?

S1: There were many flowers at the camp.

T: What colour were the flowers?

S1: Some were red. Some were yellow.

T: What about you?

S2: I saw some butterflies dancing in the flowers.

T: How beautiful! Did you catch them?

S2: Yes.

T: What about you?

S3: The birds were in the trees.

T: What did the birds do?

S3: They sang nice songs.

……

2) T: Maybe someone will say, "There were a lot of flowers in the park." According to the material, make the sentence richer.

S1: There were a lot of beautiful flowers in the park.

Tip 3：根据内容，适当发挥。

T: Maybe someone will say, "There was a hill <u>in the park</u>. There was a lake <u>in the park</u>. <u>There were</u> some trees <u>on the hill</u>." These sentence structures are the same. Can you change them? Vary the sentence structures.

S2: There was a hill and a lake in the park. On the hill, there were some trees.

Tip 4：避免句式重复，灵活变化。

T: Maybe someone will say, "There were many flowers in the park. How beautiful the butterflies were! We saw the butterflies dancing in the flowers. Some were red, some were yellow." Can you put these sentences in the correct order?

(　　)There were many flowers in the park.

(　　)How beautiful the butterflies were!

(　　)We saw the butterflies dancing in the flowers.

(　　)Some were red, some were yellow.

Tip 5：按一定的顺序去观察、描述事物。

3) T: What else did they do? Can you imagine?

S1: Sleep in the tent, sing and dance.

S2: Play chess, play cards...

4) T: After Wang Bing went back home, he wrote a composition. Can you find the key words "last week"?

Ss: Yes.

T：It's the simple past tense. We should use the past forms of the verbs.

（板书：Beginning, Main body, Ending）

Tip 6：一般过去时中，动词要用过去式。

T：He made some mistakes in his composition. Can you find them?

Ss：Yes.

S1：see—saw

S2：walk—walked

S3：eat—ate

S4：like—liked

（通过改错提醒学生注意动词形式的变化，提高他们写作时语言使用的准确度）

4. Let's compare

A camping trip

My friend and I were at a camp last week.	My friend and I were at a camp last week.
We played football and volleyball, walked in the mountains and played a lot of games. Mr Green cooked a lot of food.	The camping site was near the mountains. There were many tall trees beside our tents. I saw birds singing in the trees. We played a lot of games there. I played football with my friends on the green grass. We walked in the mountains, too. Mr Green cooked a lot of food for us. We ate a lot. We liked it very much.
I was very tried, but it was fun.	I was very tired, but it was fun.

T：Which composition is better? The left one or the right one?

Ss：The right one.

T：Why?

S1：They have the same Beginning and Ending. But their Main

bodies are different.

The left one is very simple. It is just about what they did. The right one is about what they saw and what they did. And the sentence structures are very rich.

T：Yes. An integrated composition contains three parts: Beginning, Main body and Ending. In the Beginning part, what can we write?

S2：When, who, where.（教师板书）

T：What about the Main body part?

S3：What you saw, what you did.（教师板书）

T：What about the Ending part?

S4：How you felt.（教师板书）

T：Can you write a good composition?

Ss：Yes.

T：OK. If you think you can, you can.

5. Look and say

1) T：I know, you went to Taihu Wetland Park for an autumn outing last year.

Look at this picture. When was it?

S1：It was last year.

T：Where did you go?

S2：We went to Taihu Wetland Park.

T：What did you see?

S3：I saw some tall trees, many beautiful flowers in it.

T：What did you do?

S4：I played cards, played games, ate snacks and drank some juice.

T：How did you feel?

S5：Excited.

2) T：Boys and girls, you must have been to many nice places before, just like parks, farms, zoos and so on. And last year, you

went to Taihu Wetland Park for an autumn outing. Here are two choices for you. Exercise A or Exercise B, which one do you want to choose? Think about it. Then ask and answer with these questions.

Ss：(Ask and answer the questions in pairs)

Ask and answer

A.	In the park
	On the farm
	In the zoo

B.	An autumn outing
	(Taihu Wetland Park)
	...

Composition structure

Beginning	When...?
	Who...?
	Where were you?
Main body	What did... see?
	What did... do?
Ending	How...?

6. Practice

1) T：Please write a composition about an autumn outing or a nice place you visited.

Ss：(Try to write a composition)

2) T：After you finished your composition, please read and check: the tense, sentence structures, words' spelling, handwriting and so on.

Ss：(Read and check)

3) T：(投影仪展示三篇作文，师生共同评价、修改)

Ss：(评价、修改)

4) T：Let's help each other.

① 教师出示修改符号。

② 学生互相帮助同桌修改作文,有不会写的单词可以请教老师或同学,也可以查词典。

③ 修改完作文后,互相评定等级。

(三星级作文,能运用比较丰富的语言生动地描写;二星级作文,能用三段话简单描写;一星级作文,内容简单,语法错误较多。)

5) T：Let's share.(与别人共同分享你的作文)

◆ 案例反思 ◆

上述案例中的授课对象是高年级的学生,教师布置的"写"的任务比较真实,教师不仅关注学生们写作的结果,更关注他们的写作过程,真正将培养学生实际写的能力落到了实处:写之前教师设计了很多铺垫和准备活动,既有语言方面的整理,也有文章结构方面的指导,这反映出教师对学生需求和困难的充分了解,教师只有读懂了学生的困惑,才能够给他们提供有针对性的帮助。

在语言准备的时候教师采用的是师生、生生互动的形式,促使学生在讨论、交流中回忆、整理与话题相关的语言,同时拓宽他们的思路,为最后的实践活动——"写"提供了语言上的支持;在指导文章的结构时,教师则巧妙地采用了与复述课文的活动相结合的方式,以学生熟知的课文内容为素材,通过重新组合、整理,向学生直观地演示了如何建构文章的框架。在完成这两项内容的指导后,教师没有就此止步,而是继续深入,以解读例文的形式让学生明白要完整地描述事件必须具备的几个要素——who, what, where, when,进而再通过让学生纠正片段中动词形式的错误来提醒学生注意表达时语言的准确度。

到活动最后的评价阶段,教师采用的是教师和学生共同评价的方式,这种让学生参与的评价方式能让学生有被尊重的感觉,从而发挥出他们的主观能动性。

不过,需要指出的是,没有哪个孩子喜欢看到自己的文章被老师密密麻麻的修改符号所覆盖。对于那些通过"写"的活动来复习某一类句型中的错误,教师需要及时予以纠正;但如果是运用性的作文中的错误,教师最好是有选择地更正,不要逢错必纠,毕竟,好的作文不是老师"改"出来的!

细节 11

如何激发学生玩英语、用英语的兴趣

细节阐述

由于年龄的特点,能让儿童积极投入其中的往往是那些能激起他们兴趣或者让他们有愉快体验的活动。所以,对于他们而言,兴趣是构成学习动机、促进主动学习的一个重要因素,一旦当他们对英语学习感兴趣时他们就会有说的欲望,学习效率也会大大提高。因此,小学英语教学中教师应当采取一切措施来激发学生们英语学习的兴趣,使他们喜欢学、乐于学、热爱学。在教学实践的时候教师可以尝试从以下几方面入手。

策略一:丰富课堂教学手段,激发学生"玩英语"的兴趣

在小学英语教学过程中,教师为了激发学生的学习兴趣会设计一些符合学生年龄特点的课堂活动,刚开始时出于新鲜感学生大多会兴致勃勃地参与其中,不过,随着时间的推移,"喜新厌旧"的小学生们开始对这些活动感到乏味,不再积极参与。所以,想要在课堂上始终抓住学生的"心",教师就需要不断变换教学方法,保持学生对课堂活动的"期待感"。下面介绍几种比较受学生欢迎的课堂活动形式。

方法一:小小作词家

译林版《牛津小学英语》3A Unit 1 Hello 一课中的歌曲是"Hello!"。由于歌词重复较多,且内容单调,学生唱了几遍就兴趣索然了,对此教师不妨让学生们改编歌词:把自己身边的同学、喜欢的朋友、自己的父母等填入歌曲,这样就有了 Hello Mike,Hello Miss Li,Hello Daddy……学生们觉得既新鲜又好玩,甚至乐于将全班同学的名字按序唱一遍。这不但可以促使学生主动参与,还能提升他们的学习兴趣。

方法二:小小艺术家

在教授学生关于颜色的单词时教师可以设计如下几个小活动。

活动1　如果授课对象是低年级的学生,教师可以采用让学生给代表该颜色的单词涂色的活动,这样的活动不但有效而且有趣,很容易引起低年级学生参与的兴趣,如:

black yellow red blue

活动2　对于中年级的学生,教师可以利用三原色原理,让学生通过科学实验得到一些颜色的变化规律,在发现中掌握关于颜色的单词。如:

blue＋yellow＝green　　　　red＋yellow＝orange

red＋white＝pink

活动3　让学生根据教师所读颜色的顺序给气球涂色,看谁涂得又快又好,这样使单一的听力训练变得更加有趣。如:

方法三:巧用简笔画

大多数情况下课堂气氛的活跃程度与学生学习兴趣的持久度取决于教师教学方法是否具有多样性和灵活性。在多媒体大行其道的今天,如果教师能偶尔变换一下教学手段,尝试利用简笔画促进学生学习、记忆的话,相信能起到意想不到的效果。

效果1　形象直观,便于记忆。在教授一些方位介词的时候,教师可以借助简笔画,通过寥寥几笔,让学生清楚明白地知道每个方位介词

的用途,轻松记忆。如:

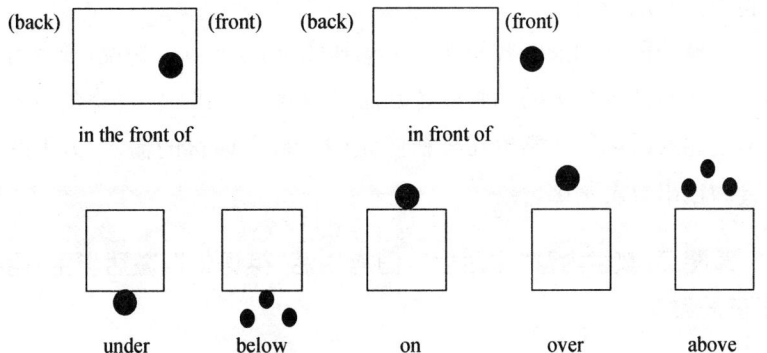

效果 2 惟妙惟肖,刺激学生学习热情。教授与运动相关的单词时,教师可以利用抽象但富有趣味性的简笔画来让学习内容变得生动而有趣。如:

效果 3 即时生成,以图说话。有时候教师在教授新的单词时,可能苦于找不到合适的途径和照片来传达单词的意思。简笔画的夸张和即时生成性能很好地解决这个问题。比如,教授单词 unhappy, terrible, crying, smile 时,教师可以先在黑板上画一个圆,然后添加寥寥几笔以呈现不同的表情,如图:

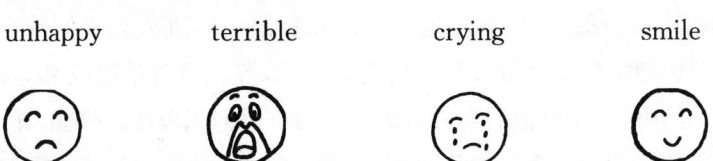

方法四:借助多媒体

随着信息技术的不断发展,电脑、白板、实物投影仪等器材在学科教学领域的使用日趋普遍。这些设备的使用不仅让抽象的语言变得形象化、具体化,而且还能够打破时间和空间的限制,为学生创设更加逼真和丰富的语用情境。

机械的朗读和操练容易让学生感到疲惫,针对这一情况,教师可以寻找一些与话题相关的动画或者歌曲,这些精美的图片、动态的效果和充满童趣的语调能让学生在轻松的氛围中接受语言的输入,为下一步语言的输出奠定基础。

策略二:教学内容"生活化",日常生活"英语化",激活学生"用英语"的思维

《英语课程标准》明确规定:要重视从学生的日常生活出发,培养学生实际运用语言的能力。这就要求教师结合学生的生活经验和已有的语言知识来设计富有趣味性、科学性的英语活动,使学生确实感到身边有英语、用英语能解决生活中的实际问题,从而对英语产生亲切感,增强学生运用英语的意识,培养学生的自主创新能力。

教学内容"生活化",要求教师尽量使用英语进行教学,给学生提供浓厚的英语学习氛围;给学生创造、提供逼真的密切联系生活的语言交际情境和创造性使用语言的机会,使课堂生活化,贴近学生的生活,让学生在熟悉的环境中探究新知,在语言使用过程中自由表达他们的思想感情。

教师通过思考,将教学内容和学生的已有知识、经验及生活阅历都结合在精心设计的教学活动中,在真实的生活情境中进行操练,加深了学生对所学知识的印象,真正做到学以致用。

日常生活"英语化"是指学生在教师的引导下,逐步具备在日常生活中使用英语的本领,并使他们认识到英语已经进入到我们的生活。教师要引导学生处处留心身边的英语知识,养成及时地吸收和运用英语知识的习惯,调动他们学习英语和运用英语的积极性。例如:让学生尝试用英文数字来表达电话号码、汽车牌照;让学生学习英语国名、世界著名景点名称、服装品牌;让学生通过认识不同国家的国旗学习英文中颜色的表达;让学生留心身边各种标志的英文写法;让学生收听国际频道的天气预报,学习表达天气的英语习惯用语等。这些活动使英语运用与学生实际生活相接轨,让学生体会到用英语的成就感、自豪感,从而激活学生用英语的思维。

▶·典型案例·◀

著名特级教师鲍当洪"Countries"课堂教学实例

片段一 利用真实情景,创设语言学习的语境,让学生自然融入英语语言的学习和运用中

Warming up

T: Hello, children!

Ss: Hello, Johnson!

T: Excuse me, Wang Yuteng, how are you today?

S1: I'm not very well.

(The boy looked ill.)

T: I'm sorry to hear that. Take care of yourself.

S1: Thank you, sir.

T: What are you doing, Wu Haining?

S2: I'm having an English class.

T: Well done! You're having an English class. You're listening to me. Is Lu Haikong listening to me, Bao Qiwen?

S3: Yes, she is.

T: Good boy! You're all good at English. You can go to other countries. Today we're going to talk about countries. China is a country. Say after me, "country".

Ss: Country.

T: Great. We know there are many countries in the world. So we will talk about some countries this class. Look. How do we spell "countries"? We change "y" into "i" from "country" first; then add "es" after "i". Understand?

Ss: Yes.

T：Wonderful.

（教师通过不同颜色的粉笔来板书单词，加深学生对country的复数形式的认知）

片段二 依托学生生活经验，注重联系生活实践，创造有利于学生英语表达的情景活动，刺激学生说英语、用英语的兴趣

Presentation and practice（Ⅰ）

1）Teach the new pattern：May I know your name?

T：Yes. We know countries. Excuse me, Wang Hao. What's your mother's name?

S1：My mother's name is... Sorry, I don't know.

（The lovely boy was too nervous to answer the question.）

T：It doesn't matter. Do you know my name?

S1：Yes. Your name is Bao Danghong.

T：You know my name. Thank you. But you should remember your mother's name. I know you love your mother. Tell me your mother's name next time. Be a good boy. See?

S1：I see. Thank you, Johnson.

T：You're welcome. Excuse me, Ye Jiachen, may I know your mother's name?

S2：Mm...?

T：May I know your mother's name? It means "What's your mother's name?"

S2：Oh, I see. Her name is Chen Yuhua.

T：May I know your grandma's name, Chen Qi?

S3：My grandma's name is Tan Lanlan.

T：Good. Look at the blackboard. Read after me. "May I know your name? My name is Jack."

Ss：May I know your name? My name is Jack.

2）Group work.

T：You did a good job. Do you want to know your classmates

well? You can ask them their father's, mother's, their uncle's name... Now please use "May I know your...'s name?" or "What's your...'s name?" to practise in your group. Now begin.

（学生进行两分钟的练习）

T：Well, now I want some of you to show us your dialogue. Who wants to have a try? OK. Lu Yuchuang, Zhang Jiahong, Liu Jiaqi, Lu Mingting and Wang Shiting, please.

（在小组练习的基础上，每组叫一位同学起来进行对话，检查新句型的掌握情况，这个练习加深了学生之间的了解和友谊）

S1：May I know your father's name, Zhang Jiahong?

S2：His name is Zhang Hua. May I know your mother's name, Liu Jiaqi?

S3：Her name is Chen Lin. What's your aunt's name, Lu Mingting?

...

（老师再请五位同学进行练习，通过旧的句型带动新的句型，精讲多练，层次清楚，过渡自然）

片段三　利用时尚元素，贴近学生生活，让学生们乐于用英语表达，为他们创造玩英语的机会

1. Presentation and practice（Ⅱ）

1) Teach the new sentence patterns：Where are you from? Where do you come from?

T：May I know your father's name, Wu Yuyun?

S1：My father's name is Wu Guoliang.

T：Great! Wu Yuyun's father is Wu Guoliang. Her father is from Zhangjiang. So Wu Yuyun is from Zhangjiang. I am from Zhuhai. Understand?

Ss：Yes.

T：Wonderful! Who can answer my question? Where are you from?

S2：I'm from Hunan.

T: Good, Zhang Ying is from Hunan. Where are you from, Ye Yanyu?

S3: I'm from Qingdao.

T: Do you like Qingdao beer?

S3: No, I don't.

T: All right. Don't drink too much beer. OK. Where are you from, Chen Mijia?

S4: I'm from Hebei.

T: Chen Mijia is from Hebei. She likes noodles very much. Where are you from, Wei Jing?

S5: I'm from Zhongshan.

T: Wow! Weijing is from Zhongshan. Zhongshan is famous for Mr Sun Zhongshan. Now, look at the blackboard and read after me. "Where are your from? I'm from Zhongshan. Where are you from? I'm from Hunan."

Ss: Where are you from? I'm from Zhongshan. Where are you from? I'm from Hunan.

（教师通过了解班级里学生的家庭情况，使学生消除了紧张感，让他们感到亲切、自然，同时也能有话可说）

T: Good! Where are you from, Zhuang Qihua?

S6: I'm from Maoming.

T: Listen. If you want to know somebody where he is from, you can say, "Where do you come from?" The answer is: "I'm from..." or "I come from..."

T: Please read after me. "Where do you come from? I come from Hunan."

Ss: Where do you come from? I come from Hunan.

T: OK. Where do you come from, Li Jiahe?

S7: I come from Gansu.

T: Excuse me, Zhu Binghui, where do you come from?

S8: I'm from Yunnan.

(通过刚学会的新句型,拓展表达同样含义的另一句型,增加了学生的知识量)

2) Game: Where is he from? Where does she come from?

T: That's OK. We come from different cities. We come from different places. Can you speak your local language? Now I want four of you to come to the front.

(分两次,每次请四位同学出来,每人讲一句家乡话,让别的同学猜猜说话的同学来自哪里)

S1: ... Where am I from?

(She spoke the local language of Hunan. Then she asked her classmates.)

S2: You are from Hubei.

S1: Sorry. Where am I from?

S3: You're from Sichuan.

S1: No. I'm not from Sichuan.

T: All right. Where are you from, Yun Xuan?

S1: I'm from Hunan.

T: Haha. You're from Hunan. But don't eat too much Hunan food. It's hot. It's not good to eat too much hot food in Guangdong.

(教师反应敏捷,马上提醒学生要注意饮食,体现了教师对学生的关爱)

S4: ... Where am I from?

(He spoke the local language of Shandong.)

...

T: Great. Ouyang Huaqing is from Hubei. So he's clever. Do you know why? Because someone says: "If a person comes from Hubei, he has 9 heads." See?

(让学生说家乡话,请别的同学猜,既活跃了课堂气氛,又巩固了刚学的新句型。教师还引用了民间的说法,起到更好的效果)

2. Presentation and practice (Ⅲ)

T：(Teach the new words: China, Britain, Australia, Japan, America and Canada)

T：Zheng Jingchen, what do you like doing at the weekends?

S1：I like sleeping.

T：Oh, you like sleeping. Maybe you're a little overweight. Don't sleep too much. Do some exercises.

T：What do you like doing, Yao Wanqin?

S2：I like dancing. I have dancing lessons every Sunday morning.

T：I see. Yao Wanqin likes dancing. She is the best dancer in our school. Can you guess? What do I like doing?

S3：You like teaching English.

T：Of course, I like teaching English. What do I like doing? Any more?

S4：You like sleeping. You should keep fit.

(在老师了解学生的爱好的同时，也让学生了解老师的爱好，体现了师生平等的教育原则)

T：That's OK. Let's keep fit together. But I like travelling the best. "Travel", understand? It means "visit". I have been to some cities in China. And I have been to other countries. Do you want to see my pictures? Where is Mr Bao now?

(老师出示一些在异地的照片，让学生根据照片来回答问题)

Ss：In Beijing.

T：Yes, I was in Beijing. In Beijing you can see the Great Wall, Tian'anmen Square, the Summer Palace and so on. There are many famous universities in Beijing too. Also in Beijing you can eat the Beijing duck. Where is Mr Bao now?

Ss：In Hong Kong.

T：Do you like Hong Kong?

Ss：Yes, we do.

T：Hong Kong is a busy city. What can you do there?

Ss：Go shopping, eat the sea food and play in the Ocean Park...

T：Great. We know Beijing, Suzhou, Jiuzhaigou, Hong Kong, Shanghai and Hunan are in China. "China". We are from China.

（老师将中国国旗贴在黑板上，写上英文 China）

T：Say after me. "China. I come from China. I live in China. I like China."

Ss：China. I come from China. I live in China. I like China.

（通过看老师在国内旅游的一些照片和师生轻松的对话，为后面学习其他几个国家的名字埋下伏笔）

T：Look at this picture. Is Mr Bao in Hong Kong, Tao Yixuan?

S5：No. You are in Dalian.

T：Sorry. Two years ago, I went to Britain to study. In the picture I was visiting London. Do you see the building with a big clock?

Ss：Yes.

T：Well done. It's the Big Ben. The Big Ben is in Britain. London is in Britain, too. This is the National Flag of Britain. Say after me. "Britain, Britain."

Ss：Britain, Britain.

T：In Britain there are many old buildings. You can see old houses and old streets. Of course there are old persons and young children, too. I was happy in Britain. I believe some of you will go to Britain to study, to visit London or to work there some years later.

T：Do you like Britain?

Ss：Yes, we do.

（教师在英国的照片引起学生的兴趣，学生还学会了介绍一个国家的句型，教师借此机会教育学生学好英语，为了解世界、走向世界而努力学习）

T: We have seen the Big Ben and some pictures of Britain. Look at this picture. Can you see Mr Bao, Lin Zewei?

S6: Yes. You're in a black coat.

T: Smart boy! They're my classmates and my teacher. Look at this man. He's my teacher. His name is Simon. Where does Simon come from? Can you guess, Yang Yi?

S7: I think he's from Britain.

T: Sorry. Simon isn't from Britain. Where is he from?

S8: He's from London.

T: No, he's from Australia. "Australia." In Australia you can see the kangaroos. Look at the picture. What animals are they?

(教师将澳大利亚的国旗贴在黑板上,并写上英文 Australia)

Ss: Kangaroos.

T: Yes! They are from Australia. Say after me. "Australia. Simon is from Australia."

Ss: Australia. Simon is from Australia.

(教师通过在英国时的照片和袋鼠的照片,使学生理解了 Australia 这个新的单词,同时对澳大利亚特有的动物袋鼠有了进一步的了解)

T: Yes, you can see kangaroos here and there in Australia. Look. What are they?

Ss: 寿司。

T: Yes. "寿司" in English is Sushi. Do you like Sushi?

Ss: Yes, we do.

T: I like Sushi too. But it takes much money to eat Sushi. Maybe you can eat Sushi in Japan. I think it will be cheaper there. "Japan". See? Where does Sushi come from?

Ss: It comes from Japan.

T: Good. Look, this is the National Flag of Japan. How do you spell "Japanese", Liu Xiaoyi?

S9：J-a-p-a-n-e-s-e, Japanese.

T：Well done! Look. How do we spell "Japan"? We take "ese" away from "Japanese". See?

Ss：Yes.

（教师根据学生的生活特点，通过他们喜欢的食物寿司引出新单词Japan，过程自然，效果好。教师还给学生介绍了一种有效的记忆单词的方法，培养了学生的观察能力）

T：What can you do in Japan, Zhu Haitong?

S10：I can go to Disney.

T：What can you do in Japan, Lin Jing?

S11：I can buy beautiful clothes and eat Sushi.

T：Would you like to take me to Japan with you?

S11：I'd love to.

（通过师生对话，检测学生对所学知识的运用，起到"学中用"的效果）

T：Good girl! You're so kind. Do you like basketball, Bao Qiwen?

S12：Yes, I do. I play basketball after school.

T：Look. Who's the strong man?

S3：Jordon.

T：What does Jordon do, Lin Jing?

S13：He's a basketball player.

T：What does he do every day?

S14：He plays basketball.

T：Right. Where is Jordon from?

Ss：He's from America.

T：Good. Say after me. "Where is Jordon from? He's from America."

Ss：Where is Jordon from? He's from America.

T：Look. When we take "n" away from "American", we can get "America".

（利用学生喜爱的偶像辅助教学新单词，直接、明了，还复习了以前学过的句型，做到"温故而知新"）

T：Well done. Guess, who's the handsome man?

S15：Yao Ming.

T：You're so smart. Is Yao Ming your favourite basketball player?

S15：Yes.

T：What are you going to be?

S15：I'm going to be a basketball player.

T：That's great. I think I will be your fans some years later. Yao Ming plays basketball in America. But he still loves China. We are Chinese. China is our motherland. See?

Ss：Yes.

（通过姚明的一张卡通图片对学生进行爱国主义教育，并鼓励有理想的同学去努力）

T：Look, this is a leaf. Which country's National Flag has a leaf on it? Do you know?

Ss：Canada.

T：Very good. This is the National Flag of Canada. The leaf is from Mr Long. He gave me the leaf before this class. He told me the leaf is from Canada. Now say after me. "Canada. Canada. Where is the leaf from? It's from Canada."

Ss：Canada. Canada. Where is the leaf from? It's from Canada.

（教师将加拿大国旗贴在黑板上，并写上英文 Canada）

T：Yes, we have learnt the new words. Look at the blackboard and read the new words.

Ss：China, Britain, Australia, Japan, America, Canada.

3. Presentation and practice（Ⅳ）

T：Well done. Among these countries I like Canada best. Why? I can see snow there. I like the white and soft snow there. I can go skating there. I can see some of my old pupils there. Understand? What country do you like? Why? Who can share with us? Good. Chen Tongyao, please.

（通过让学生听老师的表达，为后面的句型学习进行铺垫）

S1：I like Australia.

T：Why?

S1：Because my classmate Chen Fengchao is in Australia now. I want to see him.

T：Good job! Chen Fengchao went to Australia before the Chinese New Year. Do you miss him?

Ss：Yes.

T：I see. You've studied together for more than 5 years. You can write to him, call him or chat on QQ with him. Look at the blackboard and read after me. "What country do you like? I like Canada. I can see the white snow."

Ss：What country do you like? I like Canada. I can see the white snow.

（利用班上一起生活了五年多的同学移民到澳大利亚的实例，让学生表达他们的真实情感，既练习了句型，又培养了人与人之间要相互关心的美德）

T：How about you, Fang Jinyuan? What country do you like? Why?

S2：I like America. I can see the White House and the eagles.

T：Good. Now please share with your classmates. Use the sentence pattern："What country do you like? Why?" You have 3 minutes to do it in your group.

（师生之间清晰的小对话，为接下来的小组练习扫清了障碍）

T：So much for this exercise. Who wants to share with us? Let me play a game to see who is lucky today. When I beat the drum, please pass the apple and the pear. And when I stop, whoever gets the pear or apple, please share with us. Do you like this game?

Ss: Yes.

T: Let's go. Oh, Wu Haining and Wu Yanlin! You're lucky.

(通过让学生玩击鼓传花的游戏,让学生在轻松的气氛中进行新句型的操练和交流)

S3: What country do you like? Why?

S4: I like Japan. I can buy beautiful clothes and eat Sushi. What about you?

S3: Me too. I like Japan. I want to see the Fuji Mountain. I like climbing hills.

T: Well done! I know Wu Yanlin's mother very well. She likes beautiful clothes and Sushi. So like mother, like daughter. OK. Let's go on... Oh, it's your turn...

S5: What country do you like? Why?

S6: I like America. I stayed there for 6 years. I have many friends there. I want to play basketball with them. What country do you like?

S5: I like Canada. I can make snowmen there in winter.

(对话内容可以反映出学生们是在用英语表达各自的观点,是真实的交流,这种交流的感觉让学生体验到了学习语言的乐趣)

4. Have a chant

T: I think you're tired. Let's have a chant.

Tour round the world

Four, three, two, O!

Go! Go! Go!

One, two, three, four,

Go to Singapore.

Five, six, seven, eight,

Fly to the USA.

Nine, ten, nine, ten,

Travel to Japan.

Ss：...

（学生跟着节奏边拍手边读歌谣，既复习了单词，又缓解了紧张的学习情绪）

片段四　创造信息沟，以任务驱动学生语言学习的兴趣

1. Do a survey

T：Thank you. You all did well. Do you have good friends? Do you want to make new friends?

Ss：Yes.

T：Now you can interview your classmates or the teachers around you. But remember this：You are not yourself. You are another person. Look at this paper. You're Tom. You're 22 years old. You are a bus driver. You like Britain. You can ask your classmates or the teachers to make friends with them. These sentences can help you.

（老师用投影仪说明规则，使学生做到心中有数）

You can use the sentences：

May I know your name?/Excuse me, what's your name?/What's your name, please?

Where are you from?/Where do you from?/Are you from...? How old are you? What's your job? What country do you like? Do you like China?

Name	Where is he/she from?	How old is he/she?	What's his/her job?	What country does he/she like?

（教师准备了12个不同身份的资料，让学生将自己的信息告诉新

朋友,并通过对话,获取新朋友的信息。练习既操练了以前的旧知识,又给学生运用旧知识进行交际提供了机会)

T：OK. I think you have some new friends now. How many new friends do you have? Would you come here, Liu Qiyu?

S1：Yes.

T：How many friends do you have?

S1：Three.

T：Can you say something about your new friends?

S1：Let me have a try. Tommy is from Australia. He's 35. He's a driver. He likes China. Sue is 51. She's a shopkeeper. She's from Canada. She loves China. Miss Liu is a teacher. She is a Chinese. She wants to go to Japan.

T：Good job! Now please choose one of your new friends and introduce him or her to your classmates in your group.

(先让一个学生出来介绍新朋友的情况,以此做示范,再让同学们分小组就各自新朋友的情况进行交流)

2. Summary and homework

T：We have plenty exercise this class. We know the names of some countries. After class, please write some things about the country you like. You can surf the Internet, ask your teachers, your family and your classmates. Of course, you can go to the school library. OK?

Ss：OK.

(作业布置体现了新课标的要求,将课堂学习到的知识和生活实践结合起来,并通过各种获取信息的方式让学生体会学了就能用的成功感,从而激发学生学习英语的兴趣和勇于实践的精神)

T：Thank you for your wonderful actions in this class. This summer holiday I will visit Singapore. Would you like to go with me?

Ss：We'd love to.

T：Goodbye, children!

Ss：Goodbye, Johnson.

(有趣的结尾,再次让人感受到师生关系的融洽)

◆ 案例反思 ◆

鲍老师整节课如行云流水,环环相扣。学生们在轻松愉快的氛围中感受到了英语学习的乐趣。老师与学生之间的互动友好、自然,宛如"拉家常"的课堂教学过程让每个听课的学生都感受到了英语语言的魅力,在无形中刺激了学生乐于用英语表达的兴趣。

课堂伊始,鲍老师关注到一名学生的身体状况不佳,用英语"How are you today?","Take care of yourself."对学生身体状况进行了解并表达关心。这一细微之处不仅体现了鲍老师对学生的关怀,而且体现了鲍老师的课堂机智:通过和学生聊身边事,让学生自然地投入到学习环境、进入学习状态,与学生建立起融洽的关系。

课堂上,鲍老师设计了"May I know your father's name? What country do you like? Why?"等问答游戏,激活学生思维,激发学生学习的积极性,以旧知带动新知,培养了学生运用语言的能力。不仅加深了学生之间的相互了解,增进了学生间的友谊,也提高了他们运用英语进行交际,根据实际情景进行英语对话的能力。

教学过程中,鲍老师利用学生热爱的球星Jordon、Yao Ming,热衷的美食Sushi等创造了一定的语言交际情景,一下子就吸引了学生的兴趣和注意力,让学生有话可说,有话想说。此外,他为学生设计了12个来自不同地方的人物身份,让学生根据自己的不同信息去交朋友。学生需要运用英语去询问自己的朋友、同学或者老师,同时要听懂对方的英语并进行回答。鲍老师通过情景教学促进了学生个性的发展,提高了学生语言运用的能力,符合情景真实的教学原则。教学过程中鲍老师还特别注重对学生进行爱国主义教育,如在讲到姚明时,鲍老师说道:"Yao Ming plays basketball in America. But he still loves China... China is our motherland."值得一提的是,老师在教授Canada一词时,用一片来自加拿大的枫叶展开教学,他幽默的语言加深了学生对于新单词和新句型的记忆。"Like mother, like daughter."老师引用了谚语进行教学，开阔了学生语言学习的视野，提高了学生英语学习的兴趣，刺激了他们的无限求知欲。

由此可见，一节好的英语课不是教师"设计"出来的，而是教师用情感去激发学生的学习热情，用语言魅力去感染学生运用语言的信心，用与学生生活实践相结合的教学内容帮助学生达到学以致用的教学目的，从而让学生在轻松愉悦的氛围中达到玩英语、学英语、用英语的最高境界。

◆ 专家点评 ◆

在英语学习的最初阶段，出于好奇心，大部分学生都会学得兴致勃勃，但是随着学习的深入，必然会有部分学生开始打退堂鼓，这时教师的作用就显得格外重要，得想方设法激发和保持这些学生说英语的欲望。一位"用心"并且"贴心"的教师能助力学生的英语学习。所谓"用心"就是从教学安排到活动设计，要从学生的认知水平和生活经验出发，让学生有话能说，有话可说；"贴心"则是指教师要努力营造融洽的气氛，促使学生大胆开口，因为学生在尝试用新的语言表达时会表现得不自信。从上述鲍当洪老师的教学实录中我们可以发现，学生们从起初怯场、不敢说，到后来能说、愿意说，离不开老师不断的鼓励和帮助，这种友好的学习氛围让学生逐渐放松并积极投入到课堂学习中。需要补充说明的是，在课堂以外给学生创造"开口"的机会也非常重要，因为对于大多数学生而言，当他们发现英语不仅仅是默单词和背课文，而是可以真正成为与他人沟通与交流的工具时，这些活动经历和成就感就能反过来对学生说英语的欲望产生推动作用，这样，他们学英语、用英语的兴趣也会大大增强。

细节 12

如何鼓励学生开口

▶ **细节阐述** ◀

英语是研究口头语言和书面语言规律及表达技巧的学科,口语交际能力是构成良好英语素养的不可或缺的重要内容,在英语教学中具有与读、写同等重要的地位和作用。对小学生来说,学好口语是学生生活和进一步接受教育的需要。一方面,说和听的能力能帮助小学生们建立起"伙伴友谊"和"与人合作的关系",口语水平的好坏还直接影响着他们对学好英语的自信与态度;另一方面,在当今全球经济信息化的大环境中,学生需要用英语交谈和聆听,他们的理解力、创造力和想象力需要通过讨论和相互交流才能得以培养、提高和发展。口语正是他们参与这些活动必备的一项技能。

英语教师要把英语当作交际工具,注重培养和提高小学生的口语表达能力;在教学中要将语言内容和生活中的情景紧密结合,为学生创造各种实践语言的机会,努力让语言教学走向生活,在生活中学,为生活而用。

策略一:为开口说搭建舞台、编创剧本

小学英语教师首先要注重在课堂上为学生营造一个良好的英语氛围。教师带头说英语,用英语组织教学,建立和谐的师生关系,营造宽松的口语表达氛围,使学生能保持说英语的积极性。教师要主动融入教学活动,同时扮演"导演"和"演员"的角色,在轻松愉快的学习气氛中有效培养学生大胆开口、积极实践的语言学习习惯。

策略二：让模仿成为开口的第一步

流利地表达自己的第一步是通过听来获取大量的语言资料,扩大词汇量,掌握一定量的英语句型;与此同时模仿说话者的语音语调,循序渐进地提高说英语的能力。教师可利用教材中的会话原文,让学生听录音模仿,反复跟读,以使学生掌握正确的语音、语调和简单的单句会话。除课上模仿外,还要把模仿练习作为一项作业留给学生课下完成。模仿时要求学生放开声音。另外,可利用合作学习的教学模式,让学生互相帮助。

策略三：用句型激发开口的意愿

句型操练是学生交际能力的基础,句型教学不应只停留在句子的形式上,更应该注重句型的实际运用。在学生基本掌握句型的基础上,教师要引导学生在情境中运用、实践这些句型。教师在示范基本句型之后,可以给出替换词,让学生全班或分组进行替换练习。这一步完成后可以进行扩展练习,也就是在基本句型的基础上不断增减内容,从而使学生举一反三,为学生在实际中自然运用语言表达自己奠定基础。

策略四：用复述整合语言运用

英语学习的实践证明复述是一种很好的训练口语和记忆单词、句子的方式。教师应在学习完课文的基础上引导学生复述。复述练习中可以先要求学生使用一两句话来复述课文的主要内容,逐步发展到复述全部内容。教师也可以将课文内容变成问题,学生将问题的答案串联在一起便是课文内容的再现。此外,教师还可以将一些重点词汇提供给学生,让学生以这些重点词汇作为复述的线索。

策略五：其他形式多管齐下

在口语训练中,教师可充分利用学生善于模仿、好表现自己的特点,采用边看、边听、边说的方法培养学生运用语言的能力。可采用对话、角色扮演、看图说话等多种形式灵活开展口语训练。教师要注意学生的个性差异和实际英语水平,有的放矢地进行教学。对性格外向、大胆活泼的学生,在保护他们积极性的前提下,从严要求,让他们说得好、说得准。对性格内向、反应稍慢的学生,应着重培养他们敢说和愿意说的意愿,鼓励他们开口回答问题。

► 典型案例 ◄

摘自全国著名教师田湘军"Sailing"课例

教学片段一　课前热身,消除学生紧张情绪

Warming up

T：Which songs can you sing?

S1：*Little Star*.

T：Oh, *Little Star*. That's "Twinkle, twinkle, little star", yes? OK, let's begin. Twinkle twinkle little, 1, 2, go!

T& Ss：(Sing) Twinkle, twinkle, little star...

(在热身环节,田老师充分利用上课前的时间,和学生进行英语对话交流,组织演唱歌曲。通过这些自然、真实的交流,让学生在轻松的氛围中消除了开口紧张的情绪)

教学片段二　幽默对话,让学生敢于说

T：Good afternoon, boys and girls.

Ss：Good afternoon, sir.

T：I'm your new English teacher. And you can call me Mr Tian. You know, new teacher, new students. So I don't know you, and you don't know me. Yes?

Ss：Yes.

T：So I want to know something about you. OK, who can stand up and tell me something about yourself? OK, you please. What's your name, please?

S1：I'm Zhou Jian.

T：Zhou Jian. Ah... nice to meet you.（与学生握手）

S1：Nice to meet you, too.

T：Good! Sit down, please. Excuse me, where are you from?

S2：Eh, I'm..., I'm from Ma Yuting... I'm from, I'm from Nanjing.

T：You are from Nanjing. Your name is Ma Yuting. Yes? Haha... You are not from Ma Yuting.（全班笑）Yes, sit down, please. Next one? Ah... What's your favourite colour?（见学生不太理解或紧张）What colour do you like?

S3：I like pink.

T：You like pink. So your favourite colour is pink. Thank you. Sit down, please. The next.（对一男孩）Eh... what's your favourite sport? You know.（做动作）You are tall. You are strong. Yes, I think you must like sports. What's...

S4：I like swimming.

T：You like swimming. Oh, you are so strong. I'm sure when you fall into the river, you'll not sink.（师笑、生笑）So swimming, do you like swimming?

S4：Yes, I do.

T：Good! Alright. So, now, I know something about you students. Do you want to know something about me?

Ss：Yes.

T：Ask me. Ask me. You please.

S5：What animal do you like?

T：What animal do I like?（思索片刻）I like monkey.

S5：Me, too.

T：I like monkey, because I was born in the year of monkey.（模仿猴的动作，全班大笑）Alright. Any other questions? That boy please...

（田老师以平等的姿态与学生进行交流，与学生的交流风趣幽默而不失典雅。面对"I'm from Ma Yuting"这样的状况，田老师巧妙地为学生解围,使得整个教学过程更加轻松。当学生猜到田老师喜欢的动物时,他用鼓励性的话语并配合猴子的动作来调动学生说英语的积极性,一下子拉近了师生之间心理上的距离)

教学片段三　简笔画,让学生有兴趣说

Ss：Sailing, sailing...

T：Of course you don't know the meaning. (在黑板上简笔画两个三角形,组成小帆船) Now, look, ha-ha... what's this?

Ss：We don't know.

T：Is it a ship? (Ss：No.) Is it a plane? (Ss：No.) Is it a bus? (Ss：No.) What's this?

S1：A boat.

T：Yes, it's a boat! Good! It's a sailing boat. A sailing boat. "Sailing", how to spell? (学生拼读,教师板书) Sailing... (Ss：Sailing) Boat, how to spell "boat"? (学生拼读,教师板书) Good! Let's read them again. Sailing boat. (带读两遍)

Ss：Sailing boat...

T：A sailing boat sails in the sky? (做动作) No, where does a sailing boat sail?

Ss：In the sea.

T：In the sea or on the sea? It's on the sea. Alright, look! (画简笔画:一条直线) Now the sea is very very calm. It's very very smooth. Yes? But now look! (加大动作,配上怒吼声,画出波浪曲线) Now you can see, the sea is not calm. The sea is not calm. It's stormy. (板书) Read after me. (带读) Stormy...

Ss：Stormy...

T：Yes, and you can see water here, water there and water everywhere. Yes? So stormy water. But look up... (指海上面) here is the...

Ss：Sky.

T：Very good! How do you spell "sky"? (学生拼读,教师板书)

Up to the sea is the sky. What can you see in the sky?

Ss：Birds.

T：Birds, thank you. Birds.(画鸟)Ha-ha, this is a bird. Now, another one. How many birds can you see here?

Ss：We can see 3.

T：Yes, you can see 3 birds. How do you spell "birds"?(学生拼读,教师板书) Yes, so 1 bird, 2...

Ss：Birds.

T：2 birds, 3...

Ss：Birds.

T：3 birds. You can see the birds in the sky. What else can you see in the sky? That girl over there.

S2：I can see a plane.

T：You can see a plane? Oh, sorry. There's no plane here right now. Maybe later. Maybe another time. And now look here(画云彩), what can you see?

Ss：Cloud.

T：Cloud. How do you spell it?

Ss：C-l-o-u-d.(教师板书)

T：Yes, here is another cloud. And many many... clouds. Clouds.

Ss：Clouds.

T：The cloud is very...

Ss：High.

T：Yes, very high. High, h-i-g-h, high clouds(带读两遍), and the birds are...(做飞的动作)

Ss：Fly.

T：The birds are flying, yes, flying.(板书,学生跟读) Flying birds.(带读) And maybe here(画一小房子), this is my...

Ss：Home.

（田老师寥寥数笔表达出如此丰富完整的语言信息：波涛汹涌的大海上漂着一艘徐徐向前的小帆船，正带领着孩子们进入一个神奇的世界，那里有蓝天，有白云，有翱翔高飞的小鸟……从局部来看，每个单词或词组都有相应的简笔画来展现它的语言意义，如 sailing boat, flying birds, high cloud, stormy sea；从整个画面来说，可以让学生触景生情，了解到整首歌曲的内容。田老师巧妙地在英语课伊始运用简笔画，让学生积极主动地开口，快乐交流，动态生成，让课堂充满生命的活力）

教学片段四　做游戏，让学生抢着说

T：Alright. Boys and girls. Time for us to have a game. You can see a picture. But just a part of a big picture. Please guess, use this sentence pattern.（放出第一幅图）Is she...? Is she...? What is she doing? Is she...? Ah, this boy please. Yes.

S1：Is she washing her hands?

T：How clever you are! Is she washing her hands? Look!（完整显示全图）She is washing her hands. You are right! Big hands! You are so smart. Now, No 2.（放第二幅图）What is the boy doing? Is he...?

S2：Is he watching TV?

T：Is he watching TV? No, sorry, he isn't. He isn't watching TV. You please.

S3：Is he playing computer games?

T：Is he playing computer games?（做夸张动作）No, he isn't. Alright, that girl.

S4：Is he playing volleyball?

T：Is he playing volleyball?（做打排球动作）Is he playing volleyball? No, he isn't.

S5：Is he playing basketball?

T：Is he playing basketball?（做打篮球动作）No, he isn't.

S6：Is he playing football?

T：Is he playing football?（做踢足球动作，夸张，全班笑）No,

he isn't.

S7：Is he jumping?

T：Is he jumping?（动作夸张，全班笑）No, he isn't.

S8：Is he talking with her classmates?

T：Is he talking with her?（提高音调）

S8：With his.

T：Is he talking with his…

S8：Classmates.

T：Sorry. No, he isn't. Thank you. Anyway, nice try.

S9：Is he running?

T：Is he running? No, he isn't.（两手一摊）Come on. Alright.（做打乒乓球动作）What's he doing now? You please?

S10：Is he playing table tennis?

T：Yes, you are right! Look!（完整显示全图）He is playing… 1, 2, go!

Ss：He is playing table tennis.

T：Good. Try this one.（放第三幅图）Look at this beautiful lady now. Ha… what's she doing now? Is she…? Is she…?

S11：Is she dancing?

T：（做跳舞动作）Bazhahei!（全班笑）No, she isn't. She isn't dancing. This boy.

S12：Is she singing?

T：Is she singing?（做唱歌动作）Yalaso… no, she isn't. She isn't singing. Oh, that girl.

S13：Is she taking a photo?

T：Try again. Pardon?

S13：Is she taking a photo?

T：Is she taking photos? Yes, she's taking photos. Where? Where is she? She is taking photos.

S14：She is on the grass.

T: On the grass? No, sorry. She is not taking photos. She's not singing. She is not dancing. She is...（模仿马的声音,学骑马动作）who can? You please?

S15：Is she riding a horse?

T: Yes. You are right! Big hands! Wow! You are so smart. She's not singing. She is not dancing. She is riding a... horse. She is riding a horse. Alright, let's see,（完整显示全图）she is riding a horse. Hmm... now let's see the last one. This is the last picture.（放第四幅图）Look at this girl. She is a student. Now she's sitting here,（做动作）what's she doing now?（全班笑）Is she playing computer games like this?（做动作,全班笑）What's she doing now? Guess?

S16：Is she growing flowers?

T: Is she growing flowers? Ah... is she growing flowers? Wow, no, she isn't. Sorry.

S17：Is she washing clothes?

T: Is she washing clothes? Oh,...（故意装出好像是对的神态）No! No, she isn't. What's she doing?

S18：Is she bye-bye?

T: Bye-bye?

S18：By bike.

T: Oh, I know what you mean. Is she riding a bike? Yes?（做骑车的动作）Riding a bike, yes? Hmm... Is she...（做滑稽动作,全班笑）riding a bike like this?（做下蹲骑车动作,学生大笑）No, you can't ride a bike like this.

S19：Is she cooking?

T: Is she cooking?（做动作）Maybe. Yes, maybe. When you go out for a picnic. But, no. No, she isn't cooking. You please?

S20：Is she sitting?

T: Yes, she is sitting there. But what is she doing at that time?

OK, you please.

S21: Is she eating?

T: Is she eating? No, she isn't hungry at that time. She isn't eating. OK, that girl.

S22: Eh... Is he drawing?

T: He, he...（师生同笑）he or she?

S22: Is he.. is she drawing?

T: Is she drawing?（做动作）Is she drawing on the... Is she drawing on the ground? Is she drawing...（故意装出好像是对的神态）Ah... no. she isn't drawing. I am sure you don't know that.. Look at me!（蹲下边走边吹口哨，然后做丢东西的动作和鸟飞的动作）That boy please. （学生议论：噢，喂鸟）What's she doing? Is she...?

S23: Is she looking for...?

T: Is she looking for birds? Is she looking for birds? Because the birds are flying, flying, flying passing over high clouds and home again. Yes? No. Ah, would you have another try?

S23: Is she catching the insects?

T: Is she...（放慢说话的速度）catching an insect? Very good... answer. But it's not true. Alright. You don't know this word. I'm sure you don't know that. But you have tried a lot. That's good. She is feeding the pigeons.（放图片）A pigeon is a kind of bird. Yes? So feeding, "feed" means give something to the bird to eat. Give something to the birds to eat. Do you know its Chinese meaning?（Ss：Yes.）What does it mean?

S24: 她正在给鸽子喂食。

（田老师通过展示部分图片，引导学生用"What's she doing now? Is she...?"句型进行猜测游戏。在这个过程中，田老师引导学生在学习语言的同时运用所学语言，利用丰富的肢体动作帮助学生理解所学语言的含义，并学会灵活运用。愉快的游戏，随性的模仿，让学生积极

地参与课堂口语交流)

教学片段五 自编歌词,让学生自主地说

T:Yes,big hands! So today we learned something about the present continuous tense. 今天我们学了一些关于现在进行时的内容。Look at the blackboard. Hum..... read after me. Sailing...(指黑板,带读)Sailing boat... clouds... high clouds... sky... in the sky... stormy... water... the sea... bird... birds... flying birds... Here you can find I am...(边说边板书,画出横线)sailing. Yes? Sing it. I am sailing...(手放耳边,以示倾听)(Ss:小声唱)No, no, sing after me.(边带唱边做动作)I am sailing...(竖大拇指表扬)I'm sailing... Home again... across the sea.(用动作示意学生特别注意)I am walking...(根据情景已改词,做动作)I am walking... in the gym, in the gym... I am walking in the gym. I am happy to see you here.(学生还在陶醉)Big hands for me!(全班热烈鼓掌)Thank you very much. Boys and girls, now, it's time for you to compose your own songs. To compose your own songs. For example, reading.(放PPT)I am reading, I am reading...(边唱边放出每句歌词)in the classroom, in the classroom. I am reading in the classroom. I am happy to read here. Now, it's time for you to compose your own songs. Please work in groups. Do you understand? 以小组为单位,自创一首歌曲,不一定用 reading, 可以用其他动词,比如说:(做一系列滑稽夸张的动作)I am jumping...(全班大笑)I am learning. I am dancing.(全班大笑)给大家两分钟时间准备,看那一组编得更好,然后上台表演。Come on!

Ss:(小组同学开始兴高采烈地讨论。教师边小声放已学歌曲,边巡回到每一组进行交流指导)

T:Alright. Boys and girls, stop please. Now I'm going to check which group can compose their own songs. 检查哪一组编出了自己非常有特色的歌曲。Which group? OK, that girl. Your group. Stand up and come here. 10,9,8,...(加快速度数数,该小组学生站

到了台前）Alright. Good! One microphone for you, my super star.（教师唱："You are my super star."全班笑）Alright. So, shiiiii... Let's enjoy it. 3, 2, 1, go!

G1：I am sitting.（小组小声笑唱。教师参与）I am sitting... in/on the...

T：What are you doing? You are sitting, yes?（G1：Yes）Where are you sitting?

G1：On the chair.

T：On the chair, OK? Now, please sit on the chair（做动作）and try it again. 1, 2, go.

G1 & T：I am sitting... on the chair...（小组边唱边做动作，教师故意装出难受的表情）on the chair...

T：OK, stop. I am very tired. Big hands anyway. You have done a very good job. Thank you. Go back to your seat. I am sure you are very very happy. Yes? Alright. That group. Stand up. You want to have a try. Come here. 10, 9, 8, ...（学生站好）let's go!

G2：I am sleeping,... I'm sleeping on the bed...（小组边笑唱边做动作，教师参与）I am sleeping on the bed...

（田老师最后组织学生小组合作，自编歌词进行替换演唱。田老师很好地将语言学习与思维训练相结合，调动学生已有的知识，并构建起新的知识和经验，在田老师的启发下，学生的思维被充分激活，其发散性也得到了培养。学生不仅学会了这首英文歌曲，掌握了句型，而且从开口说中得到了肯定，体验了成功）

◆ 案例反思 ◆

田老师这节课的教学内容是现在进行时。授课伊始他不是以单个的动作情景导入，而是设置一个"Sailing"的情景，让学生整体感知现在进行时，然后通过之后的教学环节，让学生理解，最后巩固运用，每个环节的设计都是顺理成章。

首先，田老师以话题"Sailing"并结合简笔画导入，让学生了解航海时的情景，也为下面的听歌、做游戏等环节做了铺垫；接着，他让学生听歌曲《Sailing》并进行猜图游戏，为学生搭建语言支架，让学生顺利登上"台阶"开口表达；最后，设计自由编歌这个活动，以小组合作的形式，让每一位学生参与到语言活动中来。

田老师精湛的简笔画，丰富的肢体语言，风趣幽默的教学风格，和谐友好的师生互动，使学生始终处于积极的语言学习状态。

◆ 专家点评 ◆

在英语学习的最初阶段，由于学习的内容比较简单，加上好奇心的驱使，班级中会有大部分学生积极参与到课堂活动中。随着学习的深入，难度开始增大，部分学生由于不良的学习习惯、学习方法等因素的影响开始掉队，这直接导致了有些原本对英语学习很有兴趣的学生渐渐地失去学习的积极性，主要表现为这些学生课堂上不再踊跃发言，即使被老师叫起来回答问题也显得很不自信。所以，从中高年级开始，教师可能需要花大量的精力来保持学生的学习热情和积极性。但是无论采用哪种方法，给予学生一个有"安全感"的学习环境非常重要。细读上面的教学案例，我们可以发现，无论是热身环节时的师生介绍还是教学过程中简笔画、游戏和歌曲的运用，或者是教师口中时不时蹦出的幽默的课堂话语，都表明教师在力求创设一个宽松的学习氛围，努力消除或减轻学生学习中由于遇到困难或阻碍而产生的焦虑情绪。只有当学生感受到了这种"安全"，他们才会大胆地投入到学习的各个环节中。由此看来，教学的艺术真的就是善待学生的艺术！

细节 13

如何组织合作学习

> ● 细节阐述 ●

合作学习(cooperative learning)又称"小组学习""团队学习""分享学习",是指学生在小组或团队中为了完成共同的任务,有明确责任分工的互助性学习。对学生而言,合作是一种学习方式;对教师而言,它则是教学时采用的一种策略。合作学习不仅可以发挥学生的主体作用,促使他们主动参与到学习的进程中,而且还能提升他们与人交际的能力和解决问题的能力。英语是语言实践类科目,它的熟练程度与使用的时间成正比,小组合作学习的时候学生通过生生互动的方式可以获得比师生互动时更为丰富的语言实践机会。基于上述几个原因,《英语课程标准》中把"积极与他人合作,共同完成学习任务"列为基本学习策略之一。

一、课堂中合作学习的具体操作

1. 合理分组

科学合理的分组是合作学习的重要保障,小组在构成上应体现班级学生的个体差异性,力求使组员在学习成绩、性别、性格特征等方面具有异质性和代表性。小组可以由固定的成员组成,也可以是按照英语教学的需要分成的小组,或者是开放式小组——学生自由组合的小组。因此,划分合作小组时,教师应根据不同的教学目标和内容,采取不同的合作方式。在实践过程中,教师要确保每位组员都有事做,并担负起自己承担的责任。另外,教师还可以通过让小组成员不定期地互换角色来保持学生参与小组合作活动的积极性。

2. 合作形式

根据学习内容、学习目标以及学习者的情况,课堂上教师可以采用多种分组方式,主要有以下几种:

(1)相邻分组:位置决定组织,成组快捷简单。小组成员间座位以面对面或相邻形式为好。这样更有利于互相学习、讨论,达到充分交流的目的。

(2)自由分组:选择注定默契,学生快乐学习。当学生自己选择小组的时候,他们往往乐于选择那些相处融洽的伙伴,由于他们互相了解,彼此信任,所以在合作时能够无所顾忌,敞开心扉,坦诚交流。

(3)性别分组:性别决定组别,优势成就特色。男生和女生在组内发挥各自的性别特点,达到互相学习、共同发展的目的。如,角色扮演活动等可以充分发挥各自性别优势。

(4)正反分组:立场划定阵营,对决演绎精彩。这种分组的方式比较适合思维发展到一定层次的高年级学生,因有自己的观点,所以可以争鸣、碰撞出新知。

3. 合作评价

对小组合作学习的评价要从关注"成败"和"胜负"转向关注"进步"和"发展",把评价的重心由鼓励个人竞争达标转向大家合作达标。

(1)有对目标知识准确而熟练的掌握。基于目标词汇的认知和记忆的小组合作活动,尽管没有新的生成,但只要学生经历了小组合作学习之后能够准确而熟练地掌握目标词汇,就是有效的小组合作学习活动。

(2)有新的、有意义的内容的生成。基于目标词汇和句型等进行理解和运用的小组合作活动,判断其有效性的标准之一就是要考察活动过程中学生运用所学语言是否具有生成性的特征。

(3)有积极的思维活动过程的锻炼。在各种小组合作学习活动中,只要学生在活动过程中经历了积极的思维活动,得到了有意义的思维训练,小组合作学习就是有效的。

(4) 有愉快的情绪、情感生发的体验。有些小组合作学习活动可能新知识的生成很少,但是学生经历了教师设计的小组合作学习活动之后,兴趣提高了,合作的愿望增强了,这样的活动就是有效的。

(5) 有小组中每位学生均参与学习活动的效果。这是从学生参与性的角度来考察小组合作学习的有效性,它要求教师设计的小组合作学习活动充分关注学生,保证每一位学生在教师设计的活动中都能学有所获。

二、教师在合作学习中的角色

学生合作学习模式使教师在教学中的地位发生了根本的改变,教师是活动的组织者、引领者、促进者和合作者,具体表现如下:

1. 教师是合作学习的组织者

在合作学习前,教师布置任务,使学生有目的地进行讨论;在合作学习中,教师让学生自由发表意见,在互动中掌握所学内容;在合作学习后,教师及时对学生的展示成果进行点拨和引导。

2. 教师是合作学习的引领者

在呈现核心话题时,教师发出指令帮助学生理解,下达活动任务;当学生在活动交流中出现问题时,教师对学生进行学法指导、个别辅导,指导学生活动或解决活动中出现的问题,答案从学生讨论中来;当对知识进行归纳、解释、提炼时,教师帮助学生思考并完成学习任务。

3. 教师是合作学习的促进者

在合作学习中教师要消除学生不愿意开口的心理障碍,尤其要关注那些沉默的学生,给他们以鼓励和指导,使他们融入小组学习活动中去。教师应实时帮助学生解决困难。

4. 教师与学生是合作者的关系

在合作学习中教师与学生之间相互学习。教师与学生进行广泛的思想交流时,应有一种"学生是我的工作伙伴"的想法,问题的解决、目标的达成应建立在师生合作的关系之上。

三、课堂学生合作学习中存在的问题及解决策略

1. 问题一:课堂活动形式化

具体来说,就是"为活动而活动",学生只是坐在一起,并没有按教师设定的目标进行。有的在埋头写作业,有的在三三两两、津津有味地闲聊题外话,有的因害羞内向而沉默不语、独自发呆。事实上,小组合作学习并不是形式上简单地让学生凑在一起。这种情况已经失去了小组合作学习的意义。教师错将手段当作教学目的,没有从具体教学内容出发,忽略了教学内容和主题设计。

解决策略:

(1) 可以为不同个性和不同层次的学生制定不同的学习目标。教师应针对不同层次和不同个性的学生进行引导,在合作中调动全体学生参与学习探讨,共同商讨。

(2) 在独立思考、自主学习的基础上合作学习。合作学习目的是把小组中的不同思想进行优化整合,把个人独立思考的成果转化为全组共有的成果,共同解决问题。没有了独立思考的过程,合作就会失去真正的意义。如果教师设计的合作学习的问题没有一定难度,讨论就没有意义,就不能促进学生思维的发展。

合作学习既要重视形式多样,更要重视内容的价值。安排学生合作学习的内容,应该是多数学生感兴趣的、关心的内容。在选择这些内容时,除了教师指定,更重要的还应该是由学生自己提出。在自主学习的基础上合作学习,讨论交流时,个人都要充分发表意见。教师要鼓励学生大胆提出见解,允许学生有争论,还应从机制上让"学困生"有发言的机会,使学生通过情感的交流、思维的碰撞,切实提高学习的有效性。

2. 问题二:小组组织形式不完善

小组分工不明确,合作学习组织无序。缺乏详细具体的课前规划,分组后小组长不能起到有效组织和协调伙伴的作用,使组内成员有合作之形而无合作之实。

解决策略：

（1）提升学生合作学习的主体性，强化责任意识。在合作学习、完成任务的过程中，学生始终是活动的主要角色。教师必须选择有讨论价值的内容，明确讨论的目标，组织有效讨论，通过合理分工，强化学生的责任意识。教师随时起到点拨、提示、帮助和引导学生的作用。

（2）培养学生的合作意识，掌握协作技巧。教师应适时把一些社交技能有目的地、准确地教给学生。这些社交技能主要包括领导能力、决策能力、取信于人的能力、交际能力以及化解矛盾的能力。

3. 问题三：时间安排不合理

教师担心活动影响教学进度和任务，仅从主观出发安排活动，合作学习的各个环节浅尝辄止，在尚未起到应有作用之前就匆匆进入下一环节，学生缺少潜心学习和探究的机会。

解决策略：

（1）要给足学生思考时间。合作学习应为每个学生提供自我表现机会。为避免合作学习成为个别学生的"一言堂"，在讨论交流之前教师必须给学生独立思考的时间，引导那些反应较慢的学生也能积极思考，为语言输出做好准备。这样，既能使学生养成独立思考的好习惯，又能保证每一位学生得到运用语言的机会。

（2）要给足学生讨论时间。学生有了自己的看法，想表达，希望得到同伴的支持与认可，如果没有充足的交流时间，小组内一些语言底子相对差的学生会被迫放弃交流机会。时间久了，他们就会失去学习的自信心，只听不说，达不到生生互动、互帮互学的目的。

4. 问题四：忽视培养学生的合作精神

教师缺少有意识的引导，学生间缺乏相互倾听的习惯和自觉配合的意识，不懂彼此欣赏和尊重，缺乏积极的参与思维，不能共同分享成功的快乐。

解决策略：

（1）倾听是合作学习的重要环节，倾听也是一种学习。因此，教师要着力培养学生认真听取别人意见的习惯，使学生意识到倾听别人发言首先是一种文明礼貌行为，是对发言者的尊重，只有认真倾听他人的发言,才能使发言者感到自己发言有价值。相反,当有人发言而无人倾听时,发言者就会觉得自己的发言无关紧要,从而积极性受到挫伤。同时也要让学生意识到倾听也是一种好的学习方法,从别人的发言中会得到很多启发,从小组其他成员身上能收获更多的知识、方法。教师要逐步培养学生学会"三听":一是要认真听每个同学的发言,不插嘴;二是要听出别人的发言要点,培养收集信息的能力;三是听后需作思考,提出自己的见解,提高处理信息、反思评价的能力。

(2)教师应组织学生对合作学习进行科学的评价。倾听是一种品质,评价是一种能力,学生必须在小组内认真倾听,积极评价,使小组合作学习发挥应有的作用。评价机制的介入,可以使学生更加注重合作过程中的行为表现。评价还可以使教师获得准确的反馈信息,反思合作活动的主旨以及自己对合作目标和活动的设计,以便做出及时调整,使合作学习更有成效。

5. 问题五:少数优秀生垄断了活动

由于有的合作学习活动难度过大,优秀生垄断了有限的锻炼机会,使其余学生成了听众。教师未起调控作用,未能给"学困生"必要的帮助,致使"学困生"在活动中收益甚少。合作学习活动达不到基本的学习目标,甚至加剧了学生成绩的两极分化。

解决策略:

(1)教师应从总体学情出发,把握难易度,设计适合学生实际语言水平的合作学习活动。合作学习活动既不能只考虑优秀生的语言能力,也不能降低教学要求,而是应同时兼顾"学困生"的最近发展区,以便让每一位学生都能顺利、有效地展开活动。

(2)自愿组合,然后教师再根据学生的组合情况,并在征得他们同意的情况下作适当的调整,确保小组之间能公平竞争,让"学困生"能在自己喜欢的环境中学习,优秀生也很乐意带动他们,合作依赖,同步提高。

(3)在合作学习中要充分利用激励性评价。对学生合作的评价,不能仅仅以小组成绩为评价标准,还要评价、表扬组内个别学生对该小组合作成果的"突出贡献",让他们感受到自己在小组中的重要作用,品尝到学习的"胜利果实",享受到学习的乐趣,从而产生学习动力。

6. 问题六:教师评价不到位

教师对学生探究的各种结果不做归纳和总结评价,或评语都是"很好",放弃了教学指导应有的"肯定与否定"的责任;或是只对学生个体评价,忽略了对小组团体的评价;或只重视对结果的评价而忽略了对活动过程的评价。

解决策略:

对于学生合作活动,评价应该是多元的,只要是有益于促进学生发展的,都是可采用的。在对合作学习进行评价时,教师可以将组员自评、小组互评、教师评价结合起来。可以从以下几个方面进行评价:回答问题的准确度、小组成员的参与度、个人对集体学习的贡献、小组合作是否顺利、小组成员是否有进步、是否有创新、是否善于发现和归纳、能否提出一个好问题等。教师运用好"评价—激励"这个杠杆,可以促使学生更积极地投入到合作中来,为学生自主参与活动营造平台,令师生互动、生生交流自然流畅,学生合作有效开展。

典型案例 1

译林版《牛津小学英语》1A
Unit 10　What colour?　同题异构课

镜头一　授课教师 A 在指导学生反复指读、操练本节课的词汇后,设计了涂色的小组活动。授课教师给每个小组发了一张没有涂色的图片,让学生以组为单位给图片涂上颜色,看哪组涂得最快、最漂亮。低年级的学生大都很喜欢画画,涂得很认真。

镜头二　授课教师 B 让学生先以小组为单位讨论给图片涂上怎样的颜色,在讨论的过程中要求学生说英语,而且引导学生用少数服从多数的办法统一全组的意见。

Group 1:各抒己见,每位学生都把自己喜欢的颜色说出来,并把相应颜色的词卡放在课桌上,最后喜欢哪种颜色的学生多就涂哪种颜色。

Group 2:举手表决。一位学生说:"I like red."其他喜欢红色的学生也举手说:"I like red, too."最后喜欢哪种颜色的学生多就涂哪种颜色。

授课教师B让每组派代表把本组意见用彩色笔横线的方式表现出来,并说出:"We like red. / We like yellow. / We like..."

◆ 案例反思 ◆

小组活动的设计应以引导学生运用所学语言为目标。然而,有些教师设计的小组活动往往缺乏针对性。比如本案例中,教师A组织的小组活动非常有趣,学生也乐于参与,但由于教师忽视了学生在活动中的语言输出,导致学生虽然进行了小组活动,却缺少运用所学语言进行交流的机会,将宝贵的课堂时间都花在了非英语学习的活动上。学生没有获得更多语言操练的机会,更谈不上提高交际能力了。而在教师B组织的活动中,学生既动脑又动口,学生的学习都是在语境下进行的,这样的学生合作活动才是有效的。

➤•典型案例2•◄

山东省青岛市特级教师刘青"Festivals in China"课例

Step One　课前调查收集信息,激发合作参与动机

1) Discuss about festivals learned in the previous lesson.

2) Draw or collect pictures. Bring a photograph of you and your family celebrating your favourite festival.(课前教师要求每位学生准备充足课堂所需的交流材料,这样每个学生在课堂中都有合作学习参与的可能,不至于部分学生只是观望与等待。只有这样,课堂上的合作才会有效果,学生学习的积极性才能被相应地调动起来)

3) Do a survey and complete the form below.

T: In your group, find out your classmates' favourite festivals.(课前教师组织学生相互调查各自喜欢的节日,合作获取信息,培养学生的合作意识,使学生在课堂中更快地进入角色,同时也增强了学生参

与课堂合作的自信心)

Festivals in China	Names of classmates
Chinese New Year	
The Lantern Festival	
The Mid-Autumn Festival	
The Qingming Festival	
The Dragon-Boat Festival	

Step Two 课堂分组讨论填写表格,增加合作参与可能

1. Watching the video(观看录像,感受节日氛围)

T:We talked about some English festivals before. Today, let's talk about some festivals in China. When you watch the video, please remember how many Chinese festivals are in the video, and what they are.(教师播放节日录像片段,一方面让学生感受节日氛围,另一方面为下一个合作讨论环节做好语言铺垫)

2. Discussion

1) T:Please discuss the questions with your group and complete the form.(教师组织学生对上一环节提出的问题进行四人小组讨论,集中组内成员的智慧和经验完成表格)

2) Check the answer in the class.(教师对学生合作学习成果进行及时评价,组员将组内讨论结果与全班同学进行分享。在教师的引导下,解决那些刚才组内没有探究过的问题,全班一起探讨,重新构建新的知识体系)

① T:What is a festival?

S1:Festival is a special day.

S2:Festival is a holiday.

T:Yes, festival is a special day to celebrate something or remember somebody.

② T:What are the five festivals in the video?

Ss:Chinese New Year, the Lantern Festival, the Qingming

Festival, the Dragon-Boat Festival and the Mid-Autumn Festival.

T: These festivals are all Chinese traditional festivals. Please remember the names.

③ T: When are the five festivals?

S1: Chinese New Year is in January.

S2: This year, it's in January, but last year it was in February.

S3: Some years, it's in January, and some years it's in February.

T: You are right. It is said Chinese New Year is in a day between January 21 and February 20.

S4: The Lantern Festival is in February.

S5: Sometimes the Lantern Festival is in March.

S6: The Qingming Festival is always in April.

S7: The Dragon-Boat Festival is usually in June; sometimes it's in May.

S8: The Mid-Autumn Festival is in September.

T: Sometimes it's in October.

④ T: Look at the calendar, and then write festivals in the correct months.

⑤ T: Which festivals are always in the same month?

S1: The Qingming Festival is always in April.

⑥ T: Which festival is sometimes in a different month?

Ss: Chinese New Year, the Lantern Festival, the Dragon-Boat Festival and the Mid-Autumn Festival.

T: Some festivals occur in different months, from year to year.

Step Three　自选伙伴谈论照片,促进合作语言输出

(自选合作伙伴是为了使交谈气氛更加融洽。谈论伙伴课前准备的照片而不是自己的,可以使沟通的目的更加明确,更好地填补"信息沟")

1. What's your favourite festival?

T: I asked you to bring a photograph of you and your family at a festival. Please take it out.

　　You can choose your partner and talk about your favourite festival.（教师在活动中不停地观察合作活动：合作伙伴讨论的声音过大，教师让这两位学生互相移近一点。等讨论声音小了，教师应及时进行表扬。有些合作伙伴对任务目标尚不太明确，教师耐心地向学生说明任务的内容及操作程序。有些合作伙伴在讨论时出现语言困难，教师给予指导和提示）

2. What's your partner's favourite festival?（教师搭建平台让学生展现合作成果，组织学生描述伙伴喜爱的节日，检查合作效果，并表扬较好的合作搭档）

　　T：I will ask some of you come to the front with your partner's photograph and talk about his/her favourite festival.

　　S1：_____ is my friend. Her favourite festival is the Mid-Autumn Festival. Look, this is a picture of her family at dinner.

　　S2：Look! This is a photo of _____'s family. They are watching lanterns on the Lantern Festival.

　　S3：This is _____ and his parents. They are setting off fireworks.

3. Survey report（教师组织学生对课前合作收集的信息进行处理，反馈调查结果）

　　T：Before the class, you had the task to do a survey. Did you do that?

　　Ss：Yes. (Ss take out the survey report)

　　T：Who'd like to have a report about your group's favourite festival?

　　S1：This is my survey in our group. There are 12 students in our group. 5 students like Chinese New Year best. They are _____. 3 students like the Mid-autumn Festival best. They are _____. 2 students like the Dragon-Boat Festival. They are _____. Only one student likes the Lantern Festival. She is _____. One student likes the Qingming Festival.

Step Four　交流完成表格,培养合作探究意识

(教师引导学生共同完成表格,这是同学们之间相互学习的过程。经过教师为学生提供的一些不同形式的合作活动任务,如课前的小组合作,课中的四人合作和自由伙伴合作,学生已将合作精神融入了学习的全过程。最后,在全班生生合作和共享交流的基础上,教师充分发挥学生的主体作用,调动全体学生合作学习的积极性,共同丰富了本课的内容,学生的综合语言运用能力得到了很大的提高)

T：(Draw a form on the blackboard)

Festivals	Calendar	Special food	Activities

T：Let's talk more about the Chinese festivals and get more information about the festivals.

1. When is the festival?

T：Chinese people usually use "lunar calendar" to remember a special day. So we have two ways to tell the calendar. You can choose any one of them. (Teach the phrase "lunar calendar")

2. What is the special food?

T：It's easy for you to express.

Ss：(Say one by one from "dumpling" to "mooncake")

3. What are the activities?

T：Can you say some activities at Chinese New Year?

S1：At Chinese New Year, we eat dumplings.

S2：We watch TV on New Year's Eve.

S3：We have dinner together.

S4: We set off fireworks.

S5: We visit relatives and friends.

S6: We get money from parents and grandparents.

S7: We wear new clothes.

S8: In Guangzhou, people go to the flower markets to buy fruit trees and beautiful flowers.

4. Talk about some other festivals.

S1: At the Lantern Festival, people eat sweet dumplings and watch lanterns.

S2: We sometimes guess riddles at the Lantern Festival.

S3: We remember dead people at the Qingming Festival.

S4: We often go out to have a walk or have a trip at the Qingming Festival.

S5: In the south, people have dragon boat races on the Dragon-Boat Festival.

S6: People eat rice dumplings to remember Qu Yuan on the Dragon-Boat Festival.

S7: We eat mooncakes and enjoy the full moon at the Mid-Autumn Festival.

T: (Write some answers in the blanks and finish the form)

♦ 案例反思 ♦

　　成功的学生合作活动离不开精心的设计。本案例中，教师首先充分利用并整合教材中的素材；其次，又用好了社会这部大教材，在课前准备的时候，学生的爷爷、奶奶、爸爸、妈妈、邻居、同学、朋友、网络、图书馆都是学生合作交流的来源。而在此过程中，学生受任务驱使，会更加主动地从各个渠道寻求合作和帮助。课堂上教师通过让学生四人合作，集中组内成员的智慧和经验填写表格并在全班合作交流中讨论那些以前没有探究过的问题，最后在教师的引导下，重新构建新的知识体系。最后教师借助表格开展合作活动，不仅为学生创设语言交流的"信息沟",而且调查—讨论—汇报的过程为学生提供了反复运用所学语言的机会,促进了学生间多元信息的交流。

另外,在要求学生进行合作前教师要予以及时的帮助和指导,使接下来的学生合作的目的更加明确,让学生更好地完成学习任务。即使学生合作活动已经开始,教师也应密切关注合作活动的进程,根据学生遇到的不同困难,既可给予宏观方向的指导,又可给予具体词句的指导,必要时可以暂停合作活动,并针对比较集中的问题进行再示范,这是学生合作活动取得成功的关键所在。

◆ 专家点评 ◆

教学是一种人际交往和信息的互动,因而师生间和生生间的互动是课堂上学生最主要的学习方式。其中生生互动最直接的表现形式就是合作学习。一方面,合作学习给学生提供了安全的语言学习环境,合作活动中,成员之间可以互相交流、互相学习,使课堂教学更多地以学生为中心。另一方面,学生合作学习时每个人都有机会发表自己的观点与看法并倾听他人的意见,这有助于学生形成良好的交际沟通能力。此外,小组合作时学生间常常会就一个问题进行讨论和争辩,这个过程还能有益于学生批判性思维的形成。然而,要想充分发挥合作学习的积极作用,促使成员间建立起积极的互动关系还有赖于教师的合理安排和组织,如:教师在安排任务时要尽量给小组内的每一位成员分配任务,如果三个人能完成的任务就不要安排四个人,这样就不会有学生"搭便车"的现象发生;在成员类型的分配上,可以按阶梯式的水平层次安排:既有高于平均水平的,又有平均水平的,同时还有低于平均水平的,这样安排的目的是让学生在合作时不会因为自己和其他同学的水平过于悬殊而感到不安。

细节 14
如何实施教学评价

▶·细节阐述·◀

　　小学英语教学评价的主要目的是激发学生的学习兴趣和积极性。但传统的评价体系往往把考试作为衡量学生学习优劣的唯一依据,忽视对学生学习过程的评价;只重视评价和测试的区别和选拔功能,忽视评价为学生成长和发展服务的功能;只重视语言知识和语言能力,忽视情感、态度等其他方面;评价过程往往只有教师一方参与,没有学生参与评价。《英语课程标准》指出:评价是英语课程的重要组成部分。英语课堂的评价应根据学生的个体差异,对学生采用不同的评价标准和方法,使评价不仅仅关注结果,更关注学生的成长。

一、评价在课堂教学中的作用

1. 运用人性化的评价,让学生的学习充满乐趣

　　小学英语课程改革特别强调英语教学要关注每个学生的情感,激发他们学习英语的兴趣。著名儿童心理学家皮亚杰有句名言:所有智力方面的工作都要依赖于兴趣。小学生对学习带有明显的情绪色彩,容易感情用事,对喜欢的教师,喜欢学的内容,他们会眼睛发亮,手舞足蹈,全身心地投入。在英语教学中,会经常使用评价表,若评价表自身能吸引学生,让学生爱上它,那么评价本身也会更容易被学生接纳。这点在教学的实践中得到了证实。评价表要吸引学生,就一定要符合学生年龄和性格的特点,制作得形象、直观且充满色彩。若让学生自己设

计和制作，效果会更好。评价表有记录个人表现的个人评价表和记录小组合作学习表现的小组评价表，制作时，教师只需规定评价表的基本评价内容，其余的完全可以让学生自由发挥。个人评价表充分体现了学生的个性化，给教师提供了一个了解学生的机会，对日常教学也有帮助；小组评价表的制作是全体组员共同参与的过程，也是小组凝聚力形成的过程，一个具有强烈凝聚力的小组，对于英语的学习具有很大的促进作用。

2. 采用趣味性的奖励，让学生的学习更主动

小学生喜欢直观、具体的事物，而且对于自己喜欢的物品会有很强的占有欲，一张有趣的奖状就可以吸引学生全身心地投入到教学活动中。例如，教师在教学中，常常会画或收集一些与话题相关的图片，上完课后，这些图片往往就堆放一边或随便扔掉，这是资源的浪费。事实上，我们可以对这些图片加以利用，制作成一张张特别的奖状。

3. 给予有效的称赞，让学生的学习充满阳光

小学英语课程改革其中一项重要任务是树立学生学习的自信心。称赞是树立自信心的有效途径。孩子对鼓励与称赞的需要，就如同种子需要水一样。德国教育家第斯多惠说："教学的艺术不在于传授的本领，而在于激励、唤醒和鼓舞。"能否让孩子在英语课堂中体验成功，拥有一份自信，很大程度上取决于教师能否在评价中运用鼓励与称赞的艺术，进行有效的称赞。

同一个班的学生无论是知识水平还是性格特点都存在着差异，若教师采用同一评价标准，对于一部分学生来说，称赞会因为过于频繁而失去带来的激励意义，但是对另外一部分学生来说，称赞会因为标准过高、无法达到而失去促进作用。这两种情况都会使称赞失去效力，缺乏意义。所以教师对学生的称赞衡量的不应是完成任务的大小，而应是为了任务的完成，付出努力的多少。一节课内，能力较强的学生能背诵对话值得称赞，能力较差的学生能记忆单词也同样值得称赞，因为这个我们看来很小的任务却是他们付出巨大努力才能完成的。

二、评价在运用中要遵循的原则

1. 学生中心原则

激励性评价的主体和对象应是学生。所有评价活动的目的在于激发学生进一步进行有效的学习的欲望,比如:是否认真听讲、是否认真学与练、模仿得像不像、小组合作得好不好、表演得是否有创意,等等。一切评价活动应首先基于学生个体的学习是否有进步而进行。

2. 全面性原则

激励性评价不能仅仅评价学生的学习情况,而要以学生的各个方面表现为评价内容。如:学生的学习态度、学习方式方法、学习的自觉性、大胆发言的勇气、认真改错的态度、与别人交往的能力等。要明确的是,学生是人而不是接受知识的容器。人的一切活动,包括学习活动都要受到其意识的支配,所以教学评价就不能仅仅局限于知识的掌握程度,更要促进其兴趣、爱好、意志等个性品质的形成和发展,为终身学习作铺垫。

3. 面向全体原则

评价要关注全体学生整体、全面的发展,不能仅仅关注个别学生。每个学生都有其学习优势和弱势,对学得快的学生要及时肯定,并鼓励其带动其他人;对学得慢的学生要适当调整标准,允许他们因比"昨天"进步而获得奖励,允许他们因被帮助后进步而获得奖励等。教学评价就是要重态度、重参与、重努力程度、重交流能力等,不仅学习成绩好的学生应该获得鼓励,体验到成功的欢乐,而且成绩差的学生的自尊心与自信心也要受到鼓励。

4. 多元化原则

评价的方式必须是多样化的,既可以由教师观察学生在各种活动如讲故事、说歌谣、唱歌曲、表演对话或短剧中的表现来进行评价,也可以通过学生的自评、互评等多种方式进行。

三、评价的具体实施策略

策略一：丰富评价语言

小学英语课堂评价语有各种类型，除了常用的"Good!"，"Excellent!"，还有诸如"You're a clever girl/boy!"，"I'm proud of you."，"I'm glad you studied well!"，"You have a good head for English."，"Congratulations, you're good at English! Keep it up."等。评价语言的多样化，让孩子在快乐学英语的同时体验成功的快乐，肯定自身价值，激发无限兴趣。

（1）引导型评价。有效的引导体现在课堂中教师对每个环节的处理与把握上。对于学生不正确的观点和看法不能立即予以否定和批评，教师应巧于评价，善于引导，引导学生学会质疑，学会知识建构，进而进行合作学习，使学生们最大程度地展示自己的潜能。有效的引导，可自然纠正学生思维上的偏差，同时也可培养学生的思辨能力。

（2）幽默型评价。列宁说过，"幽默是一种优美的、健康的品质"。评价语言的运用因人而异，但评价语言的幽默度可反映出一个教师掌控课堂的能力，并是其个人魅力的体现。因此教师在运用幽默艺术的时候，一定要追求高雅，幽默是轻松的诙谐，是含蓄的机智，是挚爱的微笑，而不是油滑，不是哗众取宠，更不是恶意嘲讽。同学们在笑声中会加深对单词的记忆，而且激发对英语的兴趣。

（3）激励型评价。课堂激励型评价，使学生在心理上获得自信和成功的体验，能激发学习动机，诱发学习兴趣，进而主动学习，提高学习成绩。作为教师，我们首先要用赏识的语言多给学生表扬、激励；同时，恰当的批评和警醒，也是激励型评价的一种体现。常用的激励型评价语有："You work hard enough!" "Don't give up!" "I hope you'll persist in your efforts." "You can do it!"

（4）递增型评价。由于每个学生的知识水平、语言能力有所不同，教师在评价学生时应注意一个由浅入深、由低到高的递增型规律。如在抛出一个问题后，学生肯定有各种不同的回答，教师应有选择地加以评价,不能用单一的语言来一概而论,这样既让那些回答出色的同学觉得索然无味,毫无动力,又使那些语言掌控薄弱的同学认为这是老师的敷衍,觉得得不到尊重,因而自信受到挫伤。例如,某节英语课上,教师提问道:"Which season do you like best?"以下分别是三位同学的不同回答。第一种回答:"I like winter."第二种回答:"I like winter, because I can skate."第三种回答:"I like winter, because if winter comes, can spring be far behind?"针对上述三种不同层次的回答,教师的评价语言的递增性显得尤为重要。从第一种回答,我们可以判断出该学生在班级中属于弱势群体一员,可用评价语:"I like winter too."第二种回答说明该同学应处于班级中上游水平,我们可用评价语:"Good, you like skating. I like skiing. We have a similar hobby."对于第三种富有创意的回答,可用评价语:"Great! You're truly unique. I'm proud of you."层层递进的评价,在保护学生自尊心的同时,提升了学生的自信心,保护了学生的创新思维,也让学生感受到老师在认真听他们的回答,而不是敷衍。

策略二:抓住评价的点,控制评价的度

对学生而言,过多的夸奖并不会起到鼓励的作用,尤其是教师不假思索、脱口而出的随意性夸奖,不仅不能对学生产生积极的引导,反而会导致学生形成排斥和厌恶感。所以教师在评价学生时,首先要注意针对性,不能泛泛而谈,笼统模糊,而是要抓住学生自身所独有的特点评论,让每个孩子都能够看到自身的闪光点,树立学习的信心。特别对于"学困生",教师要善于发现并评价其闪光点,引发求知欲,为学生创设学习成功的机会,使学生获得成功的体验,克服自卑,找回自信,培养成功的信念,激发内在的潜能。

策略三:恰当使用肢体语言

肢体语言作为广义评价中的一种,起着十分显著的作用:当学生回答出色时,教师可竖起大拇指或带动全班鼓掌给予其鼓励和认可;当学生紧张时,教师可轻轻拍一下他(她)的肩或抚摸一下他(她)的头给予安慰；当学生讲悄悄话时，教师可将食指放嘴唇上给予警告；当学生回答不如意时，教师可用浅浅的一抹微笑化解他（她）内心的不安。教师动作、表情、眼神等肢体语言评价和口头语言评价的交替配合使用，能使整堂课焕发出非一般的精彩。

策略四：自评、互评相互结合

《英语课程标准》指出，评价应有益于学生认识自我，树立自信；应有助于学生反思和调控自己的学习过程，从而促进语言能力的不断发展。英语课堂中除了教师对学生的评价外，学生的自评和互评也是十分重要的。学生可根据对知识的掌握程度做出符合自身实际的评价，以此来了解自己对知识的理解和运用是否到位。对于互评，在教学实践中，教师可以采用合作评价、互评互改的方式，引导学生开展相互评价。学生在自评和互评中感受到愉悦、成功的情绪体验，提高了自身的评价能力，进而增强了学习的兴趣。

▶·典型案例1·◀

T：Now, look! (Point to the screen of a computer) What's that?

Ss：Football.

T：Good. Read after me, "football".

Ss：(Read it one by one)

T：Together, please spell it.

Ss：F-O-O-T-B-A-L-L, football.

T：Great! Who want to try?

S1：F-O-O-T-B-A-L-L, football.

S2：F-O-O-T-B-A-L-L, football.

S3：F-O-O-T-B-A-L-L, football.

(Learn 2 other words "baseball", "basketball" in the same way)

T：(Take out two basketballs) OK. Look at me, "one basketball", "two basketballs".

T：What are these? (Wave two basketballs)

Ss：They're basketballs.

T：Who can answer my question? What are these?

S4：I can. They're basketballs.

T：Can you play basketball?

S4：Yes, I can.

T：Wonderful! Please show us how to play basketball.

S4：(Do the actions of playing basketball)

T：Thank you. I think you are the best basketball player. Clap for her, please.

T：Who can play football?

S5：I can play football.

T：That's cool! Please show us how to play football.

S5：(Do the actions of playing football)

T：Very good! I think you are the best football player. Let's give him a big hand.

T：Who can play baseball?

S6：I can play baseball.

T：OK. Please show us how to play baseball.

S6：(Do the actions of playing baseball)

T：Great! Does he play baseball very well?

Ss：Yes, he does.

T：Clap for him. OK?

Ss：OK.

T：This time you can read it after the tape. （教师出示自我评价表，学生读完之后进行自我评价）

♦ 案例反思 ♦

在这个案例中教师运用了教师评价、集体对个体的评价和学生自我评价三种方式。

首先,教师激励性的评价语言在课堂上不仅能调动学生的学习积极性,增强学生的自信心,而且能活跃课堂气氛,形成师生互动的教学氛围。

其次,自我评价可以培养学生为自己的学习负责的能力,鼓励他们自己思考,使他们看到自己取得的成绩以及需要改进的地方。

最后,教师把激励性评价运用到全班,使学生得到集体的肯定,如对单词拼得正确、流利或表演生动的同学,鼓掌以示鼓励。在这样的互动过程中,学生的积极性、自信心得到了提高。

◆典型案例 2◆

译林版《英语》四年级上册
Project 2　My snack bar

1. Design new snack bars

* Choose a name in groups.

Ss choose a good name for their snack bar and show the name to the class.

If they can choose a nice name, they can get a sticker.

* Put the food and drink on the right position.

Ss put the pictures on their cards.

If they can complete this task well, they can get the second sticker.

* Set up a good price for their snack.

Make a new menu.

If they can set up a good price, they can get the third sticker.

* Have a trial opening.

Ss think about two questions: How to sell? How to buy?

If they can complete this task well, they can get the fourth sticker.

They can change the 4 stickers for a license.

2. Activity

Go shopping.(贴有顾客标记的学生们进行自由购物,贴有营业员

标记的学生们留守在自己的小店进行售卖）

3. Ticking time

Choose the best snack bar.（组内学生一起清点，计算销售额。全班同学一起推选最佳小吃店）

◆ 案例反思 ◆

1. 差异性分层

此节课之前，学生们以自荐或同学推举的方式产生四名组长，他们就英语学习能力及课堂表现而言都是班中佼佼者，产生过程是他们对自己、同学及老师对他们的肯定与评价，他们需要协助老师监督、观察活动中同学们是否在使用英语，句型及单复数运用是否正确恰当等，及时进行记录和反馈。组长们全程参与听、说、观察、记录的动态体验活动。其余学生八人一组，共五组，每组设计一家快餐店。学生可根据自己对原有知识的掌握程度、参与情况及表现积极性自评或互评出以下几类角色——每组两名服务员：他们要有较强的语言表达能力，能够综合运用卖物品的重点句型，耐心、热情地服务顾客；每组一名助手：助手可能是表达能力较弱的学生，他（她）不需要与顾客直接交流，但需要听顾客与服务员的对话后找出顾客需要的物品（这对于表达能力较弱的学生是一种非常有效的评价手段，不仅能促进他们发挥自己所长更好地参与活动，更能激励他们学习的积极性）；每组五名顾客：他们需要熟练运用购物句型来体验快餐店的服务。学生通过自我评价和同学对自己的评价，明确了各自的任务和扮演的角色，利用自己长处达成学习目标。同学们的学习情况，组长需要在活动评价表中进行体现。

2. 任务型课堂

课上教师向学生展示了原来的设施陈旧的快餐店，并提议设计新的快餐店，同时提出四个任务：第一步，为快餐店取名并展示；第二步，用相关图片及句型进行货品陈列，学生自主选择对话进行介绍；第三步，制定一份新的菜单；第四步，试营业，引导学生在活动中思考如何买东西以及如何卖东西，自主总结、整理语言知识点。每完成一个环节以小组自评或组长评价的方式给予奖励贴，得到四张奖励贴可以兑换一张"经营许可证",这张"经营许可证"体现了对学生语言综合运用能力、参与程度、兴趣专注度、拓展性思维的综合评价。

3. 创新型探索

得到"经营许可证"的快餐店可正式营业,此时顾客们可以去任意一家快餐店体验购物。最后,由四名组长和顾客共同选出最好的快餐店、服务员和助手并说明理由。

典型案例3

课堂教学中学生学习状态检测表

评价学生_____（____年级____班）

评价者	学习需求				学习态度				学习信心				努力程度				持久耐心				总体评价
	强	较强	一般	弱	强	较强	一般	弱	强	较强	一般	弱	强	较强	一般	弱	强	较强	一般	弱	
学生自评																					
同伴助评1																					
同伴助评2																					
同伴助评3																					

评价提示:1. 评价者在相应的格子内打"√"。
　　　　　2. 总体评价用文字表述,可以从四个方面选择:强、较强、一般、弱。

助评学生:_____　　　　　　　　　　　评价日期:_____年___月___日

◆ 案例反思 ◆

课堂评价可以是直接的语言表达,如 good, very good, excellent, great,也可以是量表的形式。案例中的课堂评价表如实记录了课堂上的观察结果,包括:学习需求、学习态度、学习信心、努力程度和持久耐心。其中有学生自评、学生互评。评价表在课堂教学中加入了新鲜的评价血液,增添了课堂的活力,调动了学生英语学习的积极性,促进了学生的发展。

◆ 专家点评 ◆

英语学习的终极目标是学以致用,也就是学生能用所学的语言进行交流、表达和沟通;反过来,通过大量听、说、读、写的语言实践学生的语用能力也会得到进一步的发展和提升。正是出于这个原因,英语课堂上教师经常会设计多种形式的语言实践活动。然而,通过课堂观察我们发现,有的课堂上学生会踊跃参与,有的课堂则显得气氛沉闷。其实,让学生乐于参与课堂上的语言实践活动的关键在于教师。正如前文细节和案例中阐述的,教师可以采用多种形式的评价手段来激励学生,使他们有开口的动力和欲望,并且感受到使用语言的成就感。不过,除了要用好评价的手段以外,教师设计语言活动还要做到两个结合:与学生的实际生活相结合,与学生的实际水平相结合。所谓与实际生活相结合是指教师设计的语言实践活动要立足于学生的生活实际,是他们身边看得见、摸得着的场景,这样他们就能有话可讲。与学生的实际水平相结合则是指教师要充分考虑学生的既有水平,不能要求学生一步到位,一学就会,从语言的输入到输出之间要留有足够的时间让学生理解和消化;另外,由于学生的个体差异,理解、消化的时间和进程也会有所不同,当学生遇到困难时教师要予以适时的指导和帮助,让学生在体验、探究中发现语言规律,掌握语言技能,感受使用语言的快乐!

细节 15

如何指导学生自主学习

▶ 细节阐述 ◀

当我们把目光投向那些经过了一段时间英语学习的学生时,就会发现他们不仅在学习成绩上存在差异,而且,学习的主动性方面也相差甚远:有的学生乐于参与课堂内外的活动,并且积极思考、勇于实践,有的学生却是抱着应付的态度完成老师布置的任务,有时还会有拖拉现象发生。通过观察和分析我们发现,那些对学习持积极态度的学生多是掌握了一定学习策略并且能自主学习的。学生如何才能自主学习呢?

策略一:情感是自主学习的基础

日本学者佐藤学在《静悄悄的革命》一书中写道:"学生自立、自律的学习必须在与教师的互动中,在与教材、教室中的学生以及学习环境的关系中来加以认识。"自主学习首先需要考虑的是让学生从自我情感上认同学习本身。教师要为学生营造一个"舒展"的课堂,走近学生,聆听他们的想法,感受他们的情感。这样,学生就会觉得自己是被信任和尊重的,他们就会敢于、乐于表达自己的观点。其次,教师要善于把语言学习的内容与学生的生活经验相结合,使话题的讨论立足于学生熟悉的生活场景,使学生产生情感上的共鸣,萌生学习兴趣并乐于参与学习的过程。

除了学习内容本身让学生感兴趣之外,教学活动的组织形式也需要符合学生的心理发展特点。教师应该给予学生自主的活动空间和自主的选择权:课堂上生生间的合作活动可以促进学生与同伴之间的交流,教师可设计不同的学习形式,如 pair work, group work 等,这些组织形式与活动给学生提供了学习交流空间,在互助学习的同时,可以增强他们的同伴情感体验。

策略二:在导学中培养学生规划自主学习

教师在尝试激发学生的学习兴趣后,还需要向学生提供一些方法和策略,这样才能让学生们真正地开始自主学习。例如,教师可以在作业内容的规划和指导中培养学生的自主学习能力。

1. C-I-S学习书签

C-I-S学习书签是学生作业的载体。C是common的首字母,代表了"常规作业"。I是individual的首字母,代表了"个性化作业"。S是special的缩写,代表了"特殊作业"。在"常规作业"一栏中,教师需要训练学生发现并总结如何预习和复习各个板块的知识,这需要一个阶段的持续训练,开始的时候可以采用教师说、学生复述的方式;过段时间后,教师可以鼓励学生来布置作业,并对他们的想法做出积极的评价;最后教师与学生共同完成各个板块常规的预习和复习作业。

"个性化作业"一栏,体现了教师尊重学生之间差异的理念。教师可以鼓励学生给自己布置一些额外的、适合自己的学习内容。比如学习Story time之后,常规作业为熟练朗读Story time,默写其中的单词与词组。学习能力特别弱的学生,常规作业也很难完成,那么他(她)可以在"个性化作业"一栏中写明听几遍课文,尽量读出课文,背默其中几个单词等。而学习能力比较强的学生,完全可以熟练朗读课文,那么可以忽略常规作业,在"个性化作业"一栏中多列几条课外学习内容,如开展课外故事阅读,扩充阅读量。

在"特殊作业"一栏中,教师可以根据学生的学习情况,随机地布置一些学习任务。特殊作业可以是面向全体学生的,也可以是面向某些学生的。

2. C-S-M-I 任务单

C-S-M-I 任务单是教师为帮助学生做好预习而开发的表格。C 是 confused 的缩写，代表学生在预习过程中存在的疑惑；S 是 solved，代表已经解决的内容；M 是 method 的缩写，代表了是通过什么方法解决的，I 是 interested 的缩写，代表了学生对于文本还有什么感兴趣、想知道的。

通过 C-S-M-I 任务单，学生在预习的过程中需要思考、发现问题，尝试去解决问题，记录好解决问题的方法，并可以提出自己想了解的问题。比如说在预习 Story time 的时候，学生通过预习朗读，发现有很多生词不会读，也不知道什么意思，他（她）就可以将生词记录在 C 栏中；随后他（她）开始听磁带，听了两遍之后，可能其中的几个简单的单词已经能够读出来了，他可以将这几个单词记录在 S 栏中，并在 M 栏写上方法是听录音；初步了解文本之后，在 I 栏中还可以写上一些自己想要通过教师课堂教学了解的信息。

策略三：在多元评价中促进学生的自主学习

学生都乐于表现自己，但大多数学生由于心理年龄特征的关系，很难做到自主学习，他们需要外界的适当刺激才能对学习目标进行追求。而激励行为则是一个很好的刺激方式。这种激励行为要基于课堂学习评价本身，但又需要有一定的规划性。

1. 交流启发智慧——生生互动评价

课堂教学中，学生参与学习活动并投入学习评价，是学生为主体的课堂教学理念的直接体现。

在课堂教学中，教师采用生生之间的互动评价，主要基于两个活动：一是小组合作学习。在合作学习中，学生就会根据组内同伴的情况，进行互动合作学习，在分配、执行学习任务的过程中，他们就会合理地进行相互评价。其次是小组展示后的组间评价。可以通过"我是小小评论员"等活动，对展示的小组进行点评，肯定他们的优点，也提出一点希望。鼓励相互评价也是提高学生课堂注意力的一个有效方式，要对别人进行恰当点评，自己首先得是一个优秀的倾听者。教师在教学中还可以开展评论语征集,将优秀的评论收集制作成册,来激励学生参与评论并学会评论。

这种生生之间的互动评价,让学生真正地成为课堂的主人,交流中也启发了学生的学习智慧。

2. 反思唤醒行为——自我内省评价

教师的评价与学生间的评价,都应该与学生对自我的认知产生共鸣,使其形成自我评价。例如:教师可以设置学习表现表,侧重于学生的行为认知评价。在学生的学习表现表上,首先记录的是每节课的表现分。课堂学习结束前,教师可以引导他们从以下几方面对自己的课堂表现做出评价:我对自己今天的课堂表现满意吗?我觉得自己有进步吗?此外,学生每周还可以在学习表现表中写上对自己一周学习情况的自我评价,看看哪方面做得好、应该保持,哪些方面有待改进。对那些能够比较公正、客观地评价自己表现的学生教师可以予以鼓励。

策略四:进行自主学习具体方法的指导

一般来说,懂得如何学习的学生能对自己的学习承担更多的责任,所以,教师可以在如何听课、记笔记等方面给学生一些具体的指导和建议。例如:听课的过程中,指导学生通过联想、归纳、演绎、比较等方法尝试把前后学习的知识纵横联结,形成知识的网络,这种边听边思的习惯有助于让学生在学习方面变得更加独立。至于记笔记方面教师可以做以下指导:听课时要有选择地记录,应以听、思为主,记录为辅,要记录自己的疑问,以便进一步思考,或者请教同学和老师,等等。

以上介绍的策略虽不相同,但是指向的目标是一致的,就是要帮助学生形成积极的学习态度,成为自主学习者。

·典型案例1·

案例说明:这节是复习课,教师通过多个活动帮助学生复习、巩固多个句型的过去时态。

Ⅰ. 课前5分钟

1)课前导学有两项任务:一是让学生写出熟练掌握的动词原形与

过去式。二是让学生调查并比较学校去年和现在的变化,尝试用 there be 句型说一下。

2) 学生讨论 C-S-M-I 任务单,教师巡视。

Ⅱ. **课堂教学流程**

1. Warming up

1) Daily talk.

2) Sing a song *Yesterday*.

(在这一教学过程中,教师通过问答的形式,复现了一般过去时态的基本句型,并演唱歌曲《Yesterday》)

2. Revision and lead in

1) Look and listen.

2) Look and say.

(PPT 出示学校里的质朴院的照片)

T:Which building is it?

Ss:It's Zhipu Building.

T:Was it there last year?

Ss:No, it wasn't.

(此时,教师给出关键词 this year, but, last year,引导学生来进行句子的表达)

Ss:(Read the sentence together) There is a building this year, but there wasn't a building last year.

T:Well done!

(紧接着,教师给出两张图片,一张是苹果树,一张是草根娃,都是学校改建后新增的景观。同时,教师给出关键词 apple tree, grass dolls 等,并引导学生进行同桌讨论)

S1:There is an apple tree this year.

S2:There wasn't an apple tree last year.

S1:There are some grass dolls this year.

S2:There weren't any grass dolls this year.

Ss:(Read the sentence together)

3) Discuss and show.

T: I know you have made a survey about our school's change before class. （教师请学生拿出课前准备的关于去年和今年校园变化的调查，以四人为一组进行讨论，介绍学校的变化）

Team 1:

There were 5 buildings in our school last year, but there are 6 buildings now.

There wasn't a Lingxiu Building last year, but there is a Lingxiu Building now.

此时，有一位学生举手，说道："我觉得可以有另一种说法：We had 5 buildings last year, but we have 6 buildings now."

……

教师对学生的发言表示赞赏。

（在这一教学环节中，教师通过简单的示范，指导学生如何对去年和今年的变化进行描述。随后展开两个教学活动：首先教师给出图片和关键词，学生在教师的指导下口头描述；随后，根据课前完成的调查内容，组内开展讨论并相互合作修改。这种宽松融洽的氛围有助于学生积极主动地参与活动）

3. Representation

1) Look and say.

教师PPT出示学生熟悉的人物（李老师）形象，以两张不同时期的照片引出话题："She didn't have a phone. She didn't call her friends."学生们根据教师的提示，想象二十年前李老师的生活情景，并用"She didn't..."来自由表达。

S1: She didn't have a car.

S2: She didn't have a computer.

S3: She didn't play computer games.

...

2) Interview.

S1: What did you do twenty years ago?

Did you...?

3) Learn the text.

① T:(Show the first paragraph and let the students read it)

T:(Show the following three questions:

What did she do?

How old was she at that time?

Who loved her?)

Ss:(Answer the questions)

② T:(Show four photos of Miss Li at different ages)

Ss:(Read the four paragraphs and match them with the four photos)

Then T-S have a conversation and find out the words describing different ages.

"baby child teenager woman"

③ Read and tick.

Intensive reading: the two paragraphs about "baby and child".

④ Reading.

Ss read together first.

Then Ss work in groups and try to have a fun reading.

They can read together or act the story.

The other students listen carefully and then give suggestions.

(在这个教学环节中,首先,教师选择的话题"任课老师李老师"对于学生来说是既熟悉但又有想象空间的;其次,教学组织形式多样,有同桌合作、小组学习等方式,给予了学生自主学习的空间;最后,在每个活动后的反馈中,教师通过让学生相互评价,既培养了学生的评价能力,也潜移默化地培养了学生认真倾听的习惯)

4. Consolidation

1) Group work.

T:What do you want to say to Miss Li?

2) Assessment and notes.

在课堂最后5分钟,教师带领学生朗读板书的内容,并引导学生总结归纳。

　　Q1:你觉得哪些词语对你而言有点难度?

　　Q2:仔细朗读第二列的单词,你发现什么规律了吗?

　　学生积极思考并踊跃发言,教师表示赞同;随后请学生们拿出笔记本,开始做笔记,并自我评价。

　3) Homework.

　　…

♦ 案例反思 ♦

　　复习课的目的是帮助学生归纳、总结课本知识,同时把学生带出课本,利用新的语境达到综合使用语言的目的。案例中情境来自于学生的生活经验,即学校过去与现在的变化,老师过去与现在的变化。通过讨论,教师让学生感受到周围的变化,感受到真实事物的变化,让学生在这样的情境中体验一般过去时的使用,让语言学习变得生动、富有情趣,这给学生的自主学习提供了基础。

　　自主学习能力是运用已学知识去获取新知识的能力,这个能力的获得是一个循序渐进的过程。在这个过程中,教师是一个组织者、引导者,更是一个服务者。在上述案例中,我们可以看到学生学习状态是自然、轻松的。课堂中,时而出现生生对话,时而听到齐声朗读,时而呈现小组讨论,时而闪现交流火花,这都源于丰富的教学形式。如在讨论学校变化时,教师先给出例句,再通过给出几个关键词让学生造句,最后通过小组活动让学生借助调查表有条理、有层次地说出学校过去与现在的变化;如在运用一般过去时的特殊疑问句和一般疑问句的时候,人物原型李老师来到现场,学生现场用"What did you do...? Did you...?"来进行采访活动,生动又真实;如在学完文本之后,开展小组合作学习,教师给予学生充分的选择权,可以是齐读文本,可以是分着读,可以是有的读有的表演。这样多样化的语言实践活动由收到放、由浅入深,为学生搭建了学习平台,帮助学生运用不同学习策略开展学习,达到了帮助学生学会自主学习的目的。

♦ **专家点评** ♦

  如今,学校和教师早已不再是学生知识的唯一来源,通过课堂把所有的英语知识教给学生是不可能的,基于这个原因,在课堂上教师的任务之一就是让学生能对学习主动承担责任,帮助他们掌握一些学习的策略。如细节和案例中谈到的旨在引导学生思考并学会发现问题和解决问题的课前任务单,能激励学生克服学习中的障碍的形成性评价,听课和记笔记方面的指导等,都非常值得借鉴和参考。不过,无论采用何种途径和方法,都应该以尊重、信任学生为前提。学生自主学习能力的培养是一个长期的缓慢的发展过程,课堂上教师要努力营造一个"用心相互倾听的教室",可以允许教学的进度慢一点,允许学生的发言模糊一点,但要能够听懂学生发言背后的潜在想法,让他们感到在参与课堂教学的各个阶段受到尊重并有价值,只有这样他们的身心才能处于舒展的状态,主观能动性才能得到发挥和体现。总而言之,在培养学生自主性学习的进程中教师要做的除了辛勤耕耘以外,还要静等花开!

细节 16
如何培养学生的思维能力

> 细节阐述

作为认知心理学重要分支,建构主义在小学英语教育中发挥着越来越大的影响。建构主义理论倡导情境性和交互式教学,它认为知识、技能、能力等只能通过个体自身的努力形成和建构,因此,学生才是学习的主体和教学的中心。这一理论为当今的小学英语课堂教学变革提供了理论基础,其学习观和教学观也给小学英语教师一定的启示:课堂上教师和学生的核心活动是思维,对于学生"学"的活动来讲,不论是感知、理解所学知识,还是迁移、运用知识,或者是师生、生生的互动,其核心都是思维。教师要为学生创设良好的语言学习情境,突出知识的形成过程,从而促进学生积极主动地思维。

策略一:多样化教学手段,激发学生思维意识

语言是思维的外在表述工具,思维则是我们大脑内部的语言。在学习过程中两者应该是相互促进的,学习语言的过程应该是使用目标语言进行思维的过程。作为英语教师,我们应该积极创设真实情境,促使学生用英语思维,从而提高他们的英语语言综合能力。那么,如何将课堂教学内容和思维培养结合起来,既完成教学内容又培养学生的思维兴趣呢?考虑到小学生的年龄特点、认知能力,我们可以结合不同内容创设一些简单有趣的活动、游戏。小学生对于音乐、美术、体育和手工制作都有着浓厚的兴趣,我们在教学中不妨将教学内容和这些学科结合起来。比如,在学习五官及其特征表述的时候,教师可以创设一个"Make a funny face"的游戏:教师手持五官的图片,全班同学看到后使用句型"His eyes are big. / Her... is/are..."来描述,同时请一位学生背对全班在黑板上边听边画。在游戏过程中,学生用英语描述所见、用画笔描绘所听,共同协作完成了许多 funny faces。英语语言在这个游戏中成了有效的交流工具,学生合作得开心、思维得自然、学习得有效。又如,译林版《牛津小学英语》5B Unit 6 At a PE lesson 中涉及很多动作短语,如 put... on... , touch... with... , stand in a line, turn left/right 等,在教学中教师可以将课堂转变成一节"英语体育课"。因为本课所涉及的人体部位名词学生已在 4B 中学过,所以教师在教学新语言知识时可以边说边示范动作,要求学生跟说跟做:"Put your hands on your knees."学生看到教师将双手放到了膝盖上,也学着做出这个动作并重复教师说的指令,好动的小学生这时候思维也活跃起来了。教师用同样的方法再教授 stop, turn left/right, stand in a line 等词组,学生照样很快就学会了。反复操练几遍后,教师可以试探性地说出几个"指令",如果学生迅速做出了正确的动作,说明学生已经完全掌握以上内容。小学英语教学中很多动作词汇和短语都适合使用这种 TPR 教学方式,既帮助学生脱离了母语这根"拐杖",直接使用英语思维,又为课堂学习增添了乐趣。此外,我们也可以让小学生在英语学习中算一算、想一想。比如译林版《英语》四年级上册 Project 2 My snack bar 中,教学要求是复习句型"— How much is it/are they? — It's... / They are..."。教师无需直接展示各类食品的价格让学生进行小组对话练习,而是可以设计一份特殊的菜单,上面只有个别食品价格,其他食品价格使用如"一个汉堡=三杯牛奶"、"一个蛋糕=两个香蕉"这样的方式来表达。练习过程中,学生需要看着菜单经过计算才能回答同伴提出的问题,这样,语言就成为一种载体,当学生在相互协作、共同完成任务的时候,他们思维能力得到了锻炼。

策略二:延展性阅读提问,培养学生思考习惯

英语课堂上教师常常会通过提问的形式来检测学生对文本的理解

情况,但是,并不是所有的问题都能引发学生的有效思维。小学英语教材以对话居多,且篇幅不长,在解决了生词和句型的障碍后学生理解文本通常没什么困难,这时如果教师的提问学生不假思索地就能回答,那么学生就难以养成思考的习惯。所以,教师要重视对学生提取文本信息和分析文本信息能力的培养,善于抛出让学生想一想、议一议才能回答的问题。以译林版《英语》四年级上册 Unit 3 How many? 的课文为例,文中杨玲在问海伦拥有的贴纸数量后接着说"Can I have one?",海伦的回应是"Sure.",如果教师提的问题是"How many stickers does Helen have?"或者"Can Yang Ling have a sticker?",这对于大多数学生而言是没有挑战的,也就不会有高质量的思维活动产生;但如果教师改变一下,问"Is Helen a nice girl?"这个文中找不到答案,但是似乎又能找到些线索的问题,就能激起相当多学生的参与热情。在学生们讨论并给出自己的观点后,教师可以恰到好处地补充:"Helen is a nice girl because she likes to share."通过这种方式教师能够帮助学生关注文字以外的信息。再以译林版《牛津小学英语》5B Unit 7 A busy day 的课文为例,大多数执教老师留给学生的问题是:"Can you find the sentence that is about David's busy day?"对五年级下学期的学生来说,这无疑是一个"轻量级"的问题,略加思考就能从文章中找到答案。为了让学生能真正地融入文本去思维,教师可以尝试以下问题:"Why does David have a busy day?"这样他们就能在总体把握文本内容的基础上学习寻找、提炼并分析相关信息,得出"Because he gets up late in the morning.","Because he is on duty today."以及"Because he watches a football match in the afternoon and he has no time to do his work."等开放性的结论,此时学生们的想象力和发散性思维就能得到锻炼。

策略三:情境化课堂教学,促进学生思维发展

学生在学习第二语言的时候,往往仍停留在使用自己母语进行思维的习惯中,但英语学习的目标不仅是培养学生的语言能力,也是培养学生运用英语思维的能力。因此,教师应该有效利用自己的课堂,创设合理的情境，帮助学生融入英语的环境、进行有意义的思维活动和交际活动，提高运用语言的能力。例如，在译林版《英语》四年级上册 Project 2 My snack bar 的教学中，教师想要帮助学生归纳总结学过的买卖东西时的用语。如果教师只问学生学过哪些句子可以用于购物，学生也能说出一些，但是这个过程中学生并没有使用到英语，也没有锻炼到语言思维能力。虽然知识点归纳了，但是学生也被局限在读、背的枯燥过程里。所以教师在实际教学过程中没有直接抛出 how to sell and how to buy 的问题，而是自然通过课题 My snack bar 引导学生分组进行食物的买卖。在这个活动中，教师引导学生创设了一个相对真实的情境，学生在其中选择自己喜欢的食物、使用自己所学的英语进行买卖，过程充满乐趣。之后，教师请学生说一说在刚刚的活动过程中自己使用了哪些语句，学生通过回想自己刚刚参与的买卖过程，将句子分别归入 How to sell 和 How to buy 两类中。这样，自然的情境代替了单一的课堂讨论、真实的体验代替了机械的语言记忆，当学生回想自己的购物过程时，他们是在回忆自己使用英语的情境，这也是使用英语进行思维的一个过程。再比如，教师要帮助学生复习所学过的四个单元的重点句型，其中涉及 I like, I have, I can 等不同句式，通常教学设计都会设置几个游戏或者故事，分别复习每个单元的句型，但这样就没有办法帮助学生形成一个整体的知识框架。所以教师在实际教学设计时，可以设置一个"Who am I?"的情境，要求学生通过思考和回答三个问题来介绍自己："What do you like?" "What do you have?" "What can you do?" 通过回答三个问题，学生既操练了语言，也逐步构建了"Who am I?"这个总问题的答案，使这个颇有哲学意味的话题简化到了中年级孩子能理解的程度：如何向别人介绍自己呢？只需要说说我喜欢、我拥有和我能做的事情，这样大家就能知道我是个什么样的人了，而最近学的这几个单元的句子就能帮助我讲述自己。教师通过几个简单的问题设置了一个情境，在这个情境里，每个孩子都能回答出关于自己的问题，每一个孩子都能通过回答问题构建对自我的认识，我们的教学也达到了培养语言和思维能力的目标。

下面我们来看一些帮助学生建构思维的典型课堂教学案例。

◤典型案例1◥

沪教版《牛津英语》2B Module 4　Unit 1　Activities

教师围绕单元内容 activities，在本节课中大胆创设引入了"Who am I？"的主题和小主人公 Jerry 的生活故事。教师通过"What do you like doing？/ What can you do？/ How do you feel？"三个单元重点句型帮助学生读懂了 Jerry 在生活中的各种 activities（单元句型和词汇），也理解了 Jerry 的各种生活角色（父母的孩子、朋友的玩伴、动物爱好者、绘画爱好者等）。同时教师也通过这三个基本句型引导学生对自己的生活角色进行思考，从而回答本课主题："Who am I？" 整节课教师使用了一个颇具哲学意味的问题统领单元重要句型，将它们整合上升到有意义的高度；再通过使用这些重点句型提问，帮助学生复习应用了单元重点词汇和短语。教师由上而下帮助学生建构知识和思维的框架的教学设计值得我们学习。

Step 1　Warming up

教师通过展示一组小朋友参与各类活动的图片，揭示单元内容 activities，帮助学生回顾单元语言知识；通过师生问答，鼓励学生初步使用本单元语言知识（activities 相关句型和短语）进行交流。

T：What can he do? What can she do?

　　What is the girl doing in the picture?

　　What are they doing?

Ss：He can <u>sweep the floor</u>.　She can <u>clean the table</u>.

　　She can <u>draw nice pictures</u>.　He <u>has colorful hands</u>.

　　The girl <u>is sharing ice creams with</u> her pet dog.

　　He <u>is feeding the parrots</u>.

　　They are <u>playing</u>.　They are <u>dancing</u>.

　　……

Step 2　Getting to know the roles

教师引入创设的主人公 Jerry。由于主人公是学生的同龄人而学生对他的情况并不了解,教师利用这个 information gap,鼓励学生对人物提问。由于有了前一个环节的师生问答做铺垫,这时学生基本都能使用单元句型提问。

T:And look, what is in the next picture? This boy is Jerry. Today we are going to read a story about Jerry. Before that, what do you want to know about him?

Ss:What can he do?

What does he like to do?

How old is he?

What does he like to eat?

T:You have so many good questions. Can you get the answers from the story? Now, listen.

(PPT 播放故事图片和录音:Who am I? I am a child. I am a friend. I am a helper. I am a painter. I am an animal lover. I am a dancer.)

故事提出了问题"Who am I?"并通过列举 Jerry 的各种生活角色解答了这个问题(我是谁? 我是个孩子、是个玩伴、是个小帮手、是个画家……)。教师通过这个环节引入本课最重要的一个问题"Who am I?"

T:In his story, Jerry asked "Who am I?" and he told us about his different roles.

T:Jerry is a helper. How about you? What can you do to help others?

S1:I can help others wash the dishes. I can help throw the trash. I can help feed my parents' dog.

通过这个环节的教学,教师还能让学生初步感知生活中的不同角色和生活中的各种活动之间的关系,为下一步帮助学生把本单元学习的 activities 短语按角色归类(如角色 helper 主要对应 wash dishes, feed pets, throw the trash 等活动)做铺垫。

Step 3　Learning to talk about a role

教师进一步展示 Jerry 的故事，从 Jerry 的一个生活角色(child)具体展开，通过讲述作为 child 的 Jerry 参与的各种活动(画线部分)帮助学生进一步感知活动可以按不同生活角色归类。

T：In the story, Jerry says he is a child. Actually, Jerry wants to tell us more about that. Let's listen carefully.

"Who am I? I am a child. I am Dad and Mom's good boy. I <u>like running</u> with Dad. I <u>like reading</u> with Mom. I can <u>have fun with them</u>. I feel warm in their arms."

接着教师要求学生诵读并尝试复述故事内容。对于小学生来说，这个要求显然很高，于是教师巧妙地将故事内容整合成三个问题(见下图)，学生回答了这三个问题也就完成了复述。其实，Jerry 作为 child 的故事就是根据三个问题而精心编排的，三个问题正是本单元学习的三个句型。学生很容易就能在故事内容和三个问题间建立逻辑联系，并能使用单元语言知识参与故事的复述表达。在这个过程中，教师帮助学生运用语言知识、建立逻辑思维，也促使学生初步思考本课话题 "Who am I?"。教师用话题"Who am I?"引出各个生活角色(I'm a child/ help/friend 等)，引领并提升单元主题 activities，在帮助学生归纳并运用本单元语言知识的同时，也从情感认知的角度给学生提供了一个很好的思维范例。

T：Now I will check your memories. When you retell the story please look at the three questions：

> What do you like doing?
> What can you do?
> How do you feel?

Ss：(Answer the questions and do the retelling)

T：(Do the conclusion) So we can see Jerry is a child. He likes doing these things and he can have fun. He feels warm.

教师进一步拓展 Jerry 的其他生活角色，给出的生活角色小故事都重复使用之前三个问题的模式,促使学生围绕三个单元重点问题,应用单元语言知识进行复述。学生独立阅读和理解文本,逐渐把握各种生活角色和活动间的关系,掌握如何表述生活角色,领悟本课话题"Who am I?"。

T：But actually, Jerry has other roles. You and your deskmate will do two different short passages. But each passage has one word missing. Can you find it?

Who am I? I am a _____. I like playing with my friends. We can share our toys. We are happy together.	Who am I? I am a _____. I like helping others. I can set the table at dinnertime. I am so proud when I help.

1. Read the two passages of different roles.
2. Highlight the roles on the thinking map.
3. Write down the answers of the three questions.
4. Talk about the roles without the passages.）

Ss：(Work on the project)

T：who can talk about the roles? Now let's share.

Ss：(Talk about the roles)

从上面的教学活动中,学生已经对生活角色（roles）和活动（activities）之间的关系有了感知,也对表达模式有了了解,教师顺势将话题引导到学生自身,激发学生对自我进行思考和表述：

T：Jerry is a child, a friend, a helper. What about you? Among the three roles, who do you think you are? Circle the one you think you are and talk about it.

Ss：(Try to talk)

T：You see, besides the three roles, Jerry has more roles. He is a painter, a dancer and an animal lover. How about you? Are you a painter, a dancer or an animal lover? Please choose among the three roles and circle one. Write something about it.

Ss：(Follow the instructions)

教师按照学生选择的生活角色将学生分组,进行小组活动,使同一个生活角色的表述能得到充分有效的讨论,也借此培养学生在课堂中的交流协作能力,借鉴整合他人思维,完善自己的自我介绍。

T:(按学生所选角色给学生分组)Now you can share your information with your group members and take notes if necessary.

Ss:(Work in groups)

T:Your idea excites me. Actually, Jerry also has his ideas about these three roles. Check the answers in the box on your desk and get more information to make your introduction better.

Ss:(Check and better their introductions)

接着教师要求学生进行组际交流,促使学生不局限于一个生活角色的表达和思考,能对"Who am I?"有个全局的认识,帮助学生最后能真正地多角度地讲述"Who am I?"这个话题。

T:Now please go to the other groups to choose one friend to tell him about your introduction.

Ss:(Do the inter-group activities)

T:You can see Jerry has many roles. And let's go through all his roles' story together.

Ss:(Read after the tape while watching the picture show)

T:Up till now, we have learned Jerry's six roles. And you have chosen your roles in your life. So it's your turn to make your story "Who am I?" and if you want to talk about more roles among these six ones, you are welcome.

Ss:(Talk about their roles by themselves)

T:(Ask some of the students to come to the front to talk about their roles)

最后教师还设置环节请学生与听课教师互动,给学生创造了更多的表述机会,也使听课教师都参与到话题的讨论中来。

T:Please share your stories with your friends and the teachers here.

Step 4　Conclusion

T：Today we learned a story of Jerry's roles. But in our life we can have many other roles. We can be a singer, a neighbor, a music lover and a sports lover. Let's leave them to the next period.

（阐述本课教学的主旨：生活角色不局限于课堂讨论的几种，我们的生活可以丰富多彩，我们的活动可以各种各样）

◆ 案例反思 ◆

这堂课的教学中教师站在建构主义的理论高度为学生搭建了一个语言和思维的支架(scaffold)，如图：

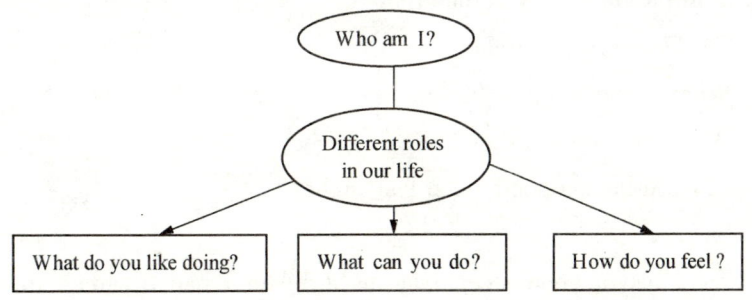

学生在这个框架下理解文本，领悟自我在生活中的不同角色，领悟生活角色和单元三个重点句型之间的逻辑联系。学生在这个框架下思考问题，定位自己的生活角色并使用所学单元语言知识回答三个问题，从而充实了生活角色的表述。在教师的步步引导下，学生对于单元语言知识的复习不是简单的再现，而是有意义的再构。根据不同生活角色，单元教学中的activities得到了有意义的归类，使得这些语言知识和学生的生活经验联系起来，实现了学生对于语言知识的内化和应用。此外，教师还通过小组合作，引导学生协作互助，改善自己对生活角色的理解、对语言知识的掌握；通过组际交流，促使学生不局限于对某个生活角色的单一思考，真正做到了以学生为主体，自主合作，在真实情境中交流。

典型案例 2

译林版《英语》六年级下册　Unit 1　The lion and the mouse

这是一节伊索寓言的故事教学课。与以往小学英语教学常见的对话语篇不同,本课教学内容是一个故事。课文按时间顺序讲述了这个经典的寓言故事,而教师在教学中抓住了故事人物的情绪变化线索,引导学生在理解人物情绪的基础上领会故事内容和寓言的深层含义;也通过故事人物的情绪线索,帮助学生体会和表演故事。

Step 1　Pre-reading

Skill building 1：Accumulation

T：How are you today?

What is the weather like now?

What was the weather like yesterday?

Did you have a good sleep last night?

Ss：…

T：I had a good sleep last night. And I had dreams. In my dream, I came to a place. (Show a picture of a forest)

Where was I?

What could I see?

Ss：You could see trees. And sunshine.

T：Yes, it was very beautiful. And I was very happy. I walked happily by the trees and I saw many animals. They came together in the forest to have a story party. I was very lucky to hear one of their stories. Do you like to know it?

Ss：Yes!

(教师在师生交流中自然展开教学,将学生引入课文情境:森林。教师在 PPT 图片和音效的配合下向学生展示了森林的美丽;学生在轻松自然的交流和欣赏中初步感知了本课需要学习的词汇:forest, happily, walk by 等)

Skill building 2: Prediction

T: OK. Let's begin our story time. First of all, are you curious about my story?

Do you have any questions about my story? Can you ask questions about the story? (Use PPT to show key words of the questions: who, where, when, what)

Ss: When did the story happen?

Who were in the story?

Where did the story happen?

What is the name/title of the story?

T: (Help and elicit the answers from the students)

Ss: The story happened in a forest in the past. There were a lion and a mouse in the story.

The name of the story is "The lion and the mouse".

T: (Use PPT to show the title)

(教师引导学生对故事进行预测和提问，帮助学生形成良好的阅读思维习惯，学会使用 what，who，where，when，how 等特殊疑问词了解故事梗概。教师在图片和音效的配合下引出故事主人公——狮子和老鼠，同时揭示课题)

Skill building 3: Depiction

T: Let's see the two major roles in this story: the lion and the mouse. (Use PPT to show pictures of the two animals)

What kind of feelings do you have when you see the lion?

How can we describe the animal?

Can you give me some adjectives?

S1: Strong, large...

T: What about its teeth and claws?

S2: It's very sharp.

T: (Teach "sharp") And what about the mouse?

S3: I think it's very small. It's very cute. It's very soft...

T: Yes. It's very small and cute. And we say it's very weak. (Teach "weak")

They are so different. But at the end of today's story, the two animals became good friends. (Use PPT to show pictures)

Do you want to know what happened?

Ss: Yes!

(教师进一步引导学生对比故事的两个主人公,请学生说一说看到狮子时候是什么感受,从而引出描绘狮子的形容词:strong, large, sharp 等;又通过图片形成的视觉对比冲击,请学生说一说哪些形容词可以描绘这只小老鼠,引导学生说出并学习 small, cute, soft, weak 等形容词。接着教师告诉学生这两个反差如此之大的动物会在故事的结尾成为好朋友,引发学生的思考和好奇心,进而进入课文教学)

Step 2 While-reading

Reading strategy 1: Understanding the feelings

T: Look at the picture. How did the mouse feel when he saw the lion?

S1: He felt afraid.

T: How did the lion feel when he saw the mouse? Can you look at the pictures and have a guess? You can discuss with your partners.

Ss: Happy, sad...

(教师问学生当老鼠遇到狮子的时候是什么感受,学生很快给出答案:害怕、恐惧;教师又问学生狮子看到老鼠是什么感受,学生经过思考给出了不同的答案。教师顺势给出四张故事图片,图片中狮子或大笑或哀伤,这让学生感到很好奇。教师引导学生快速阅读课文,找出描述狮子情绪的词句)

T: The lion, as you can see in the pictures, had many feelings in today's story.

(Use PPT to show the four pictures of the story and ask students to observe the feelings of the lion)

Sometimes he is happy and sometimes he is sad.

Now can you go through the story quickly and circle the words that show the feelings of the lion.

Ss: Angrily, laughed, loudly, sadly, happily…

T: When we feel something funny we laugh loudly.

（教师要求学生将这些图片和词汇配对，培养学生的读图和思维能力）

Now can you match the four feelings with the four pictures?

Ss: (Do the match work)

T: We can see in the story, the lion at first got angry and then he felt funny. Later on, he was sad but at last he became happy again.

What happened to make the lion change his feelings?

Let's learn the story together.

（教师进一步引导学生思考狮子是如何经历生气—好笑—悲伤—开心的情绪转变的，故事又是怎样随着狮子的情绪变化而起承转合的。学生经过这个环节中教师的引导，已经能够初步感知狮子的情绪变化，也能理解狮子的情绪变化与故事的情节变化之间的关系）

Reading strategy 2: Comprehending through feelings

[Part 1]

T: Now please listen to the beginning of the story. (Play the tape of the beginning of the story)

At the beginning of the story, the lion was angry. Why? What did the mouse do?

S1: The mouse walked by and woke the lion up.

T: Can you do the action "walk by" and "wake up"?

Ss: (Try to act and through acting, try to understand the meanings of the two phrases)

T: (Teach the two phrases)

T: What did the lion do then?

S2: The lion wanted to eat the mouse.

T: What did the mouse say?

S3: "Please don't eat me. I can help you some day."

T: Yes. And he said it quietly. Now can anyone say these sentences like the mouse?

Ss: (Try to say the lines of the mouse)

T: Can you add the actions?

Ss: (Try to act out the mouse)

T: Great! Let's read this part together.

(教学故事的第一部分时,教师要求学生思考狮子生气的原因和生气的结果;思考老鼠面对狮子时说话的语气、动作等。教师的所有提问都由狮子的情绪展开,帮助学生通过理解狮子的情绪理解故事情节的发展,帮助学生通过理解狮子的情绪模仿和表演故事)

[Part 2]

T: The mouse begged the lion. And what did the lion say? Please read the next part of the story.

S1: "You're so small and weak! How can you help me?"

T: Then what did the lion do?

S2: He laughed loudly and let the mouse go.

T: Exactly. Can you act the two actions?

Ss: (Try to act "laughed loudly" and "let sb go")

T: (Teach the two phrases)

T: Can you act the lion?

Ss: (Act the lion out with the lines)

(帮助学生学习故事第二部分时,教师引导学生自主思考狮子大笑的原因。当学生理解了狮子大笑的原因之后,教师鼓励学生表演这段故事,也请学生思考他们的表演方式如何体现狮子在这段故事中的情绪变化)

[Part 3]

T: What happened to make the lion feel sad? Please read the next part of the story.

This time you can ask your own questions and find the answers by yourself.

(Divide the students into two groups. One group read carefully to ask questions while another group read carefully to prepare to answer the questions)

G1: (Follow the patterns: What did... say?/What did... do?)

What did the lion say?

What did the two men do?

What did the lion do?

Did that help?

G2: The lion said sadly: "How can I get out?"

The two men caught the lion with a large net.

The lion bit the net with his sharp teeth.

That did not help.

T: (Teach "get out", "catch with", "net", "bite with" and ask students to act these actions out and say the lines with these actions)

(在第三部分的故事教学中,教师将学生分成两组,一组阅读本段故事后提出问题,另一组阅读本段故事后回答上一组同学的提问。这样有效地避免了故事教学的疲乏感,也激活了学生主动思考、归纳信息的能力。提问小组的同学必须在完成阅读后思考什么样的信息值得提问、如何提问;回答问题小组的同学必须阅读并将获取的信息归纳记忆,才能回答提问小组的问题。通过这种自主学习、交流协作的方式,故事信息被充分挖掘,人物情绪得到充分的理解)

[Part 4]

T: What happened next? Can you read the rest part of the story by yourself? This time this group ask questions and that group try to answer them.

Ss: (Read the rest part of the story)

G1: What did the mouse do? What did the lion do? What did the lion/mouse say?

G2: The mouse saw the lion and made a big hole in the net with his sharp teeth. The mouse said, "I can help you." The lion said, "Thank you!"

T: (Teach "net" and "make a hole" and ask the students to act out the lines with actions and feelings)

T: Let's see the end of the story.

Ss: From then on, they became good friends.

T: (Teach "become" and "from then on")

(教师继续通过小组分工协作，完成第四部分的故事理解。学生在教师的指导下尝试表演部分语言和动作)

Reading strategy 3: Integrating

T: As we have learned the story, would you please order the following sentences into the right order?

Ss: (Do Exe 1 on the worksheet)

T: (Check the answers with pictures of the story)

(通过完成排列句子顺序的练习，教师帮助学生整理故事思路，完成故事文本的整体教学)

Step 3 Post-reading

1. Lines with emotions

T: Let's go back to the lines in the story. (Use PPT to show lines with emotions)

Lines are not just sentences and words. They are said by the actors and they have feelings and they need actions.

Can you try these lines again this time with feelings and actions?

Ss: (Work in groups and present in the class)

T: Great! When we say these words and sentences with feelings and actions, they become lines. And the story becomes a play.

(教师带领学生整体感知故事的台词，帮助学生思考台词和一般语言的不同：台词是融合情感、动作的舞台语言，从而进一步指导学生小组合作"演绎"文中人物的台词，帮助学生将故事转变成一个小剧本)

2. Getting to know something about a play

T: Let's get to know something about a play. What makes up a play?

Ss: The roles. The lines. The feelings. The actions.

T: And we need narrators. Now work in groups of six. Act out the play according to the worksheet.

(学生分组分配角色,通过自己对这个故事的理解和思考,加工表演故事。实际教学中学生确实在这个环节给了教师很多惊喜,他们对主人公的语言、情绪、动作都有着自己独特的理解和表演方式)

3. Integrating skills: Make our own play

……

4. Moral education

T: What can we learn from this story?

Ss: ...

T: All have strong points.

　　Don't look down upon those who look weak.

　　Be kind and helpful to others.

　　They can give you a hand when you need.

(学生表演结束以后,对这个寓言故事有了更多自己的体会,教师接着从情感教育的层面向学生提问:我们能从故事中学到什么呢?请学生讲一讲通过这节课的学习、体会、感悟和表演后自己对这则寓言故事的寓意的理解。教师最后做归纳和升华)

◆ 案例反思 ◆

案例中教师基于自己对于文本的理解,抛开时间顺序的教学方式,引导学生关注文本故事中人物的情绪变化。在教学过程中,教师处处以情绪为切入点,帮助学生把握故事情节的发展、人物语言和动作及其内在联系,使得学生最后能结合自己对故事中人物情绪的理解,有感情地表演这则寓言故事。在教学设计上教师跳出了理性的按时间顺序学习故事的方式,带着学生从更感性的角度走进故事、靠近人物。在故事学习中,学生常常需要思考:为什么故事中人物会有这样的情绪?为什么会说这样的话?应该用什么语气来说这样的话?要用什么动作来传达这样的情绪?这样的问题也许和语言知识的学习并没有直接联系,但是却能真正帮助学生用英语学习文本、用英语思考问题、用英语演绎故事。

◆ 专家点评 ◆

美国学者贾尼斯·萨博曾列出智慧学生的特点,其中包括:能够提出问题,能够表达有力的观点,能够抽象概括,能运用知识,善于反思,等等。学生这些品质的形成离不开教师的引导。可是,当下的英语课堂,我们看到的多是语言知识的传输,学生在知识积累的同时鲜有学习过程的体验和思维能力的发展。不少教师认为英语学习主要是读读课文,背背单词,再记点语法,谈到思维的培养则好像有点无从入手。其实,要培养学生的思维,教学方法和技巧是关键。以词汇教学为例,当教师直接展示图片,呈现其发音、拼写和意义时学生思维的流量相对比较少,但要是变换一种方式,让学生通过对教师描述的内容进行判断、选择而最终加以理解的话,就是迈出了发展学生思维能力的第一步。同样,阅读教学时教师设计的问题要避免总是让学生沿着规定好的路线去思考,要做到把思考的主动权交给学生,教师则抓住对学生提问的契机来激发他们真实的思考,继而借助对问题个性化的解答来推动学生对文段的深入理解。至于语法教学,教师应该改变"只有通过教师讲授,学生才能学会"的观念,宜采用先感知、理解再模仿运用的做法,给予学生一定的空间和时间,相信他们能够依靠自己的努力去发现语言运用的规律。所以,能呈现学生真实的学习过程的教学就是促进学生思维发展的教学!

细节 17

如何促进学生语用能力的提高

▶ 细节阐述 ◀

英语教学的一个重要目标是把语言的知识目标和能力目标相结合,让学生学会用英语做具体的事情。这种用英语做事的能力就是语用能力。语用能力的提高是以语言知识的获得为基础的。举例来说,当学生要向他人介绍自己时,就必须先掌握与这一话题相关的词汇和句型结构;而如果要想描述自己曾经的一段生活经历则必须具备与时态有关的语法知识。不过,语言知识并不能保证语用能力,这是因为它们的发展和内化是相对独立的,也就是说,即使学生英语的语言知识掌握得相当扎实,在真实的跨文化交际时,他们牢固的语言知识也并不一定能有效地被激活成语用能力。

然而,现实的情况是,不少教师已经习惯于把自己的讲解作为学生学习语言的主要途径,教师争分夺秒地向学生灌输一个个语言知识,大多数时候,课堂上学生的主要任务是"认真听讲",即使让学生操练也多是机械的对话和练习,学生一直说的都是别人的话,很少有表达自己思想的机会。时间久了,这些学生尽管学了不少语言知识,语言技能的长进却不大,真正到需要与人交流的时候不是说不出什么就是没什么可说。语言学习的这种"高耗低效"的现象并不是我们愿意看到的。那么,如何扭转这个现象,促进学生语用能力的提升呢?有效的解决途径是要实现从强调教师的"语言教授"到重视学生的"语言学习"的转变。让学生在体验、感悟与实践中学习语言,在比较真实的语境中学习用语言进行交际。

策略一：真实交际　意义输入

第二语言的习得理论认为,在语言学习的过程中,学生主要关注语言使用的目的和语言表达的意义,而不是语言的形式。同样,以建构主义理论为基础的教学主张语言是通过使用来学习的。因而,课堂上教师要尽可能多地创造出为实现真实的交际目的而使用语言的机会。这个真实包含三个方面的内容:真实的内容,真实的语言和真实的交际。所谓真实的内容就是教师要说"真话",如果教师说"Look at the picture of my new house.",那么他(她)呈现的就应该是自己家的照片,而不是一看就知道是从网上下载的"假"图片,这是因为只有真话才能激起学生探究、学习欲望。即使为了便于学生理解而创设的"虚拟"情境也要合情合理。另外,课堂上教师要尽量使用真实的语言,也就是这个语言是会在某个现实生活的场景中被人们使用的。有些句子看似语法正确,实际生活中却很少或几乎不用,如:"Good morning, Teacher."最后是真实的交际。对于初学者来说,只有在一定交际情境下的有意义的输入才能有利于他们获得语用能力。不过,课堂上并不是所有师生间一问一答的形式都能被认为是真实的交际,假如老师明知对方是六年级的学生还要问"What grade are you in?",这就不能算是真实的交际。真实的交际应该存在于交流双方有信息差的时候。这样,课堂上的这种交际体验会被学生逐渐迁移到日常生活中,并在真实的交际中发挥作用。

策略二：创设情境　促进迁移

把语言知识从语境中提取出来解读不仅晦涩难懂而且没有意义,有效的解决办法是教师把语言学习置于语境中,注重语言的实践。教师可以使用实物、图片、视频等创设真实或接近真实的语言习得情境让学生感悟相关语言项目的意义,然后通过增加运用的频率强调该语言结构,引导学生仔细观察并关注其用法,继而帮助他们在使用的过程中进一步体会这个语言项目的表意功能。

在创设语境的时候教师要突出它的准确性和真实性。首先是准确性，也就是创设的语境要能够贴合对应的语言项目，很好地诠释其意义。以进行时态的教学为例，教师常常通过一边做某个动作，一边用进行时态的句子描述的方法呈现。但是，某些瞬间动词的发生是在刹那间的，学生不容易察觉这个动作正在进行。如：教师说"I'm opening the box."，往往教师的话没有说完，盒子已经是打开的状态了，这种情景创设就会造成学生对进行时态的不解或误读。其次是真实性，也就是说课堂上教师创设的语境要尽可能地基于真实的信息交流的目的，只有这样学生才能将课堂学到的语言迁移到实际的生活中加以运用。例如，教师可以在呈现将来时态 be going to do 时虚拟一个人物 John，并且告诉学生："John always writes himself a list at the beginning of every day. What is he going to do today? What's he going to buy?"同时还给学生列出 John 的待办事项。这样，学生就被置身于教师创设的语境中，一旦当他(她)在日常生活中遇到类似的场景就很容易把学到的语言进行迁移使用。

策略三：意义操练　注重表达

英语教学的最终目的是为了让学生获得语言的技能，做到准确、有意义和得体地运用语言形式表达思想和情感，而练习是获得技能的唯一途径和方法。一般情况下，语言的练习多为教师完全控制下的形式：练习前教师一遍遍地口述例句，等学生听熟后给出提示词，要求替换句中的部分成分。虽然类似这样的机械性练习能加深学生对短语结构的印象，但是它忽略了语言的表意和使用功能，学生不知道这个句子是如何在生活场景中发挥作用和表达意思的。所以，小学英语课堂要以意义操练为主，教师要善于把枯燥的语言练习与真实的生活相结合，突出它在语境中的表意功能。还是以 want to do 的结构操练为例。教师可以设计这样的背景：假如你要去一个孤岛单独生活一天，请说出你最想在孤岛上做的两件事情。有了这个背景，学生就不是在说别人的语言，而是在表达自己的想法。

另外，课堂上教师还要给学生提供激活语言知识的机会。教师可以模拟真实或者接近真实的生活场景让学生置身其中,然后再用语言去完成各种任务,如制定节假日计划,了解同伴的爱好,描述自己生活的城市的面貌,等等。学生在完成这些任务的时候就会把注意力放在如何使用语言来完成事情上,萌生出语言运用的现场感。

策略四:尊重差异　多维评价

研究表明,每个人的学习方法和风格都不一样,在一部分学生身上奏效的方法可能并不适合另一部分学生;某些教学活动或许更适合视觉型学生,而另一些可能更适合动觉型学生——简而言之,就是学生用适合自己的方法学习更易实现高效学习。因此,教师应该尊重不同的学习风格,努力寻找契合不同学习风格的教学手段与方法。例如,使用多种教学辅助手段,不断变换教学方法和活动,把多样的设计蕴含在学习中:单独学习和小组合作讨论学习相结合;听录音与看图片相结合;角色扮演与故事复述相结合,等等。这种对差异的尊重是"以人为本"的理念的具体表现。而"以人为本"理念的另一体现则是实施多维评价。多维评价与单一评价的区别在于它既关注知识技能,又关注过程方法以及学生正确的情感态度和价值观的形成。实施多维评价时教师需要对学生日常学习过程中的表现、所取得的成绩以及所反映出的情感、态度、策略等方面的发展做出全方位的评价。多维评价常与形成性评价相依相伴,与以"一锤子买卖"为特点的终结性评价最大的区别在于,这种过程性的评价与学生的学习同步进行,不仅能反映学习的过程,而且能对学生起到激励和激活的作用,帮助学生树立"I can do it."的自信。

典型案例

说明:本课教学内容为译林版《牛津小学英语》6A　Review and check,这是一节复习课,通过教学要求学生能在回顾、复习前三个单元的基本句型的基础上将所学到的语言知识运用到听、说、读、写的各项活动中。

Step 1　Greetings

T:Good morning, boys and girls, nice to see you. I'm your

new English teacher today. First I'd like to know something about you.

T：May I know your name?

T：What do you usually do after school/on Saturday and Sunday?

T：I think… is your hobby.

T：When is your birthday?

T：What would you like as your birthday present?

T：I've learned something about you. Do you want to know something about me? You can ask me questions.

	English teacher
Name	Lisa Ye
Birthday	Month：the seventh month of the year Date：the twelfth day of the month
Hobbies	Reading books, watching cartoons, doing word puzzles
Birthday presents	Books, CDs, word puzzles

从上面的对话内容来看，这节课的执教教师应该是借班上课，在正式进入教学前，教师利用与学生首次见面、相互熟悉的机会恰到好处地复习了前三个单元学习的句型，让学生在自然的语境中实践了语言，同时还拉近了师生间的距离，给学生创设了宽松、融洽的学习气氛，可谓一举两得。

Step 2 Word revision

1) T：As you know I like doing word puzzles. Would you like to play word puzzle games with me? Now let's have a look.

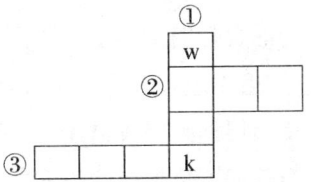

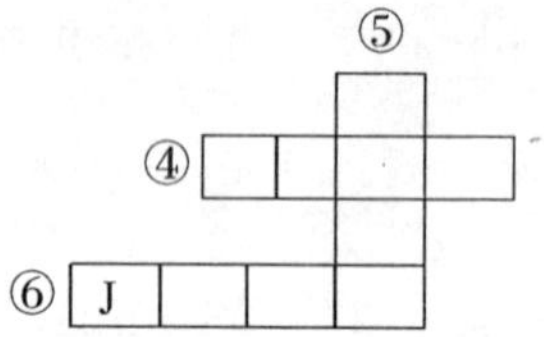

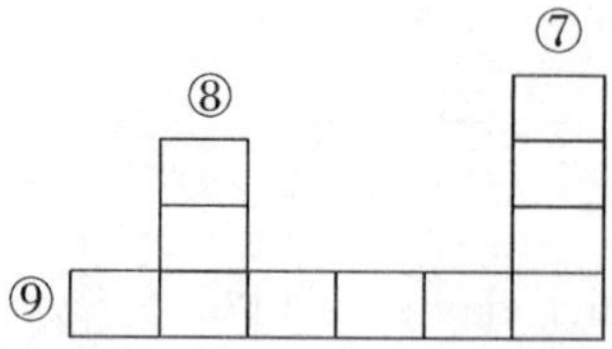

（提示句子）

① My grandpa often takes a _____ after dinner.

② Excuse me, can I _____ you a question?

③ The sign means you shouldn't _____ the flowers.

④ What does it _____?

⑤ —What's the _____ today? —It's Oct. 23rd.

⑥ _____ is the sixth month of the year.

⑦ It means "Danger" and you _____ stay away from it.

⑧ Miss Li was in the office ten minutes _____.

⑨ The watch was on the desk a _____ ago.

2) T: Now please look at the given phrases and sentences and try to tell the right words.

① a hand phone _____

② I have three letters. My first letter is in the word "him" but not in "his". My second letter is in the word "at" but not in "it". My third letter is in the word "any" but not in "and". _____

……

在这个环节教师采用 word puzzles 的形式帮助学生复习单词。教师首先要求学生根据所给句子的提示,在方格中填入合适的字母,使其横行、竖行皆能组合成单词;然后又要求学生根据解释或描述写出相应的单词。这样的任务设计能够让学生体会到词汇是如何在语言交流中发挥作用的。

Step 3　Preposition revision

T：(Show a picture of Su Yang) A girl's birthday is in the 11th month of the year. Who is she? Look，it's Su Hai. Today Su Hai is telling her class about her family's birthday. Let's read the passage.

> *It is Wednesday afternoon. The children are having an English lesson. Su Hai is telling the students about her family.*
> Su Hai：My dad is an English teacher. His hobbies are collecting stamps and taking photos. November the twentieth is his birthday. My mother works in a hospital. She likes music very much and her birthday is in the ninth month of the year. Su Yang and I were born on the same day—the first of March, 1998. But I was born at six and my sister was born at six twenty. We both like PE.

Read the passage above and try to answer the questions：

1. When is Dad's birthday?
2. What would Dad like as a birthday present?
3. When is Mum's birthday?
4. What would Mum like as a birthday present?
5. When was Su Hai born?

T：(Show PPT) Let's read the three sentences. Do you know how to use "in", "on" and "at" correctly?

教师考虑到抽象地讲解三个介词的不同使用特点，学生难以理解，因此，在设计PPT时，用了下列图画：

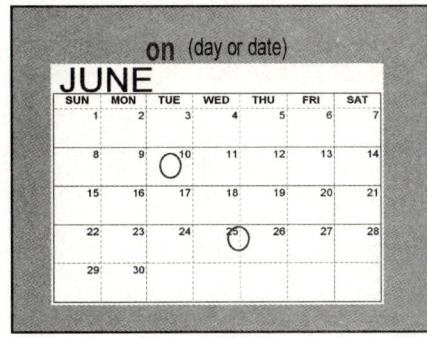

```
         in ( a period of time )
in the morning ┕━━━━┙
           six    twelve

in October ┕━━━━━━━━━┙
         Oct.1st      Oct.31st

in 2015 ┕━━━━━━━━━━━━━━━┙
      Jan.1st              Dec.31st
```

Exercise：

1. I usually go to school _____ half past six.
2. My brother often plays football _____ Sunday.
3. Christmas is _____ December.
4. I like swimming _____ summer（夏天）.
5. Children's Day is _____ June the first.

在语法教学的环节，教师没有要求学生记忆语法条文，而是借助阅读后回答问题的机会，巧妙地引出关于 in，on，at 这三个介词不同用法的话题，然后通过直观形象的演绎，帮助学生区分、归纳它们的用法。在检测环节，教师又将含有这些介词的短语放在句中让学生选择填空。自始至终，语法的学习没有脱离语境。

Step 4　Revision of "should" and "shouldn't"

T：You did a good job! I'll give you a sign. Which sign should I give you?（PPT 出示分别表示赞赏、不满、愤怒的标志）

Ss：...

教师通过对学生前面所做练习的评价图案自然过渡到本课最后一个复习内容：should/shouldn't。

T：Look at the pictures. Which signs can help them? Please choose the right ones and tell the meanings of the signs.（PPT 显示不同的人物在医院、教室、非停车区域等想吸烟、饮食、停车的图片和文字）

这个练习要求学生先根据图片选择合适的标志，再用英语说出标志的含义。设置的语用场所均是学生比较熟悉的,如:医院、教室、停车场等。目的是让语言的实践与日常生活更加接近。风趣、幽默的图案很容易激起学生的表达欲望。

T:Look at the Invitation. Mike's birthday is coming. He would like Yang Ling to go to his birthday party. But it is the first time for Yang Ling to go to an American birthday party. So Mum is telling Yang Ling what to do and what not to do at an American party. Please read and then complete the sentences.

Not-to-do list
1. Don't be late.
2. Don't take the dogs or the cats.
3. Don't make noise when you eat.

To-do list
1. Keep the fork in the left hand.
2. Keep the knife in the right hand.

You _____ go to the party late.
You _____.
You _____.
You _____.
You _____.

教师通过创设中国学生杨玲要参加美国同学 Mike 的生日聚会,而向妈妈咨询关于西方国家聚会礼仪的语用情境,要求学生根据 Not-to-do list 和 To-do list 的内容,用句型"You should..."和"You shouldn't..."向杨玲提出建议。这种有意义的生活化的语言输出形式有助于学生产生语言使用的现场感,促使他们将语言迁移到日常生活的交流中。

Step 5 Sum up

T:Can you tell me what you have learned in this lesson?
Ss:...

Step 6 Homework

1) Finish the dialogues on Pages 34—36.

2) Surf the Internet and try to find more information about the differences between Chinese parties and Western parties, and then try to write a short passage. You can use the following modal verbs:

"should","may","must" and "can"。

课堂总结,是教师和学生对一节课的高度梳理和概括,是学生把学到的零散知识进行整体建构并内化为自身知识的一个重要环节,能收到"课已尽而意无穷"的效果。家庭作业的布置则重在考查学生的语言运用能力,如第一项的完成书本上的对话,第二项的上网搜索中西方聚会的不同特色,把了解到的信息用英语写下来,以此锻炼学生的书面表达能力。

◆ 案例反思 ◆

日常的英语复习课多以语言知识的整理与归纳为目的,很多教师设计练习和任务时会注重考查学生语言知识的掌握程度,所以,无论从内容还是形式上来看都比较单一而且机械化,不仅难以激起学生的学习积极性,而且对学生语用能力的培养帮助不大。这节六年级的复习课以促使学生将学到的语言知识顺利地转化为语言技能为目标,给我们提供了一个比较理想的范例:从单词的检测、句型的巩固练习到语法的学习与反馈,都与语意和语用密切联系,而且没有脱离生活化的语境。学生在课堂上完成任务时获得的语用经历和体验有可能在未来的某个时候迁移到相似的生活场景中,转变为语用能力。

另外,尽管所涉及的词汇、句型等语言项目是学生已经熟知的,在这节课上它们却出现在新的语境和上下文中。通过阅读它们,学生可以接触到书本以外的鲜活、多样的语言材料。当需要输出时,学生使用的语言也有可能更为丰富。

综观这节课,教师将知识目标和能力目标相结合,分别从听、说、读、写等方面为学生提供了多样的语言学习和实践的机会,这种做法对发展学生的语言运用能力是大有裨益的!

细节 18

如何进行文化意识的渗透

▶ 细节阐述 ◀

在小学英语课堂教学中,文化主要是指"日常"文化,包括西方的一些生活习俗、节日习俗、小典故和小忌讳等。文化的学习在英语教学中具有非常重要的作用。一方面,在英语学习过程中,小学生会对不同于自己国家的异国文化习俗产生强烈的好奇心,希望能更多了解它们,教师可以充分利用学生的这种好奇心来激发他们的英语学习兴趣;另一方面,小学生能否使用英语进行成功的交流,很大程度上也取决于他们对英语语言所蕴含的文化的理解程度。所以文化的学习应该伴随着英语学习的始终。

策略一:循序渐进逐步渗透　以点带面有效渗透

小学英语课堂文化教育所引入的文化内容应该与学生所学的语言内容密切相关,应贴近学生的日常生活。对于不同年级的学生,应根据其英语语言水平的差异,按照由浅入深和循序渐进的原则,进行文化教育和熏陶。例如,译林版《英语》三年级下册 Unit 6 Colours,教师在教授完颜色词汇时,为活跃课堂气氛,增强学生了解英语文化的兴趣,可以结合西方文化中颜色的不同含义来讲解颜色词汇,如蓝色代表忧郁、紫色代表高贵、白色代表纯洁、黄色代表紧张等,也可以请学生对比中国文化里颜色代表的意义。但三年级学生词汇量和理解力有限,若在三年级课堂中渗透更多、更难的颜色习语,不仅不能达到活跃课堂气氛的目的，还会给学生造成语言理解的障碍，削弱学生的学习兴趣。又如，在教学译林版《英语》四年级上册 Unit 1 I like dogs 时，教师可以根据四年级学生的语言水平适当补充相关动物词汇的短语，如 a lucky dog, a white elephant, rain cats and dogs, a black sheep 等；而一些比较难的动物习语可以在教授译林版《英语》五年级上册 Unit 3 Our animal friends 时再补充。

　　同时，文化学习要注意避免补充的内容过多、过杂，要结合课堂教学内容对相关的英语文化进行介绍，不应过多地涉及其他内容，为补充而补充。文化学习的目的就是通过介绍某个文化背景知识帮助学生更好地理解课文文本，培养英语学习兴趣，起到以点带面的作用。如，教学译林版《英语》五年级上册 Unit 8 At Christmas，在介绍圣诞节时，教师应集中介绍西方圣诞节的来历和习俗等，这样可以帮助学生更好地理解 Story time 中人物在圣诞节所做的各种事情；但是不应该引入其他西方节日的来历和习俗等，这样内容庞杂，也偏离了教学目标。

　　语言教学与文化渗透并重是小学英语教学的必然趋势。在小学生学习英语的初始阶段，教师在课堂中将语言与文化有机地结合起来，并按照科学的方法和原则进行文化渗透，对加深学生对英语国家文化的了解，帮助他们更好地学习理解文本，进一步提高他们学习英语的兴趣起着至关重要的作用。

策略二：在比较中感受文化　在实践中融入文化

　　小学英语课堂的文化教学应注意结合小学生的心理特点、认知水平和生活经验，在教学中教师要灵活运用各种方法进行渗透、要善于利用各个教学环节进行传达。例如，译林版《英语》五年级上册 Unit 6 My e-friend 的 Culture time 的教学中，教师可以首先展示中文地址的表达方式，然后请同学们试着用英文再写一遍地址，最后出示正确的英文地址表达方式，通过请学生比较中文地址和英文地址在表述时顺序上有什么不同，使学生了解地址的英文表达顺序是从小到大，而中文则是从大到小。又如，在学习日期表达时，教师可以提问学生："我们平时是怎样表达日期的，顺序是怎样的？"然后再问学生："英语中的日期表达方式跟我们国家是一样的吗?"通过这种提问,让学生主动关注两者的不同之处,将两种文化进行对比,明白西方国家的日期表达与我们是相反的。运用对比的方法,可以促使学生自己发现问题答案,让学生直观地了解汉语和英语两种语言表达方式的不同,从而使他们在交际中正确灵活地运用。

同时,小学英语课堂教学中的文化教学更多讲求在做中学、在实践中体悟。例如,在教授数字 13—19 时,教师讲解数字 13 在西方文化中是个不吉利的数字,很多场合都要避讳。随后教师设计了一个读数游戏,要求学生看到屏幕上的数字时说出英文,但是遇到数字 13 时要说"Bomb"。在游戏过程中,学生体会和内化了数字 13 的西方文化意义。再比如,译林版《英语》六年级上册 Unit 1 The king's new clothes 的 Culture time 中介绍了不同国家的衣着,教师结合单元主题,设计出四个含有不同 dress code 的请柬,要求学生分组按照所收到的请柬中的着装要求选择合适的衣物出席各个场合,这不仅调动了学生的积极性,也使学生在完成任务的过程中体验和融入了文化。在低年级英语教学中,也有很多对话环节适合进行有效的文化渗透:教师对每个帮忙的同学都说"Thank you",渐渐地小朋友就适应了西方文化里频繁地说"Thank you"的文化习惯,这时候教师又对每个说"Thank you"的小朋友用"You are welcome"回答,通过听和模仿,慢慢地小朋友也就学会了怎么回应别人的感谢。

策略三:挖掘教材文化因素　利用课堂渗透理解

小学英语教学语言素材相对简单,我们应该如何发掘文化元素呢?其实现行的很多小学英语教材都包含了一些常见的文化主题,所以小学英语课堂教学的文化内容主要是结合教材文本进行挖掘。教材文本是教师进行文化教学的最好载体,每个单元内容中都包含了一定的社会或人文文化。教师只要做一个有心人,细心挖掘,积极创设良好的英语氛围,因势利导,积少成多,就能为学生打开博览英语文化的世界之窗,提升学生对英语文化的理解。

例如,在学习厕所的词汇时,学生学习了 toilet 和 restroom 两个词,这时候教师可以引导学生课后查一查资料,看看哪个词在美国用得更频繁、哪个词在英国用得更广泛。在资料查找过程中,学生可能还会发现厕所的其他表达方式,如 washroom, ladies' room, men's room 等。借助这个自我学习的过程,教师也可以请学生小组合作整理一个厕所词汇小专题在班级交流一下。这样既提高了学生的学习兴趣和词汇量,也加深了学生对西方国家文化的理解。这样的各国文化差异在英语中还有很多,例如温度单位的不同表达、餐具和食物的选择等,教师可以在课内设置 Culture time 板块,帮助学生体验文化,扩大词汇量。

➤• 典型案例 1 •◀

译林版《牛津小学英语》6A
Unit 7　At Christmas　Part A　Read and say

　　本段对话通过 Jim 一家在圣诞节互赠礼物这一情境引出主要学习内容,伴随着圣诞歌曲 *We wish you a Merry Christmas* 的音乐,PPT 呈现几种常见的圣诞元素,如 bells, stockings, Santa Claus, cards, songs, presents 等,教师开始教学:

　　T: Do you know this song? What's it about?

　　S1: It's about Christmas.

　　T: Yes. When is Christmas?

　　S2: It's on the 25th of December.

　　T: What do people usually do at Christmas?

　　S3: ...(根据图片提示回答)

　　T: Right. These are some Christmas symbols.

　　(教师对每种圣诞元素加以讲解,通过谈论收到的礼物过渡到课文的教学)

　　　　……

　　本节课结尾,教师设计了一个模拟互赠圣诞礼物的环节。学生在歌曲中走下座位,把事先准备的礼物和卡片送给自己的朋友。

S1：Hello, ×××. This present is for you. Merry Christmas!

S2：Thank you. I like it very much. Merry Christmas!

...

T：Good. Everybody has got a nice present. In western countries, how do people send and receive presents? Here are some tips for you.

（PPT呈现西方国家送礼和受礼的基本知识和图片，学生饶有兴趣地观看）

◆ 案例反思 ◆

这个案例中教师将圣诞文化贯穿整节课，从开始的圣诞歌曲、圣诞元素到最后小结西方送礼和受礼的习俗，教师用圣诞元素带领学生走入课文学习，最后又用圣诞活动把学生从课堂引向生活，引导他们去了解圣诞节、感受圣诞节、体会圣诞节的文化内涵。学生在学习语言知识的同时也接受了圣诞节的文化熏陶，在阅读课文之余也体验到了过节的快乐。实践得真知，通过和同学的交流和互动，学生在相对真实的语境中应用了所学的文化知识，能够更好地掌握语言并融入文化。

▶·典型案例2·◀

译林版《英语》六年级上册

Unit 1　The king's new clothes　Culture time

教师通过提问帮助学生回顾单元故事情节，并从故事里国王不穿衣服而受到众人嘲笑自然过渡到穿错衣服一样会受到大家嘲笑，从而引出这个教学环节的主题：西方文化中如何正确穿衣。

T：Do you remember the story of the king? Why was he laughed at?

S1：Because he didn't wear anything when walked on the street.

T：That's right. People will be laughed at if they wear nothing. But if you wear the wrong clothes, you will also be laughed at. Why? Let's look at some pictures.

（教师出示图片1：沙漠中一个西装革履的男士）环境和人物衣着的强烈反差引起了学生的兴趣，学生大笑，并指出在沙漠中我们应该根据地理和气候穿着合适的服饰。教师顺势渗透：衣着首先要考虑到气候因素。

T：Can you see a man dressed like this in a dessert?

Ss：(Laughing) No!

T：If we should travel in a dessert, what clothes do we need?

Ss：Jeans, T-shirts...

T：Yes, because it's very hot and dry.

Now we know we should dress according to the WEATHER.

（教师出示图片2：一个牛仔打扮的人出现在教室里）教师结合学生的生活，通过图片产生的强烈视觉冲击，让学生感受到穿衣服还要注意场合。

T：Can we dress like a cowboy when we are in school?

Ss：(Laughing) No!

T：So we should dress according to the PLACE.

（教师出示图片3：旧时代的绅士穿着燕尾服走在街上）教师用幽默的语言提醒学生：这是旧时代人们的着装，如果你现在这样穿，人们还以为你拍电影呢。学生在笑声中也悟出了穿衣必须符合时代。

T：Look at those gentlemen. They wore the clothes of their own time. But if you dress like this today, people may think you are shooting a film.

Ss：We should dress according to the TIME.

T：Exactly. When we choose our clothes, we should think about the weather, place and time. How can me wear the right clothes? We should learn the dress code.

教师在这个环节并没有选择直接讲解，而是给出了四封请柬，要求学生根据请柬中的 dress code（着装规则）和提示图片来选择合适的衣服出入各种场合。

T：Now we know we should dress according to the occasions.

But do you know the dress codes?

I have four invitations here. Each group will have one. You can find the dress codes on the invitations and you can discuss with your group members to find the right clothes.

Ss：(Work in groups and discuss the dress codes on the invitations)

学生完成讨论并选好了衣服以后，分组展示，看看哪一组选对的衣服最多、解读的着装规则最正确。

T：(Further explain the different dress codes of different occasions：

1. Cocktail
2. Black tie
3. White tie
4. Wedding)

在评论学生选错的衣服时，教师也顺势渗透 over-dressed 这个概念，指出日常生活中西方人穿衣服比较休闲，没有人会穿得非常精致隆重。如果你穿得过于隆重，那么你就是 over-dressed。穿得随便是不礼貌，穿得过于隆重也是不合时宜的。

♦ 案例反思 ♦

Culture time 是译林版《英语》教材在小学高年级阶段新增的一个板块，教材通过这个板块引导教师结合单元文本内容进行相关的文化知识传授。在教授这个板块时教师需要结合自己对单元内容和相关文化知识的理解，做有效、有益的补充和拓展。本案例中，单元 Culture time 只给出了两幅图片：美国牛仔和身着苏格兰短裙的苏格兰男士。教师应如何结合本单元故事皇帝的新衣和这两幅图片进行文化介绍呢？教师想到国王不穿衣服被人嘲笑，而穿错衣服也会被人嘲笑，并就此将这个单元的 Culture time 适当改编，衍生出了西方常见的一些场合的着装要求(dress code)。通过学习，学生可以基本理解、掌握请柬上的 dress code 并能够说出各个场合所需的正确服饰，这对于学生今后的生活和社交是一个有益的补充。在实际的教学过程中,学生通过对比图片中人物衣着和环境、场合的反差迅速领悟到了教师所要传达的西方社交礼仪信息:要在不同的时间、地点、场合穿着不同的衣服。在接下来的教学活动中,教师设计了有效的小组活动,让学生在实践合作中,相互学习、讨论、发现一些着装的要诀。在发挥了主观能动性的情况下,学生对于自己"寻找得来"的文化知识印象就特别深刻。

◆ **专家点评** ◆

实践证明,英语学习者需要综合运用语言规则和文化规则才能正确、得体地使用语言,形成运用英语进行交际的能力。可见,语言和文化是密不可分的,它们相互渗透,"你中有我,我中有你"。课堂上文化学习的作用主要体现在两个方面:首先它能够为语言的学习创设情境,促进学生对语言的理解和运用,例如教材中常见的 At Christmas, Halloween 等。除此以外,文化学习还能够提高学生对中外文化异同的敏感性和鉴别能力,促进他们的思维发展。

不过,课堂上要将语言学习目标和文化目标有机地融合在一起,起到"润物细无声"的效果,需要以教师自身深厚的专业素养和文化素养为基础,所以,教学之余,老师们要注重平时的积累和学习,只有这样才能在教学的时候有东西可以挖掘、有内容可以渗透。

细节 19

如何开展文化比较

> 细节阐述

语言和文化息息相关,它的表现形式受到社会习俗、生活方式、行为方式、价值观念、思维方式等的制约和影响。不同民族间的文化差异也必然在其语言中得到充分的体现。即使是同样使用英语的国家,其文化方面也存在着诸多的差异。对于学习英语的中国学生而言,如果能对这些差异有所了解,就能更好地认知和掌握这门语言,成功地进行跨文化交际。因此,《英语课程标准》中就文化意识的培养作了如下要求:"教师应当结合教学内容,引导学生关注语言和语用中的文化因素,了解中外文化的异同,逐步增强学生对不同文化的理解力,为开展跨文化交际做准备。"为了落实课程标准的要求,教师就要善于将文化教学的内容贯穿于英语教学中,把文化的差异比较纳入到语言教学的多个方面。

策略一:利用词汇教学,进行文化比较

词汇是语言中文化载荷量最大的部分,许多英语的词汇受历史、风俗和地理等的影响,蕴涵了丰富的文化知识和内涵。教师在教授这些词汇时就最好将这些相关的知识介绍给学生。以汉语"猪"和"猪肉"两个相互关联的词语为例,后者是在前一个词的基础上衍生而来的。但是英语中"猪"(pig)和"猪肉"(pork)却是完全不同的单词,这是因为它们源自不同的语言。pig 来自古英语,而 pork 来自法语,起源于

1066年法国对英格兰的征服。因此,山野间这些动物的名称用的是饲养它们的英格兰人的语言,而餐桌上的食物的名称则源自统治英格兰人的法国人的语言。有了这个背景知识,学生就能理解为什么"牛"(cow)和"牛肉"(beef),"羊"(sheep)和"羊肉"(mutton)有不同的名字了。

另外,同样是使用英语的国家,在许多单词的选择使用方面也存在着差异。例如,"罐头",英语中称为 tin,而美语中则称为 can;"糖果"在英语和美语中分别是 sweet 和 candy。还有,英国人眼中的 the first floor,如果在美国,人们通常认为是 the second floor。词汇教学中融入这些文化差异的介绍不仅可以让语言学习变得更为鲜活、有趣,而且更加易于学生记忆。

策略二:利用对话教学,进行文化比较

中英文化有相通相似之处,但也存在着巨大的差异,这尤其体现在日常的交往、习惯、风俗等方面。现行小学英语教材中的对话多与它们有关。因而,教师需要有意识地指导学生尽量避免以母语的思维方式去理解英语文化现象。以下面一段对话为例:A:Would you like to come to my birthday party this weekend? B:Yes,I'd love to. But I'm afraid I have no time. 按照英语表达的习惯,连词 but 后面的内容才是说话人的言下之意,所以,这样的回应其实是在婉言谢绝对方的邀请。但如果学生不了解这一点就容易把它理解为回答的人有意愿参加这个聚会。可见,对话教学时,教师如果能引导学生对两个国家不同的习俗加以比较,就能帮助他们在未来的某个场合与人交际时得体地运用语言。

策略三:利用语法教学,进行文化比较

与汉语相比较,英语的逻辑形式和结构有很大的不同。教学中经常可以见到学生使用"中文思维+英文形式"的语言结构,究其根源,就是不同的文化和思维方式给学生带来的障碍。比如,在阐述理由时,汉语习惯说"因为……所以……",把结论放在后面;但英语表达更倾向

于先说结论,再说原因,也就是常把 because 放在后面,并且 because 和 so 不在同一个句子中出现。又如,当学生见到句子"Where is my knife and fork?"时往往会感到疑惑:为什么 be 动词的形式没有改为 are？原来,这和英语国家人们的用餐习惯相关。在他们看来用餐时刀和叉是一个不可分割的整体或组合,自然就用单数形式了。一旦学生了解了这种思维方式,就能更好地理解语言的形式,避免发生使用不当的情况。

策略四：利用话题教学,进行文化比较

学生学习英语固然要了解英语国家的文化,但也不能忽略对自己国家文化的学习。现行小学英语教材的话题涉及学校生活、健康饮食、交通规则和节日等内容,教学时教师可以采用对比的方法,将英语国家的文化和我们国家的进行对比,发现异同,并将这些信息传递给学生。例如:学习关于 Christmas 的话题时,教师可以先从日期、月份入手,引导学生了解、对照各个国家新年时间的不同,然后借助图片或视频资料向学生介绍 Christmas tree（圣诞树）、stockings（长筒袜）、Christmas card（圣诞卡）等具有代表性的圣诞物品,并结合介绍中国新年常见的 red packet（红包）、fireworks（烟火）和 lion dance（舞狮子）等内容,让学生在比较中熟悉不同国家的人民庆祝新年时习俗的差异。为了帮助学生深入了解这种差异背后的文化渊源,教师甚至可以再补充有关节日的起源和历史变迁等内容,最终,让学生感悟到,无论对于哪个民族而言,新年都是家人团聚、憧憬美好未来的时刻。又如:在学习有关 birthday 的话题时,教师可以播放一位来自英语国家的孩子介绍自己生日的视频资料,让学生边看边思考自己是如何过生日的；接着再采用小组讨论的方式,说出两者的相似和不同之处。这种将不同文化相互渗入的方式,不但可以促使学生加深对我们国家文化的了解,而且还能提高他们对不同文化的敏感性。

最后需要指出的是,在进行文化意识的渗透时,教师应该根据学生的年龄特征和认知能力,采取适当的方法逐渐扩大文化知识的内容和范围,为学生未来的语言学习之路奠定基础。

➤•典型案例 1•◄

教师完成"A letter to a penfriend"的教学内容之后,布置了一个给美国友好学校的学生写信的任务,同时还要求用英文书写信封上的地址。有学生按照中文的书信格式填好地址并呈现给大家时,教师提问:"Do you think the students can get the letter?"这让大部分学生感到不解。这时,教师解释:不同国家之间有很多文化、习惯、思维方式的不同,这种不同会反映在生活的各个方面。寄往英美等国家的邮件,信封上的地址要按照收件人姓名—街道—市(郡)—州—国家的顺序排列,并且寄件人和收件人的地址应该分别位于信封的左上角和中间略偏右的位置,如下图:

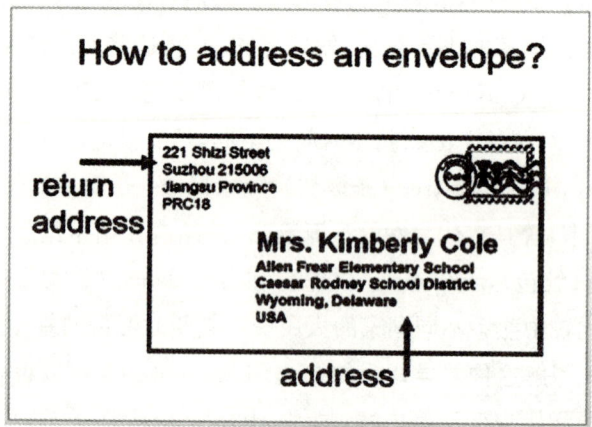

在上述教学环节中,教师没有直接告诉学生美国人如何填写信封,而是先让学生尝试。毫无疑问,依据既有的生活经验,学生的书写方式一定是中式的。学生完成后,教师的提问很自然地会引发学生的疑惑,此时教师再向学生呈现美式信封的规范写法,不仅有助于加深学生的印象,而且也巧妙地将文化的比较融入了教学中。

➤•典型案例 2•◄

教师在完成关于昆虫的单词 ant, butterfly, firefly, butterfly, bee, cricket, cicada, grasshopper 的教学后,出示了一些包含有昆虫

的英语俗语，要求学生根据句意来填空：

1. Even an _____ can hurt an elephant.
2. As busy as a _____.
3. Unlike the singing cicada, the silent _____ burn itself.
4. Different seas, different fish; different fields, different _____.
5. It is not summer until the _____ sings.
6. Happiness is like a _____.

这些句子中要求填写的单词均是这节课上学生学到的有关昆虫名称的单词。学生可以根据上下文的提示，同时联系昆虫的生活习性猜出空缺部分的昆虫名称。这个练习一方面能帮助学生有效地复习并巩固所学内容，另一方面也向学生展示了英语的语言文化。而且，当学生在阅读这些句子的时候还会下意识地和自己国家的表达习惯进行比较，从中领悟到两种文化间的异同之处。

➤·典型案例 3·◄

这节课的主题是 Chinese New Year，但是教师并没有局限于这个话题，而是设计了如下情境，即：圣诞老人来中国给 Bobby 送礼物时恰逢中国新年来临，所以，圣诞老人向 Bobby 了解中国新年的风俗……

● **Practice**

T：Bobby is a good boy and Santa will give him some presents. What presents will Santa give him? Watch the video and answer the questions.

T：Here is Santa. He would like to know about Chinese New Year. Can you tell him?

S1：People usually have a big dinner.
S2：We can watch fireworks.
S3：Children always get red packets.
S4：…

● **Consolidation**

T：When is Chinese New Year in 2015?

Ss：It's on the 19th of February.

T：What are we going to do at Chinese New Year?

Ss：...

● **Culture time**

T：People do different things in China and the USA at New Year. Can you tell the differences between Christmas and Chinese New Year?

Ss：...

T：Both Christmas and Chinese New Year are full of fun, love, happiness and wish.

文化比较，一个听起来有些严肃的话题，经过这堂课的教师的精心设计和整合后立刻变得富有生活气息了。上述片段中，人物形象Bobby和Santa分别代表了两种不同的文化，通过他们的互动和交流，自然地引出了中西方文化的比较，这种方式与学生的生活经验非常贴合，所以，学生就会有话想说，有话能说，从而收到比较好的教学效果。

◆ 案例反思 ◆

一位外语教学专家曾经说过："采用只教语言不教文化的教学法，只能培养出语言流利的大傻瓜。"《英语课程标准》中也强调在语言学习的同时要了解英语国家文化与本民族文化的差异，提高对中外文化差异的敏感性和鉴别能力。上述的三个案例中，教师将文化的元素分别融入词汇、句型和话题的教学中，使语言和文化的学习形成一个有机的整体。而且，教师在进行文化渗入时，并没有局限于让学生了解英美文化，而是把中国文化也融入其中，帮助学生在比较中加深对祖国文化的理解。

另外，教师多样的、生活化的任务设计让学生的视野和思维都能够得到拓宽，学会以包容的态度对待不同的文化和习俗。

所以，教师应该充分认识到文化在语言学习中的重要作用，不仅要帮助学生了解外国文化，更要引导他们学习和弘扬自己国家的文化，提高对不同国家间的文化差异的敏感性，获得跨文化交际的意识和能力。只有这样，学生才既能享受到英语学习的乐趣，又能得体、恰当地使用语言！

细节 20

如何提升学生的跨文化交际能力

细节阐述

文化是一个国家或民族的历史地理、风土人情、传统习俗、生活方式、文学艺术、行为规范、价值观念等。语言与文化密不可分,语言有丰富的文化内涵。袁昌寰指出,语言与文化的密切关系主要表现在三个方面:第一,语言是文化的重要组成部分。从文化的内涵来看,文化包括一个民族在长期的历史进程中创造的物质财富和精神财富两个方面,而语言正是精神财富的一个部分。第二,语言是文化的载体。语言反映一个民族的文化,解释该民族文化的内容;透过一个民族的语言我们可以对一个民族的文化具有全面的了解。第三,语言与文化相互影响,相互作用。

《英语课程标准》中也明确指出:"在学习英语的过程中,接触和了解外国文化有益于对英语的理解和使用,有益于加深对中华民族优秀传统文化的认识与热爱,有益于接受属于全人类先进文化的熏陶,有益于培养国际意识。在教学中,教师应根据学生的年龄特点和认知能力,逐步扩展文化知识的内容和范围。在起始阶段应使学生对中外文化的异同有粗略的了解,教学中涉及的外国文化知识应与学生的学习和生活密切相关,并能激发学生学习英语的兴趣。在英语学习的较高阶段,要通过扩大学生接触外国文化的范围,帮助学生拓展视野,使他们提高对中外文化异同的敏感性和鉴别能力,进而提高跨文化交际能力。"

王宗炎教授指出:"跨文化交际是双方的交流,而不是单方面向一方面学习。"在进行西方文化知识教学的同时,我们更应该加强对中国传统文化的教学。充分掌握汉语与汉语文化也是英语学习和提升英语交际能力不可分割的重要组成部分。

在课堂教学中,提升学生的跨文化交际能力可以采用以下几种策略。

策略一:多角度传授文化知识

对于中国大部分学生来说,课堂是学外语的主要场所。因此,在教学中需要适度渗透有关文化知识的教育。文化知识的教育应该与英语教学相结合,不能为了传授文化而传授文化。教师可以根据课堂教学的需要及文化知识的表现形式自主选择导入的方法。

方法一:注释法。可以对教材中具有文化内涵的内容进行注释和讲解。比如,当教学中涉及 Halloween, London 等一些国外的节日和较为著名的外国城市时,教师可以通过注释法告知学生节日的由来及日期,或者是一些著名城市所在的国家及其地理位置等信息。采用这种方法有很强的针对性,但是比较零散,缺乏系统性。

方法二:比较法。它是指在教学中对中国文化和外国文化进行比较,从而发现两种文化中的异同,加深学生对两种文化的理解,有效地培养学生的文化意识。比如,译林版《英语》教材中的 Culture time 板块经常会涉及一些文化对比。五年级下册 Unit 1 的 Culture time 板块内容为"Coffee is popular in Western countries. Tea is popular in China.",六年级下册 Unit 3 的 Culture time 板块内容为"Chinese people often have some porridge and steamed buns for breakfast. Western people often have cereal, bread, eggs and sausages for breakfast."。在教学上述内容时,教师可以适时对学生进行饮食文化的对比教学。

方法三:融入法。它是指直接把外国文化或者中国文化的内容作为教学的材料。比如:译林版《英语》六年级上册 Unit 8 Chinese New Year,主要围绕中国传统节日春节以电子邮件的形式介绍了主人公一家在春节前的打算。这样可以把语言学习和文化学习有效地结合起来。

方法四：体验法。教学中可以通过具体的语言实践让学生学习和了解外国文化，例如看英语原版的电影、卡通片，阅读英语原版文学作品，举办圣诞晚会等。译林版《英语》小学高年级的教材编写中将第一单元设置为童话故事的教学，比如，"The king's new clothes"，"The lion and the mouse"等，教师可以给学生播放原版的卡通片，以此来激发学生的学习兴趣，让学生体验到原汁原味的英语语言。

策略二：双向交流，发挥跨文化交际的真正作用

交际就要发挥其双向交流的作用，学生不是单方面学习外国的先进文化，而是也要运用英语向外国人传播我国的传统文化，培养跨文化交际中的平等意识。

小学生的价值观与道德观都处在形成的过程之中，他们思想活跃，容易受到新鲜事物的影响，又缺乏一定的鉴赏能力。因此，教师在教授外国文化的过程中，要善于引导，帮助学生形成正确的价值观、道德观和世界观；引导学生吸收外国文化中有益的部分，培养其扬弃能力，使母语文化的学习与外国文化的学习相互促进，相得益彰。

以节日文化为例。受到西方文化的影响，许多学生对外国的一些节日诸如 Christmas, Halloween, April Fool's Day 等非常感兴趣。他们会在圣诞节这天制作贺卡，相互赠送礼物；会在万圣节的时候玩"Trick or treat"游戏；会在愚人节的时候做一些恶作剧。但是，学生们往往更加注重这些西方节日的外在形式而忽视了节日文化本身的意义。此外，在这些西方文化的冲击下，很多学生对中国传统节日反而失去了兴趣。诸如重阳节、端午节等一些十分有教育意义的节日却无法吸引学生。面对这种情况，教师在教学过程中应当引导学生建立正确的价值观，树立祖国文化意识，形成一定的文化鉴赏能力，接受西方文化中的精华，并发扬中国传统文化的精髓。比如：在介绍节日文化时，教师可以利用中西方节日文化的对比进行教学，教师教授有关西方节日的文化知识，同时要求学生自主收集中国节日文化的信息进行分享。这种自主学习方式,可以激发学生的学习兴趣。又如,西方人通常爱喝咖啡,而中国人较爱喝茶。在介绍饮食文化时,教师可以借机介绍一下中国几千年的茶文化,民族自豪感便会在学生心中扎根,这也为学生进行跨文化交际增加了语言知识的储备。对于英语语言的学习,教师应当注重引导学生发挥其语言工具性的特点,为学生创设一些利用英语进行交流的机会,如:开展 English Corner 活动;开展以"Chinese festivals"为主题的 English Salon,以英文小报、英语演讲等形式推荐中国的传统节日文化、饮食文化;利用学校资源,建立与国外学校的联谊,让学生结交 penfriends,利用 e-mail、Facebook、Twitter 等方式进行文化交流。

　　文化意识是在语言知识教学的潜移默化中培养起来的。外国文化与中国文化的相互作用与影响是在教师的不断引导和渗透中实现的。它需要教师深挖教材,找到文化异同的切入点,利用教学机智对学生进行适时的教育。

典型案例 1

PEP《小学英语》
五年级上册　Unit 5　Part B　Let's learn

　　本课时的教学重点是方位词,教师在教学过程中别出心裁地插入了一个 Chinese Zodiac,为课堂教学增添了一个亮点。

　　在教学完词组 in front of 之后,教师拿出一个橘子,把自己作为参照物,就方位进行提问。

　　T:Where is the orange?

　　Ss:It's in front of you.

　　T:Where is the orange now?

　　S1:It's over the teacher.

　　T:Yes.(教师手一动,橘子就藏到了教师的背后)Where is it now?

　　S1:It's...(该学生侧着脑袋,苦苦思索想要表达的方位词;再看其他学生,也都在苦思冥想)

T：Mmm... it's behind me.（看到学生们的模样,教师终于说出了答案 behind）

T：Look! What are they?

Ss：They are animals.

T：What animals are they?（黑板上呈现十二生肖的图片）

Ss：They are mouse, ox, snake...

T：Who is behind the mouse?

S2：The ox is behind the mouse.

T：You are so great. You know, the twelve animals can be the names of years. Please give the correct order of them.

Now, you may discuss in groups and put them in order.

Ss do the guessing game in groups.（教室里开始热闹起来。有的同学背着从课外学来的"子鼠、丑牛、寅虎、卯兔……"来排序）

T：Now, let's look at the blackboard together.

Ss：The ox is behind the mouse. The tiger is behind the ox. The rabbit is behind the tiger...（当十二生肖以正确的顺序出现时,学生一片欢呼）

♦ 案例反思 ♦

该案例中,教师在认真研读教学内容的基础上,以中国特有的生肖文化作为训练学生英语语言表达的素材,可谓用心良苦。学生非常乐意接受这样的语言素材。教师在学生既有知识的基础上,让其以另外一种语言表达形式表达出来,这不仅让学生的语言得到了训练,更加激起了学生的学习兴趣,加深了学生对中国传统文化的了解;让学生充分感受到语言学习的乐趣,体会到中外文化的相互交融、相互影响;也极大地鼓舞了学生用英语传播中国传统文化的信心,提升了学生的文化修养,培养了学生的爱国精神。

·典型案例2·

著名教师刘小菁"London is the capital of England"课堂教学实例

这是外研社《新标准英语》(三年级起点用)第四册第二单元的内容。本课的主题是"Talk about London",教学目标是让学生了解有关伦敦的著名建筑及历史古迹,学会用英语描述某个城市。单元用两个课时完成,所选案例为第二个课时。第一课时中教师安排学生自己动手,利用书籍和网络等收集有关London的资料,并自学课文。第二课时中,教师先请学生根据自己收集的资料进行汇报,谈谈他(她)所了解的伦敦,同时教师予以补充;接着教师请学生描述我国的首都北京;最后,教师结合学生的生活环境,把视角投向他们所生活的城市和校园,要求学生用所学的句型编一段话。

Ⅰ．Warming-up

1. Greetings

...

2. Sing a song *London Bridge is falling down*

Ⅱ．Presentation

T：Where is London Bridge?

Ss：It's in London.

T：Where is London?

Ss：It's in England.

T：OK, now let's talk about London.

(学生用所收集的资料进行汇报)

S1：London is the capital of England.

S2：It's beautiful and big.

S3：This is the Thames River. There are lots of boats on it.

S4：This is the Big Ben. It's a very big clock. And it's famous.

S5：This is London Bridge. It's tall and wide.

（根据学生的汇报，教师板书以下句型：

London is the capital of England.

It's beautiful.

This is the Thames River.

There is/are...）

T：You are so good. Boys and girls, we are going to London.

（教师播放介绍London著名建筑和景点的录像，并趁机补充学生未提及的描述性词汇）

T：Look, this is <u>the Thames River</u>.（教授画线的词汇）

It's long and wide.

This is the <u>Big Ben</u>.（教授画线的词汇）

It's very tall and old.

This is the <u>Hyde Park</u>.（教授画线的词汇）

It's very beautiful.

This is <u>Tower Bridge</u>.（教授画线的词汇）

It's very famous.

Ⅲ. Practice

1. Talk about Beijing

T：London is the capital of England. Which city is the capital of China?

Ss：Beijing.

T：Yeah, let's talk about Beijing.

（学生自由谈论北京，描述北京的著名建筑及景点，教师帮助解决词汇问题）

S1：Beijing is big and beautiful. It's clean. There is 天安门广场。（教师补充：Tian'anmen Square）

S2：There are Ming Tombs in Beijing. There are lots of tombs.

S3：There is 长城（教师补充：the Great Wall）in Beijing. It's very long.

（教师还可视情况补充如下词汇并板书在黑板上：Forbidden

City, Summer Palace, Beihai Park, Temple of Heaven Park...)

2. Talk about other cities

T: I'd like to say something about other cities. Would you please guess where it is?（教师接着描述重庆的著名建筑及景点，借助多媒体演示，让学生猜测是重庆的哪个地方）

1) T: It's beautiful and old. And it's famous.

(PPT 展示出重庆市朝天门一角)

S1: This is Chao Tianmen. There are many boats on the river.

(PPT 展示出重庆市朝天门全貌)

T: Yes, this is Chao Tianmen. It's...

S2: It's beautiful and old.

S3: It's famous, too.

2) T: It's long and wide.

(PPT 展示出长江大桥一角)

...

3) T: It's clean and beautiful.

(PPT 展示出学校的一角)

...

S1: This is our school.

(PPT 展示出学校全貌)

...

Ss: Yes. This is our school. It's clean and beautiful. And it is very famous in Chongqing.

（学生分组讨论，利用自己收集的所感兴趣的其他国家首都的资料进行描述和汇报）

Ⅳ. Consolidation

T: Let's say it together.

London is my city.

And it's pretty.

There's a river.

And it's wide.

There's a bridge to the other side.

There's a tower.

And it's tall.

T：Now, would you please compose a rhyme about Chongqing or our school?

（学生分组比赛，自编关于重庆的歌谣。看哪组编得最快最好，并进行表演）

R1：This is Chongqing.

And it's very nice.

This is the Yangzi River.

And it's wide.

This is Gele Mountain.

And it's tall.

I like Chongqing.

And welcome to Chongqing.

R2：This is our school.

And it's very beautiful.

This is our classroom.

And it's clean.

This is my bag.

And it's nice.

I like our school.

And welcome to our school.

（学生在表演歌谣中结束新课）

◆ 案例反思 ◆

教师在介绍世界著名城市及其文化的同时，引导学生关注自己国家的文化特色，让学生在文化比较的过程中逐渐理解、尊重和包容不同文化的存在，帮助他们拓宽视野，形成科学、开放的跨文化认知与理解的观念。

教师将教学内容与学生的生活实践有机结合起来,为孩子们创设了真实的语境,让学生能够体会到"学了就能用"的成就感,能够运用所学语言进行交际。教师还通过各种形式,激发学生的学习兴趣,培养学生勇于实践的精神。

此外,教师深刻挖掘教材,利用教材这个载体,渗透文化,创设场景,培养学生的发散性思维、文化意识及跨文化交际能力,关注到了语言教学的社会文化目标和思维认知目标。

◆ 专家点评 ◆

语言教学中进行文化教学的目的是让学生了解多个国家的文化内容,通过比较学会尊重、包容不同的文化,并加深对祖国文化的理解。日常教学中,在处理外国文化和中国文化的关系的时候有几个误区要予以避免:① 教师的文化介绍仅局限于英语国家,不涉及非英语国家。② 教师对外国的文化、风俗、习惯等内容津津乐道,却很少有对自己国家文化的介绍。③ 文化的教学远离学生的日常生活。前面的案例呈现了对中外文化进行教学时较好的处理方式。案例一中,教师结合所教的话题,和学生一起感受了中国的生肖文化,由于它和学生的生活经验密切相关,易于激发他们的学习兴趣,收到了很好的效果。案例二中,教师从单元的主题"Talk about London"展开,逐渐把视角转向中国的城市,在讨论的过程中,学生感受了中外文明的不同,这是一种"润物细无声"的教学。当然,如果后续的教学中能增加世界其他著名城市,甚至是非英语国家的城市介绍,就可以进一步开阔学生的视野。

参考文献

[1] 中华人民共和国教育部. 义务教育英语课程标准(2011年版)[M]. 北京:北京师范大学出版社,2012.

[2] 王蔷. 小学英语教学法教程[M]. 第2版. 北京:高等教育出版社,2010.

[3] 程晓堂,刘兆义. 小学英语[M]. 上海:华东师范大学出版社,2008.

[4] 程晓堂. 英语教师课堂话语分析[M]. 上海:上海外语教育出版社,2009.

[5] 林立. 英语语法教学[M]. 北京:外语教学与研究出版社,2013.

[6] 程晓堂,孙晓慧. 英语教材分析与设计[M]. 北京:外语教学与研究出版社,2011.

[7] 程晓堂. 英语阅读教学[M]. 北京:外语教学与研究出版社,2012.

[8] 胡春洞. 英语教学法[M]. 北京:高等教育出版社,1990.

[9] 赵国忠. 中国著名教师的精彩课堂 小学英语卷[M]. 南京:江苏人民出版社,2008.

[10] 郑文. 小学英语教学课例——实录与评析[M]. 杭州:浙江教育出版社,2012.

[11] 刘青. 走进名师课堂——小学英语[M]. 济南:山东人民出版社,2009.

[12] 崔刚,孔宪遂.英语教学十六讲[M].北京:清华大学出版社,2009.

[13] 惠幼莲,洪子锐.小学英语新课程教学法[M].长春:东北师范大学出版社,2006.

[14] 周彬.课堂密码[M].上海:华东师范大学出版社,2012.

[15] 周成平.新课程名师精彩课堂实录[M].北京:中国科学技术出版社,2006.

[16] 禹明.小学英语教学活动设计案例精选[M].北京:北京大学出版社,2013.

[17] 岳蔚.小学英语教学精彩片段和课例赏析[M].宁波:宁波出版社,2013.

[18] 庞维国.自主学习:学与教的原理和策略[M].上海:华东师范大学出版社,2004.

[19] [美] David Nunan. 英语语言教学理论与实践[M].张晶晶,任晴,王春梅,译.南京:译林出版社,2008.

[20] [美] David Nunan. 语法教学实用技巧[M].陶懿,郭秀茹,译.南京:译林出版社,2007.

[21] [英] Ricky Lowes & Francesca Target. 帮助学生自主学英语[M].李进,译.南京:译林出版社,2007.

[22] [英] Jeremy Harmer. 朗文如何教写作[M].邹为诚,译.北京:人民邮电出版社,2011.

[23] [英]斯科特·索恩伯里.朗文如何教词汇[M].王琦,译.北京:人民邮电出版社,2011.

[24] [英]斯科特·索恩伯里.朗文如何教语法[M].邹为诚,译.北京:人民邮电出版社,2011.

[25] [美]林瑟.儿童英语教学实用技巧[M].郭艾青,译.南京:译林出版社,2007.

[26] [日]佐藤学.静悄悄的革命:创造活动、合作、反思的综合学习课程[M].李季湄,译.长春:长春出版社,2003.

[27] [英] Tricia Hedge. Teaching and learning in the language

classroom[M].上海:上海外语教育出版社,2002.

[28] 吴丽华.小学英语高年级词汇教学新模式的实践探索[J].中小学外语教学(小学篇),2015(12):1—5.

[29] 程晓堂.关于英语语法教学问题的思考[J].课程·教材·教法,2013(4):62—70.

[30] 丁海英.从一节研究课谈小学英语阅读教学的有效设计[J].中小学外语教学(小学篇),2012(12):11—16.

[31] 江萍.小学英语会话教学的实践与研究[J].中小学外语教学(小学篇),2012(2):12—15.

[32] 蒋芳芳.提高学生口语表达能力的探索[J].中小学外语教学(小学篇),2012(4):22—25.

[33] 楼银君.把握情境要素　打造给力课堂[J].中小学外语教学(小学篇),2012(4):13—17.

[34] 罗立胜,张莱湘.英语语音教学的回顾及对目前英语语音教学的几点建议[J].外语与外语教学,2002(10):21—23.

[35] 褚金丽.我国小学英语语音教学的现状及反思[J].中小学外语教学(小学篇),2005(12):2—5.

[36] 华伟.小学低年级学生英语认读能力的个案分析与思考[J].中小学外语教学(小学篇),2008(9):13—16.

[37] 高晓霞.谈小学英语课堂思维空间的创设[J].中小学外语教学(小学篇),2005(07):15—17.

[38] 沈丹莹.小学英语初始阶段认读能力培养的探索与研究[J].中小学外语教学(小学篇),2005(7):43—46.

[39] 祖瑞.厘清关系,发展学生英语自主学习能力[J].中小学英语教学与研究,2009(1):15—20.

[40] 程晓堂.论自主学习[J].学科教育,1999(9):32—39.

[41] 叶莲芳.例谈小学英语语法教学的四种有效方式[J].江苏教育:小学教学,2016(3):42—43.

[42] 王晓华.小学英语教学中学生思维能力的培养[J].小学时代(教育研究),2011(8):28.

[43] 郭有吉.小学英语应该如何进行语音教学[J].小学教学研究,2012(10):91—92.

[44] 张素云.小学英语语音教学的问题及思考[J].山东师范大学外国语学院学报:基础英语教育,2009(4):65—69.

[45] 朱珠.在小学英语课堂中渗透文化背景知识[J].英语广场(学术研究),2013(11):149—150.

[46] 王桂琴.小学英语课堂话题教学的实践研究[J].新课程:小学,2012(2):103—104.

[47] 黄敏.试析小学英语教学中文化意识的有效渗透[J].校园英语,2014(14):72.

[48] Stahl, S. A., Duffy-Hester, A. M., & Stahl, K. Theory and research into practice: Everything you wanted to know about phonics (but were afraid to ask) [J]. *Reading Research Quarterly*, 1998,33(3):338—355.

[49] 英语句型教学有效性探微[EB/OL].[2014-05-13]. http://www.xzbu.com/9/view-5157640.htm.